Men in Black

Men in Black

John Harvey

The University of Chicago Press

JOHN HARVEY teaches English at Cambridge University. He is the author
of *Victorian Novelists and Their Illustrators* (1970), three novels,
and many scholarly articles.

The University of Chicago Press, Chicago 60637

Reaktion Books Ltd., London WIP IDE

Copyright © John Harvey, 1995

All rights reserved. Published 1995

Printed in Great Britain

04 03 02 01 00 99 98 97 96 95   1 2 3 4 5 6

ISBN 0–226–31879–6 (cloth)

Designed by Humphrey Stone
Jacket designed by Ron Costley

Library of Congress Cataloging-in-Publication Data
Harvey, J. R. (John Robert)
Men in Black/John Harvey,
       p.   cm.
Includes bibliographical references and index
 1. English literature—History and criticism. 2. Costume in literature. 3. Black in
literature. 4. Men in literature. 5. Man—woman relationships in literature.
6. Symbolism of colors in literature. 7. Clothing and dress—Psychology.
8. Clothing and dress—Great Britain—History. I. Title.
PR149.C67H37 1995
809′.93355—dc20   95—4585
                                                                      CIP

The University of Chicago Press acknowledges permission from Grove/Atlantic Inc.
to reproduce quoted matter from *Reservoir Dogs* by Quentin Tarantino on the back
jacket and as an epigraph.

This book is printed on acid-free paper.

Contents

Acknowledgements

I am most substantially indebted, for criticism, advice, tips, castigation, to those who very generously consented, at differing stages of its development, to read and comment on my manuscript: David Armitage, John Beer, Derek Brewer, Peter Burke, John Burnett, Philip Collins, Don Cupitt, Gerard Evans, John Gage, Graham McMaster, Leonée Ormond, Aileen Ribeiro, Jonathan Riley Smith. But I have I think gained and learned from every conversation I have had with friends and acquaintances on the topics of this book. My greatest debt is to my wife, Julietta Harvey, for her alert reading and criticism and suggestions.

MR PINK:
Why can't we pick out our own color?
JOE:
I tried that once, it don't work. You get four guys fighting over who's gonna be Mr Black.

Quentin Tarantino, *Reservoir Dogs*

1 Edgar Degas, *The Cotton Market, New Orleans*, 1872, oil on canvas. Musée des Beaux-Arts, Pau.

Introduction: Clothes, Colour and Meaning

In Degas's *The Cotton Market, New Orleans* (illus. 1), the radiant fluff of new cotton on the table, which seems made of the white light that illumines it, contrasts distinctly with the black figures of the connoisseurs and potential buyers. One of them holds up to a colleague a spray of new cotton, with a movement he might make in a different kind of painting – offering a chalice to someone he admires (but his stance here is less celebratory: he has one foot up on the seat of a chair). Everywhere in the painting different blacks play against different whites: top-hat, shoe-leather, darkness (the fireplace); cotton, paint, paper, daylight (the window). With its calm recession of people and rectangles, its space and high ceiling, its even clear light, the painting sees a certain grace in the world of business. The men in their black suits are at their ease, assaying, appraising, comfortable in acumen; the black man in black, leaning on a sill, appraises the appraisers. It is the world of men and money, in which a dazzling raw material (which would, a few years earlier, have been tended on the plantation by the enslaved parents of the negro) is traded before being transformed into clothes – into such radiant white shirts as all the men are wearing, notably the clerk in shirt-sleeves on the right, writing in a ledger with a fastidious expression. (Later, thrown away as rags, the same material might become paper, or newspaper.) And the painting reflects the values of clothes. The men's black has its formality, however much the men are at ease. It reflects position, whether they are owners or employees; it reflects also their impersonality of expertise. They owe it both to themselves and to their situation to wear this common colour so. The man in the light jacket, at the end of the table, is not of them: he is perhaps a grower, waiting with a concerned stare to know the price the cotton may fetch. He has the produce, but they, at this point, have the power.

The people not shown are women, though the cotton on the table will be transformed chiefly into dresses for women, especially into muslin, which many of the women attached to these men will be wearing, in their world: at home, in their gardens, or out (accompanied). They will be wearing mainly white – in the New Orleans sun they will be radiant at least as the new cotton here – as the men are wearing mainly black. And if their white shows both that they are not in service (unless the white is an apron), and also is virtue, more precious than the costliest muslins, made from the best cotton trade prices can fetch, still the men's black will pull rank. It has gravity, authority.

One could be struck by the quiet assurance men's black has here. For, five hundred years earlier, in Europe, such a group of men, dressed almost all in black, might well have been monks or friars: the radiant white table might carry sacred things. They would have been clerics – or they would have been mourners. Five hundred years earlier still they would, simply, have been mourners: and then the white long shape on the table, which has, broadly, human proportions, would have been the body, wrapped in its white winding-sheet. They would not, then, have sat so casually; and they would not have been only men. There would have been both men and women in black, grieving together. For if this book is about one gender and one colour, it is because the curious metamorphosis that has occurred in the use of black cloth – that is, the empowerment of black – has occurred primarily in men's dress (for obvious reasons), while women have tended, almost until the present century, to be left with the grieving and penitential use of black. Even when brilliant, rich, powerful women have worn magnificent black in the past, they have usually needed the pretext of mourning to do so. And what has seemed to me a curious point of interest for study is the way in which, through time, the use of this colour – the colour that is without colour, without light, the colour of grief, of loss, of humility, of guilt, of shame – has been adopted in its use by men not as the colour of what they lack or have lost, but precisely as the signature of what they have: of standing, goods, mastery. The subject, in other words, involves more than externals. It relates to the relations between people in society, and to the relations between men and women; and to the way in which people display externally what in some ways is a 'dark' interior of human motivation. There is a residual mystery in the process: the connection between black and death is never wholly left behind. Though black has developed dull and workaday uses, as well as smart ones, there has recurringly been a sinister element in the use men have made of black.

This is a study, then, in the meaning of colour and clothes. What kind of meaning is the meaning of clothes? That clothes in some sense *mean* is clear from the difficulties one runs into, as soon as one tries to imagine a choice of clothing that would really have no meaning. Even clothing that says 'I don't care what I wear' does say that, it does not say nothing. But, as the last example suggests, it is easy to be casual about how precisely it is that clothes mean, or signify, or signal to us. Indeed, casualness marks a good deal of ambitious generalizing about 'the language of clothes', as it marks Alison Lurie's illuminating, loose-limbed book of that title:

Especially in the case of persons of limited wardrobe, an article may be worn because it is warm or rainproof or handy to cover up a wet bathing suit – in the same way that persons of limited vocabulary use the phrase 'you know' or adjectives such as 'great' or 'fantastic'.[1]

Neither an exact nor an attractive equation of verbal and actual poverty – as if a person huddled in a downpour is in the same case as someone improving their feelgood factor by saying 'Great!' and 'Fantastic!' non-stop. And though Lurie says, somewhat breezily, that 'if clothing is a language, it must have . . . a grammar', her offer to construct that grammar is both sketchy and arbitrary. So she says a case can be made 'for considering trimmings and accessories as adjectives or adverbs', and cites buckles on shoes and buttons on jacket-cuffs as 'modifiers in the sentence that is the total outfit'. But it is hard to see that they are adverbs, since she does not identify the verbs. Perhaps they can be called adjectives, but they could just as well be called parentheses, subordinate clauses, interjections or punctuation marks. An accessory like a badge might be so important as to be the subject of the sentence.

As to adjectives in clothing, one could, it is true, call colour an adjective, a usage that would at least correspond to the way, in words, we mostly speak of colour. But colour is also compared by Lurie to tone and pitch of voice. This is reasonable, of course: the underlying point is that colour in dress is neither an adjective nor a tone of voice, because if clothes have a language, it is not a language that corresponds in this close way to verbal language; and, by extension, it cannot carry meanings in quite the way that words do.

If one turns to a more systematically scientific linguistics of dress, such as that proposed by Roland Barthes in *The Fashion System*, one finds a great deal of attention and analysis given, precisely, to the differences between the way in which clothes mean things and the way in which language does. By setting the actual language of dress, as in fashion writing, beside the clothes the writing describes (he identifies, playfully, the unit of 'the vesteme'), Barthes is able to be exact about the very different ways in which clothes, and words, signify. Thus, while recording the oppositions that mark items of dress with meaning (oppositions of weight and lightness, openness and closure, emphasis and neutrality), he records also the major difference:

Everything in language is a sign, nothing is inert; everything is meaning, nothing receives it. In the vestimentary code, inertia is the original state . . . a skirt exists without signifying, prior to signifying; the meaning it receives is at once dazzling and evanescent: [fashion writing] seizes upon insignificant objects, and . . . strikes them with meaning, gives them the life of a sign; it can also take this life back from them, so that the meaning is like a grace that has descended upon the object.[2]

In *The Fashion System* Barthes is mainly concerned with that broad but especially evanescent meaning – most of all like a grace that descends and is withdrawn – of 'fashionableness' (he notes that 'in Fashion, *black* is a full colour'). It may be that in other contexts one can find a more durable structure of dress-meanings, as must be the case with any sort of uniform, as Nathan Joseph, in particular, has argued. But it does appear that what Barthes calls 'the vestimentary code' is unlike most codes in that its meanings are (in his word) fragile. Umberto Eco has preferred to use the term 'undercode' for the way clothes signify, meaning that they work through an aggregate of cues and clues, rather than by agreed clear signs.[3]

Indeed, the way in which clothes 'mean' is not so much like verbal meaning as like the kind of meaning involved when people say 'I know what you're saying', and then place their own construction, in their words, on your words. The 'meanings' of clothes are 'constructions' placed on them, and are not readable in a dictionary sense, as verbal meanings are. These meanings are based on the perception of specific choices (or abdications of choice) as to material, colour, cut, newness, but there is a high degree of ambiguity as to the purpose of such choices. Any meaning in the clothes will, moreover, be either corroborated or qualified by the posture and movement of the body inside the clothes. There is an inescapable 'multivalence' in dress: and this is especially so with the 'meanings' of colours, which are easily also misread – as for instance with the colour red. Is it politically active, or sexually inviting, or simply cheerful, or maybe cross?

This is to say that a study of the way in which clothes work as signs must take good account of the way signs work as signs, which is not only by way of agreed codes (as in red/green lights), but also by indeterminate historical association (as with various forms of directional arrow – a sign with no counter-sign – most of which retain the barbs of real arrows and spears), and also by the unconscious or half-conscious semaphore of gestures. Gestures can be voluntary or involuntary, and may be read as signs by others whether they are intended as signs or not (as with blushing). So unsureness, nervousness, a modest social background, may be legible in dress where no such sign was intended: while, in the clothes of an affable host for instance, the combinations of colours chosen, each with their several ambiguities, may send a variety of signals at once, all together the sign of aware life in the wearer of the clothes. Indeed the ambiguities, puns and equivocations of dress are so subtle and multiple that a science of them would need to be not so much a clear-coded semiotics as a science of inferred contradictory implication. And commentators expert in the semiotic field, such as Susan Kaiser, have distinguished many levels of dress communication, tracing, at one extreme, 'the most complex kinds of appearance messages – rife with ambiguity, emotion, expression'.[4] At times one wants not so much a linguistics as a poetics of dress.

One might ask how, given these multiplicities, one could talk with any decision about the larger meanings of dress. Yet certain main meanings do accrue, thickening over time by accretion of usage. This is especially so of the colour black, which is remarkable, as Anne Hollander has observed, in its 'combined symbolic and optical power'.[5] It is a colour without colour that speaks loudly because it is conspicuous, even if it says 'Don't see me! I efface myself.' The 'associations' it carries are the memories of the occasions on which it has been worn. Indeed, the associations of black have been stamped so deep that it is easy to think of it as having something like a permanent meaning. So even Roland Barthes, departing for a moment from a concept of meaning defined by immediate binary oppositions, says the colour black is 'naturally associated with formal wear'. It is so, but was not always so, and at the present time it has other values also, which come into play in (for instance) leather-jackets. Fashions change, and so do meanings; and the colour black, naturally emphatic, has been used at different times to mark off individuals or groups in quite different ways – from the unbereaved, from the worldly, from Catholics, from women. In the more local worlds of folk costume, black may be used to mark off the old from the young, the married from the unmarried, and even, in Moravian Slovakia, other men from millers.[6] To allow that meanings alter is not to agree with Barthes that meaning departs entirely like a departing grace. Meanings change but older meanings cling, with something like the tenacity of a stain on cloth. The colour black itself has recurred in fashion, with increments of meaning over the centuries that have become, by our own time, both formidable and paradoxical.

In sum, the meaning of a colour is to a great extent the history of the colour. It is a meaning that is made by movement through time. This is a point that should be stressed with the colour black, which is a paradox-colour, as perhaps should be expected of a colour that is no-colour. For black tends to play a double game with time. In general one might say that fashion in dress is change and movement: newness matters, and, in our own time especially, the incentive is to wear tomorrow's clothes today, and never to be caught in yesterday's. Fashionableness is always a moment within a movement, and the larger changes of dress (as from stiffness to looseness, less silk more linen, tailor-made to off-the-peg) are indices of currents of change in society. Black fashions, however, have tended to endure: to be anti-fashion fashions with a power to persist, and sometimes death-fashions unwilling to die. Black may thus seem the colour of social immobility: though (I hope to argue) its work may also be to hide, and thus assist, surreptitious social change.

That meaning in dress is made of movement in history is apparent in the process that has come to be called power-dressing – as when anyone not in a governing group chooses to wear the clothes the governing group has long worn. At issue here are the more intimate, and more potent, aspects of dress. For while dress may shield a private vulnerability, there are also ways in which, in choosing to wear certain clothes, one may be not so much adopting a cover, as conjuring a new persona for oneself. One may be devoting oneself more wholly to an emotion (like grief), or to a mood (like a fun or party mood), or to a character (as of a businessman of probity and acumen). In all of these a kind of magic is involved, as if, by arraying oneself in their colours, one were inviting the genius or daemon of fun, of love, of piety, of business, to possess one body and soul. Our outer dress does inner work for us, and if clothes 'mean', it is in the first place to ourselves, telling us we are or may be something we have meant to be. Especially dress helps us, if it resolves an uncertainty as to who or what we are. In the 'collective selection' theory of dress, as developed by Herbert Blumer and refined, recently, by Fred Davis, fashion follows fashion as communal interest veers both to address and to dress new loci of unease.[7] We find our clothes, our clothes find us: they save us from being lost. At home in dress, we enjoy its touch, its crispness, smoothness, softness, texture, its feel on the skin it fits: these pleasures serving the larger pleasure of being at last, or hoping we are, our more glamorous and more potent self. In dressing we enter an inheritance, which may include a new self, which we feel to be a 'true' self, revealed or rather realized by the donning of these good clothes.

It is because it works in this inward and intimate way that power-dressing can have – what nineteenth-century commentators detected – a sinister aspect, as if, by adopting certain externals, one can interfere with one's soul; the more so when the dress of wealth and financial authority (the black frock-coat with black cravat, for instance) already carries, in its colour, associations of spirituality and spiritual power. Much dressing is power-dressing, and power-dressing is by its nature political. It is likely to involve putting on other people's clothes, normally the clothes of people higher up the social gradient – who, in their turn, may strike back with new clothes. The whole theory of fashion of Georg Simmel centred on the proposition that subordinates imitate superordinates, who for their part are anxious to differentiate themselves, in a continual large-scale process of overtaking and dodging, seen by Simmel as occurring at every social level.[8] And since such dressing involves people's fundamental sense of their selves – we might say it is one way in which they construct their 'subjectivities' – the politics concerned is a politics not only of income and class, but a politics, in a sense, of the spirit.

It is a politics, also, of gender. If, as Judith Butler says, gender is performative, something that we do, then it is certainly something that we do in the way we dress: this is clear in the attempted special magic of cross-dressing. And studies of dress have long recorded the way in which the inflections of gender alter as moral and material economies change. In particular, dependence and independence are registered in the character of movement dress allows. Much of the work that dress performs is, in Fred Davis's terms, 'ambivalence management'. Markedly this is so in the clothes of gender, which in our society will not rest, but fondly and warily circle each other in a restlessness of mutual miming and of dis-identification. (So, to take a minor example, when men were slope-shouldered, like First World War soldiers, women adopted padded shoulders to enhance the trim feminine waist: men adopted padded shoulders, adjusting them to a strong-arm style: and women returned to rounded shoulders, since padded shoulders had a 'masculine' squareness.)[9]

Especially, gender may be expressed with colour. Luce Irigaray has claimed indeed that 'the incarnation of the divine, of man, of woman, *cannot be imaged without colour*'.[10] This is true, though it is also true that this incarnation of man, of woman, which in a sense is what dress performs for us, has at certain crucial periods been represented not so much by the strong colours she mentions (for instance, red, purple, gold), but rather by those paradox-colours, which we treat both as colours and as non-colours, or anti-colours, black and white. As, for example, in the ballrooms of the nineteenth century, at those sumptuous festivities of social brokerage and symbolism where the two genders massed to confront each other *as* genders and *as* sexes – the men in black, the women mostly in white – with the intention of dancing in pairs. It is an antithesis perpetuated, in our far post-Victorian and polychrome world, in weddings and wedding-photos still.

One must be careful of facile connections: yet one may be tempted to relate the women in white to those studies in gender that find a social wish to read feminity as absence (as for instance does Luce Irigaray, who, in a fresh poetic chiming with a nineteenth-century image, also reads the feminine as the white angel of a veiled mother). As to the strong colours often used in women's dress, whether cyclamen or saffron, whether azure, green or rose, they may reflect the freedom for those 'personal' feelings, and also for play and for display, which came to be reserved as a feminine prerogative. The show of both the whites and colours may tempt one, then, to relate the men in black to those other gender-readings – such, for instance, as that of Nancy Chodorow – which see masculinity as defined in terms of negation, and defined in particular as negation of the feminine: especially in the developing industrial age when fathers, more than ever and for longer, were absent from the home. Such readings may be the more attractive when one considers at the same time how the colour black (the colour of loss, of negation, the colour with which one annuls one's self) had already come, in its centuries-long appropriation by men, to represent the responsibilities of the shrouded male self. At issue fundamentally is the active part that is played by negation in human life and in social life, and in making men and women 'what they are'.[11]

By the same token, black may be engaged in the negation of the gender distinction itself, as when Josephine Baker or Marlene Dietrich appear in black top-hat and tails (the man in black as a beautiful woman) or as when Michael Jackson dances, in gold-trimmed black, 'androgynous and ageless', to be then mimicked by Madonna, wearing a man's black suit and monocle. Such figures, in theatre, Marjorie Garber has claimed, enact a free knowledge our culture desires, 'that gender exists only in representation'.[12] Garber does not discuss the role of black dress in such theatre, though that role is clear in many of her illustrations, where it says yet more loudly what black often says: Don't see me, and, See me. I show you here what is not to be seen. Gender negates, I negate negation. I am death and freedom beyond man and woman. I am what is not. I am no self and sheer self. I am undivided power.

Such black is the cloak of a play-identity, which is very much 'vested' in the cloak: a charged identity of a third order, and one with a powerful internal polarity. This is not to say that sexual polarity is only to be found in a cross-dressed figure. It has long been a principle, important in psychology, that there is an element of masculinity in the feminine, and of femininity in the masculine. The costume scholar Elizabeth Wilson has said of both Marlene Dietrich and Greta Garbo – of them, not of their clothes – 'that the mysterious quality of their allure comes in part from a hint of manliness at the very heart of their feminine presence'. There is a sexual polarity within the dress of each gender. For the contemporary designer Vivienne Westwood 'there are certain polarities operating in whatever I do, very strong ones – between masculine and feminine (how much femininity goes into men's clothes, how much masculinity can go into women's clothes)'.[13] Negation, in gender, is never total, and the most four-square masculine dress may incorporate still a feminine retort: lace at the cuffs, a corseted waist, or (at the present time) a necktie in the colour-spectrum of women's blouses and dresses. These gender antitheses, within the dress of gender, give the dress of both the genders a mobile electricity.

Not that the polarity is ever equal: fashion has not aimed at the transcendence of gender, or ever, truly, at androgynous dress. On the contrary, as Jo Paoletti and Claudia Brush Kidwell concluded, following a broad survey, 'not only has truly androgynous dress never existed for adult men and women, but the closest we have ever come to androgyny is for women to dress like men'. The proposition sounds drastic, though it is possibly not surprising if negation plays a much larger part in men's dress than in women's.[14]

I realize it may be read as my own negation of the feminine, that in this book I concentrate on the clothes of men: there is a particular mystery in what men have done with black. A truly full account of dress, culture, colour and gender would be too huge to be contained within one book, especially since, as each new study shows, dress itself is as complicated as our social life. One might indeed say that dress is the complication of social life made visible – made indeed 'material', in fabric – unless one preferred to say (to adapt a phrase from Stendhal) that dress, like painting, consists of *values* made visible. We live in a world permeated by values – gender values, social values, political values, ethical values – and in our style of life we see them. We see them in all our 'furniture', including our clothes. And we don these values, put them on, to promise a behaviour (a promise we may not keep).

The close value of clothes is clear, if we observe, in ourselves or others, the ways in which we touch our clothes. The touching may be preening or grooming, but people can also draw a support or comfort from the clothes that meet their touch. There is a dynamic in the relationship between people and their clothes, and other people in *their*

clothes. People may toy, for instance, with the taking off of garments –
coats, jackets, jerseys – not in striptease, or sexual flirtation, and yet
after all in a kind of flirtation. How much do we take off? How much do
we let go or keep? Shall I show you another side of myself? Clothes start
us guessing, and play at claiming and giving.

Dress exists in a realm between flags and art. As art, dress is also
performance art, for playing both safe and dangerous games. The
clothed person is a persona we perform: and the man in black, like the
woman in white, is a whole family of personae. Dress thus serves, in
Elizabeth Wilson's phrase, to 'stabilize identity': and the identity that
dress makes firm is both single and shared.[15] The persona is more
impersonal than we are, and may indeed seem hardly ours. For as soon
as we start to choose our dress, we find that already we have been
dressed: by parents, school, the company, by class, gender, race, faith.
We dress to join groups, and to escape other groups and the past; we
also dress dissociatively, to mark us off from types we want not to be
mistaken for. We may dress old, we may dress young. We may dress up
to 'our betters', we may dress down, in a placatory 'status demurral'.
Broadly, as Nathan Joseph has put it, 'one dresses for the requirements
of an event', though much of the choosing may be unconscious,
intuitive, our instincts having entered the choice of our dress.[16] Within
the persona there is polarity, as between masculine and feminine
elements, and as between the unique and the common, the formal and
the easy. The persona may indeed be double, a persona and a counter-
person: as with someone in uniform (but much dress is uniform) who
wears the item at an angle, with style, or with visible disaffection. There
is also a polarity between our clothes and us, between the persona and
the person, who may be fearful, or soaring, or in pieces, or most private.
For in the end it is true that clothing hides: there is a 'subjectivity'
within the postures within the clothes that is intangible, incalculable,
and will never give all its secrets to others; its secrets are proof that it is
a self, even when it keeps some secrets from itself.

Such discussion may omit the largest social context of all: for it is
often pointed out that the whole large rapid metamorphosis of dress,
the phenomenon of Fashion, is itself, in origin, a peculiarity of Western
culture. In traditional societies, dress was largely prescribed and slow
to change. It seems there is a connection between the mobility of
fashion and both the mobility and the 'knit' of society. In a close-knit
social group, dress itself will stabilize, as it does still in schools, armies,
institutions. As the weave loosens, dress also will change: so it is
perhaps not by chance that fashion originated, as it appears, in
Europe's loosest-knit state, or non-state, the territories of Burgundy. It

is in the present most broken-up and atomized period that fashions change faster than ever before, coming now from many centres, and from minorities and sub-cultures as well as from the *couture* houses. One might be tempted to relate this change to an increasing individualism, as more individuals dress in more individual ways. This cannot, however, be the entire explanation, since people do not dress in wholly individual ways, especially in the age of mass-produced dress. Rather, more or less wittingly, people follow fashions. One might then read the increasing rapidity of clothing-change as not only the product of individual choice, but as an ever more urgent clutching for community. Our clothes have also a clutch on us. Styles of clothing carry feelings and trusts, investments, faiths and formalized fears. Styles exert a social force, they enroll us in armies – moral armies, political armies, gendered armies, social armies. And this, markedly, has been done by black.

It is because of the largeness and complexity of the issues that, in discussing the nineteenth century especially, I have referred extensively to the testimony of novelists. For their famed skill is precisely in reading the inner meaning of externals. In particular I have taken as my chief window on the period the novels of Charles Dickens. This is not to disparage the more direct documentation, in fashion journals, the press, the memoirs of the dandies, of which I seek also to give an account. But there are larger questions raised by nineteenth-century black than are ever acknowledged in the overt fashion literature, and it is precisely novelists like Dickens, or Charlotte Brontë, who are at once most sentient and most exact in tracing in people's dress, as in their words, their pushes of assertion and bids for control. Their work is fiction not fact, and must be checked against the other testimonies, or the other fictions, of history, but it may still register better than other sources facts of the large spiritual politics of the time that were reflected in the inner and outer person together. I do not mean to privilege exclusively novelists: writers such as the 'prophet' John Ruskin and the poet Charles Baudelaire are corroborative witnesses. And, on the literary side, it is important for critics to be fully alert to dress, since in the novel in many periods, as in the cinema and television now, dress may be a vital part of characterization, and may carry a burden of broader meaning.

At issue here is a particular insight, which it seems became seriously feasible only in the latter years of the eighteenth century: the notion that God was exclusively a human invention, and, in the form especially of God the Father, represented not something divine, rather a fearful hypostasizing of human fears, jealousies and punitive passions. One can see this idea on the verge of realization (but staying within that verge) in the lives of figures such as William Cowper, who terrorized themselves and perhaps even drove themselves mad with the sense of their sinfulness. The melancholia of Dr Johnson has something of this character. By the time of William Blake, however, the idea is available that the God the Father many people believed in might be not so much Jehovah as Nobodaddy, a communal human invention, which the believers then used not only to terrify but to torment both themselves and others. Once one is free to think in these terms (which it is possible to do, as Blake later was able to, without prejudice to a good God one might still believe in), one is equipped to question not only the self-tormented individual conscience (what has happened, in history or in people's history, to make people *want* to hurt themselves so much?), but also the large purposes served by religions in societies. These purposes have much to do with social power, and may include much that is repressive, even tending to emotional, social and sexual terrorism. Involved in this policing is the politics of piety, the utilization of severe pieties to hold in order a society under stress. All of this may sound remote from issues of dress, but it is precisely an idea running through both Dickens's and Charlotte Brontë's work that black dress may involve a form of black preaching, an unending sermon audible everywhere, while what is being preached is principally a social and political gospel. It was not so hard for Dickens or Charlotte Brontë to have these thoughts, for the hard work had been done by an earlier generation of radical anti-clerical thinkers. Equally, it must be to the novelists' credit that they did not so much think the idea through, as see it through – through the clothes people wore in the world around them.

They certainly convey the sense, which history may confirm, that clothing articulates a political will, both reinforcing the wearers and binding them to something larger, and not only inviting but exacting a certain form of attention from others. Individuals may be enlarged by their dress, so they become to an extent, and in little, the group: so that a man in black (or in white, or blue, or khaki) may be a one-voiced version of a crowd in that colour, and may thus be assisted to be more ruthless and less human, as crowds may be. In other words, like-dressing may be a means of invoking the powers of crowd psychology without needing to get the members of the crowd physically together: thus making the crowd, or group, or 'élite', or social class, or church, or 'church', more formidably powerful.

If the closing section on the twentieth century does not make the same use of a novelistic 'window', but seeks rather to see from a more dartingly mobile and changing perspective, this is only in part because, since the time of Dickens, the novel has developed new priorities, while the interpretation of the appearance of the age has been undertaken by other, more visual media, notably photography and film. The other consideration is that the twentieth century hardly has a dominant colour, in the way the nineteenth century did, for men. One might rather see our century as decidedly parti-coloured, even when not pursuing a polychromatic dream-coat idea of itself. At the same time, dead-black is hardly itself dead – indeed, it was in our century that the darkest side of men's black came to its climax, in the years approaching the Second World War. More recently, and worn now if anything more by women than by men, black has returned to high fashion in so many ways and so often that one might be tempted to think of black as something like the ultimate fashion, from which *haute couture* continually departs, riding different rainbows, only in order to give the necessary fresh impact to the new ensuing resurgence of the fashion for black. 'Black is back' said a T-shirt last year. In such quick changes, meaning falls from garments. Still, if black has remained the staple of fashion, it is not only because it is a strongly marked colour, but also because it keeps a residue, a memory, of the different assertions black has made in the past. We find new ways of playing with death's colour, in finding the angle at which we stand to life.

2 'The Tailors Monthly Pattern Card of Gentlemen's Fashions for January 1842, approved of by London Fashionables of the Club of St James's Street and decided on by a committee of celebrated London Fashionable Tailors', hand-coloured engraving, published with *The Gentleman's Magazine of Fashion*, January 1842.

1 Whose Funeral?

I begin in the nineteenth century both because it was in this period, more than ever before, that men wore black; and also because it was in this period that the blackness of men's dress was perceived as problematic – something that men puzzled at, even as they dressed in black. Clearly black served for gender-coding: what disturbed commentators of the time was not this, but rather the way in which, more and more, it appeared men were opting for the dress of death. Alfred de Musset found 'le deuil' (the mourning) men wore 'un symbole terrible'.[1] So did other commentators, recording the new fashion with troubled wonder, as if a sombre mystery were unfolding steadily in everyday dress.

Previously men, like women, had dressed in many colours. In the Middle Ages men dressed splendidly if they could afford it. Even the poor wore varied colours – brown and green, a red or blue hat – as medieval illuminations show. In the Renaissance there was a fashion for black, but still black was far from being worn by everyone. And men wore colours in the eighteenth century, and into the first two decades of the nineteenth. But from this point on men's dress becomes steadily more austere and more dark, and if one consults the fashion journals one can see colour die, garment by garment, in a very few years. By the early 1830s the evening dress-coat and the full dress coat were normally black (though they might, for instance, be dark blue). In the early 1830s trousers might, in the summer, be white (they had ceased to be coloured), but by the later 1830s 'black trousers or pantaloons were the rule'. Even the cravat did not hold out for long: in 1838 *The Gentleman's Magazine of Fashion* recorded that the white cravat 'was driven from all decent society by George IV. He discarded the white cravat and the black became the universal wear.' For some years the waistcoat was a last redoubt of colour, but in May 1848 *The Gentleman's Magazine of Fashion* observed 'the materials for dress waistcoats are black or white watered silk or poplin'. The same changes occurred simultaneously in France, where, in 1850, the *Journal des tailleurs* noted that formal menswear now consisted solely of 'un habit noir, un pantalon noir, un gilet blanc et un autre noir; une cravate noire et une autre blanche': Théophile Gautier regretted in his essay 'De la Mode' that men's dress had become now 'si triste, si éteinte, si monotone'.[2]

Not everything was black. Trousers and waistcoats might still be white or off-white, and in the frock-coat dark green, dark blue and dark brown fought back in some years and retreated in others. But all the bright colours were gone beyond recall, the tone was dark, the dominant colour was black. The 'Tailors Monthly Pattern Card of Gentlemen's Fashions for January 1842' (illus. 2) contains some dark blues and browns, but most of the garments are black, each of the Gentlemen is wearing some black items, and the Gentleman in the centre wears a black hat, a black frock-coat, black trousers and black shoes. The opera-goer to his left wears an elaborately brocaded opera-coat, which again however is wholly black, accompanying his hat, trousers and shoes. One can demonstrate the chromatic narrowing that has occurred by comparing the smart clothes people wore in those years with the 'fancy-dress' they might wear to balls. For fancy-dress consisted of the clothes worn in other countries, and worn at other times; and as illustrations of the period show, such clothes are full of colour, that is what makes them 'fancy dress'. Otherwise colour, in any strong sense, was restricted to the military, especially to 'dress' uniform, which thus became the serious mode of fancy-dress.

The young gentlemen of 1842 are technically Victorians (Victoria came to the throne in 1837), but they are not yet grave Victorians: they are young, doll-faced, men about town. And since fashion-plates glamourize in a youthful direction, it took fashion-art a little while to register the new mood of gravity and moral uprightness, which later came to be synonymous with 'Victorian'. Such a figure may, however, be seen in a fashion-plate of 1851 (illus. 3), where the seated man, though young-faced and cherry-lipped, as the genre required, still visibly has jowls, grizzled whiskers and a fair measure of white hair. It is not clear whether he is to be construed as the father or grandfather of the girl and boy: fathers could in any case be grandfatherly. But he sits with the stiffness, the buttoned-up-ness, the rigid verticality that Dickens attributes to many of his characters – features that the artist has attempted to render dashing. The young gentleman also wears black, as he will for much of his life. In the background, the year being 1851, stands the Crystal Palace in Hyde Park.

It was a great change. Men wanted to dress in a smart kind of mourning, and as a result the nineteenth century looked like a funeral. It was seen as a funeral by writers of the time. Baudelaire said of the

3 Fashion-plate, hand-coloured engraving, from *The Gentleman's Magazine of Fashion*, January 1851.

frock-coat: 'Is it not the inevitable uniform of our suffering age, carrying on its very shoulders, black and narrow, the mark of perpetual mourning? All of us are attending some funeral or other.' Balzac observed that 'we are all dressed in black like so many people in mourning'. The same thought was independently expressed in England by Dickens, who then extended the conceit from the clothes people wear to buildings, even cities. In *Great Expectations*, when Pip arrives in London, he finds Barnard's Inn wearing 'a frowsy mourning of soot and smoke', and as to the black-clothed, black-jowled Mr Jaggers, his own 'high-backed chair was of deadly black horsehair, with rows of brass nails round it, like a coffin'. A powerful macabre imagery runs through Dickens, and especially through his late novels, which sees life in England, and life in London, as being one ghastly funeral, a funeral that is nightmarish because it never comes to an end. In *Dombey and Son*, the light that enters Dombey's office leaves 'a black sediment upon the panes'.[3]

It is perhaps because they are the centre of a funereal world that real funerals, actual interments, take such a strong hold on Dickens's imagination. They are terrible in the labour they make of their mournfulness, no good way of meeting death. In the description of the funeral of Pip's sister in *Great Expectations* we see what is alive in Dickens protesting, in the high-spirited play of fancy with which he both evokes and evades the dismalness. There is a hard-bitten, an exasperated, catch in his voice:

The remains of my poor sister had been brought round by the kitchen door, and, it being a point of Undertaking ceremony that the six bearers must be stifled and blinded under a horrible black velvet housing with a white border, the whole looked like a blind monster with twelve human legs, shuffling and blundering along under the guidance of two keepers.

Both the humour and the pall are over everything, even over the new, rapid, noisy railway system, which, for all its coal-dust, smoke and soot, might be thought one of the less sepulchral features of Victorian England. But in 'Mugby Junction' there are 'mysterious goods trains, covered with palls and gliding on like vast weird funerals, conveying themselves guiltily away from the presence of the few lighted lamps, as if their freight had come to a secret and unlawful end'.[4]

Baudelaire and Dickens have the same vision of their suffering age. In the light of this concurrence one may ask, what had the nineteenth century suffered? What was being mourned?

Baudelaire gave a political explanation: 'And observe that the black frock-coat and the tail-coat may boast not only their political beauty, which is the expression of universal equality, but also their poetic beauty, which is the expression of the public soul.' For him the black frock-coat was the uniform of the democratic spirit, of all the democratic bourgeois. He said 'a uniform livery of grief is a proof of equality'. Democracy had killed a precious individuality, and following that death democratic life could only be 'an immense procession of undertakers' mutes, political mutes, mutes in love, bourgeois mutes'.[5]

For Baudelaire, black, like death itself, was a leveller. And the association of black dress with democracy is persuasive, if one thinks not only of France, but of nineteenth-century America, where black was very widely worn. Black was so dominant in the United States that Dickens, for example, was thought garish on the strength of light trousers, a coloured waistcoat, and blackly glittering boots. The *St Louis People's Organ* complained in 1842: 'He wore a black dress coat . . . a satin vest with very gay and variegated colours, light coloured pantaloons, and boots polished to a fault. . . . His whole appearance is foppish, and partakes of the flash order. To our American taste it was decidedly so; especially as most gentlemen in the room were dressed chiefly in black.'[6] Black was fashionable in England too, however, where the democratic commitment was less strong, to say the least. The politics of the move to black are complex.

In what way was the change political? J. C. Flügel, in *The Psychology of Clothes*, asks what were the causes of 'the Great Masculine Renunciation', and finds them in 'the great social upheavals of the French Revolution':

It is not surprising . . . that the magnificence and elaboration of costume which so well expressed the ideals of the *ancien régime* should have been distasteful to the new social tendencies and aspirations that found expression in the Revolution.[7]

He argues that these tendencies and aspirations promoted simplification and uniformity of dress. There must be a measure of truth in this. What Flügel does not explain is why these tendencies and aspirations led to darkness and to blackness – hardly a natural corollary, even if one allows that the forces that will turn a society upside down are likely to be severe. Nor, in fact, was the process of change a simple matter of the vanishing of finery as the guillotine fell. Both the plain fashion, and then the dark and black fashion, were not actually set in revolutionary France. They were set in England, and only later taken up elsewhere. The plain style had its origins not so much in social levelling as in the practical requirements of the English gentry, travelling not in carriages but on horseback. And as to blackness, the first item of menswear to go black was not the daytime frock-coat of the democratic bourgeois, it was evening dress, the 'dinner-jacket' of high society.

The dinner-jacket epitomizes the change that occurred, for up to a certain date in the early nineteenth century, men's evening wear changed freely and could be in many colours. Then, in the later 1810s, the smart began to wear black in the evenings, and evening wear has stayed black ever since. The present century, it is true, has seen the occasional white coat at dinner: but black has remained dominant, and indeed the dinner-jacket or tuxedo that is worn today is not a great deal different from what would have been worn 170 years ago. It was, especially, a fashion for gentlemen, propagated for instance by the novelist Edward Bulwer-Lytton, Baron Lytton, author of *Pelham, or the Adventures of a Gentleman*. For Pelham, only one colour will do. 'I do not like that blue coat', his mother tells him, 'You look best in black – which is a great compliment, for people must be very distinguished in appearance in order to do so'. And when Pelham prepares to go out for the evening at Cheltenham, he commands his man:

'Don't put out that chain, Bedos – I wear – the black coat, waistcoat, and trousers. Brush my hair as much *out* of curl as you can, and give an air of graceful negligence to my *tout ensemble*.'

If 'negligence' should seem a surprising component of evening-dress smartness, we may turn up Maxim VII in the set of 22 maxims on dress given in chapter 44 of *Pelham*:

To *win* the affection of your mistress, appear negligent in your costume – to *preserve* it, assiduous: the first is a sign of the *passion* of love; the second, of its *respect*.

Black for Pelham, then, is romantic, or Romantic, as well as distinguished. He will be a man in black, or a man in dark coloured clothes, at all times of day. So he notes, as he attaches his jewellery in the morning, 'I set the chain and ring in full display, rendered still more conspicuous by the dark-coloured dress which I always wore'. Circulating in black, as did his author also, Pelham is elegantly, yet dashingly, gloomy: the novel was an international bestseller, and helped broadcast the fashion. There is scant sign of democracy about Pelham's black, it is much more distinguished, *distingué*, though associated also with the leisured melancholy of the Romantic hero: the graveyard pose, the mysterious past, the blighted heart, the blazon of death, with all the genteel Hamletizing that was in those years *à-la-mode*.[8]

The fashion for Romantic melancholy passed away, but evening dress stayed the same and stayed black, and to explain how the fashion originated is not to explain how it was fixed. And it is the fixing of black that is in question, for black fashions may come and go, but in 1820 or so black came and did not go. As to Bulwer-Lytton and the black dinner-jacket, the consideration to turn to, as shedding relevant darkness, is that Bulwer-Lytton was a dandy: for it was not directly in a trundling of tumbrils, but rather in a stalking saunter of dandies that the plain and then dark styles were launched as fashion.

Bulwer-Lytton, or rather his creation, Pelham, was picked out by Carlyle in *Sartor Resartus* as the 'Mystagogue, and leading Teacher and Preacher' of 'the Dandiacal Sect'. Nowadays the word *dandy* might conjure the image of a colourful fop, but that is the wrong image. In the eighteenth century, the beaux and later the macaronis may have been elaborate and polychromatic: what the dandies introduced was a restrained and sober smartness. The first dandy was Beau Brummell (though the word 'dandy' was applied to him after his apogee). He lived for elegance, going for his coat to one tailor, for his waistcoat to another, for his trousers to a third. The detail most often re-recorded is that he gave a good part of the morning to tying his cravat right: when one visited, there would be a pile of cravats slightly crumpled on the floor, while the valet explained 'These, sir, are our failures'. But his clothes were simple: just trousers, waistcoat and coat, in the sparest style but of the best material and of perfect cut. 'Cut' itself, close, sharp and smart, acquires, with the dandy, a pre-eminent importance, hence Pelham's Maxim XIV, 'The most graceful principle of dress is neatness'.[9]

In the evenings Brummell would appear in a black waistcoat and tight-fitting black pantaloons: in contemporary prints he cuts so sharp a dash, he can even seem a trace satanic (illus. 4).[10] On his advice, his friend the Prince Regent wore black in the evening: and it is with the fashion-setting friendship of Brummell and 'Prinny' that one may return to the politics of dress. For though Brummell was both the Regent's and the Regency's glass of fashion, he had no blue blood in his veins. His grandfather was in trade (or possibly in service), his father was a form of civil servant, and if he was a dandy he was not exactly a snob. When a gent said to him at an assembly 'I vote for cutting all grocers and valets who intrude themselves into good society', his reply was cool, level, and evidently effective: 'My father was a very superior valet, and kept his place all his life.'[11] The reply confirms what his dress asserted – the smartness, the elegance, the perfection of taste, which was as available to the non-aristocrat as to the aristocrat. It was the style, conspicuously unflashy, of an impeccable self-respect, of a self-respect not tied to rank. He never aped the aristocrats, and on the contrary the times were such that the aristocrats,

4 'Beau Brummell in deep conversation with the Duchess of Rutland', detail from *Sketch of a Ball at Almacks*, 1815, hand-coloured etching.

and even the prince of the realm, doffed their plumage in order to ape him.

Though Brummell himself did not wear black in the daytime, he eschewed colour of any strength, and his successors – such dandies as Lord Alvanley and 'Golden Ball' Hughes – wore more regularly a black coat and black trousers, and would have been difficult to distinguish from modern undertakers. The black style of dandyism so caught on that it was copied in France, where Bulwer-Lytton's *Pelham* was cited in the *Revue des deux mondes* as 'le manuel du dandyisme le plus parfait et le plus pur'. In Delacroix's portrait, of 1826, of Louis Auguste (later Baron) Schwiter (illus. 5) one can see the conspicuously austere 'dandy' style and the fashionable melancholy converging: the portrait reflects Delacroix's admiration for the English portraitist Sir Thomas Lawrence, and Lawrence's ability to capture, as well as gaiety, 'la nuance la plus délicate de mélancolie'. The brighter coloured dandies, such as Count d'Orsay, with his sky-blue cravat and primrose gloves, come later in the century; and even d'Orsay wore, in his later years, to the great approval of Jane Carlyle, 'a black satin cravat, a brown velvet waistcoat, a [darker] brown coat and almost black trousers'. Dandyism kept returning to black, though with varying additions: the young Disraeli wore 'a black velvet suit with ruffles, and black stockings with red clocks [stitched patterns]'. When Dickens gives us a dandy, a superannuated dandy, in old Mr Turveydrop in *Bleak House*, there is no touch of colour in the picture, and little decoration. His clothes are dark; his smartness is all in his stiff deportment.[12]

The Dandy, then, is the figure who makes simple, and dark, and especially black clothes fashionable through the early decades of the nineteenth century. So, in 1838, the Paris paper *Le Dandy* advises 'English black is the shade most worn', and again, 'the black English suit with silk buttons is always required for *grande tenue*'.[13] It would be natural to see a connection between the spare style of the dandies, and the sober or sombre style of the middle-class merchants, of the 'democratic bourgeois', who were definitely in the ascendant through these years, especially since the English merchant class had been notable, for two centuries, for its Protestant, dissenting, sometimes Calvinistic, allegiances. And Brummell's background too was to some degree in trade: but still, any connection between the dandy and the businessman must have been of a chilly and indirect kind. The dandy style is not positively bourgeois (the dandy is by definition idle), but it does show it was no longer smart, in either the English or the American sense, to show one was an aristocrat. The dandy style renounces plumage, but is still a form of display: thus, the display of wealth is still present, subtilized into such evidences as the quality of the material on close inspection, and the meticulousness of cut (though Schwiter, in the Delacroix, seems not so sharp-cut as Brummell). The dandy style declines the assertion of rank, but is still a style more of assertion than of conciliation, asserting a character equivalent to rank, the character of the 'gentleman' – a term that had many inflections, but which steadily tended to emancipate itself from the ties of money and blood. Pelham's Maxim XVI runs: 'Dress so that it may never be said of you,

"What a well-dressed man!" – but, "What a gentleman-like man!" '
Gentleman-likeness is an attribute that, while far from classless, is still an honourable quality not identical to rank, which gives Pelham the advantage in his encounters with the more tawdry baronets and viscounts. In the novels of Dickens and Thackeray the idea of the 'gentleman' does become emancipated from dress and rank, and comes to mean a scrupulous modest honourableness that anyone might (in theory) possess. What the dandy style appears to show is that operation of fashion where you win by anticipating your competitor: it practises a form of, as it were, bourgeois chic, which includes beating the bourgeois at his own game. It shows, perhaps, how the rising figure of the grave, precise Protestant businessman, often, in England, of dissenting background, came finally to weigh with a dominating gravity on the consciousness of the world of the fashionable. His austere and chaste clothes are absorbed and transcended by being turned into fun clothes, and a new style of display.

At the same time it is cold fun, and a cold display. In the sterile person of Brummell himself, and in dandyism in general, there is a marked degree of narcissism and male coquetry; the dandy is a cold fish, compared to the eighteenth-century beau. The famous dandies were not famous as rakes. Those who knew Brummell 'never knew him engaged in what is called a *liaison*'; and though the Count d'Orsay shocked contemporaries by the terms on which he lived with both Lord and Lady Blessington, he was otherwise found sexually harmless. He had, according to the novelist Camilla Toulmin, 'a touch of effeminacy quite different from that woman-like tenderness which adds to the excellence of a man'.[14] Though Brummell, Bulwer-Lytton and Disraeli were not thought effeminate, other dandies were: the person of the dandy was sexually ambiguous, and both his black and his bright-coloured aspects were to be consummated in the aesthete–dandies of the later nineteenth century, most notably Oscar Wilde. The early dandies could thus be seen as pioneers of gender, exploring an identity that puzzled contemporaries by seeming at once both manly and feminine. This identity was maintained in a state of considerable ambivalence to women, and, in a figure such as Brummell, in an ambivalence with regard to sexuality itself. The dandy observed an aesthetic of strictness: and if the style had its roots in a strain of ascetic severity in English middle-class life, it certainly kept up – in a quite secular form – the severity. An important item of Brummell's toilette was the intimate washing and scouring of himself, to a degree that prefigures the later, Victorian obsession with scrubbed cleanliness. And the style of dress he inaugurated is constrained, even constricted.

5 Eugène Delacroix, *Louis Auguste Schwiter*, 1826, oil on canvas. National Gallery, London.

What Dickens emphasizes, in the ageing Mr Turveydrop, is the extreme stiffness, tightness, unnaturalness, and even pain, that his vanity exacts of him:

He was pinched in, and swelled out, and got up, and strapped down, as much as he could possibly bear. . . . As he bowed to me in that tight state, I almost believed I saw creases come into the whites of his eyes.

'He had', says Dickens, 'everything but any touch of nature'. When Carlyle guys the dandies as the fanatical adherents of a mock-religion in *Sartor Resartus*, he inevitably presents them as an ascetic and severe sect – 'a certain touch of Manicheism . . . is discernible enough' – to be compared also with fasting monks on Mt Athos. The element of severity is striking, in a cult that was also, as Carlyle stresses, a vanity: it would seem indeed that the odd fervour of 'the British Dandy' was what principally moved Carlyle to write *Sartor Resartus*, the great mock-metaphysic of Clothes.[15]

Dandyism played with discipline, and self-discipline, and the style was, not surprisingly, popular with the military. Brummell had been a military man: he was a cornet, then a captain, in the 10th Hussars. Brummell himself did not face cannons; but an outer dandy smartness was also worn as an accent of courage by those who repeatedly did confront death. Wellington was thought a dandy, and at Waterloo wore a white cravat, leather pantaloons, and a large cocked hat *à la Russe*. Wellington in turn had to reprimand the officers of the Grenadier Guards for riding into battle, on a day of foul weather, with their umbrellas raised.[16]

If certain bourgeois severities had an indirect influence on fashion through the dandies, they had also – the dandies apart – a powerful direct influence. For as well as the French Revolution, there was another great revolution that affected fashion, the Industrial Revolution. The families that prospered in the manufactures in the North of England have traditionally been regarded as sober, thrifty, industrious; they were frequently Nonconformist, learning in the dissenting academies skills in mechanics and applied mathematics which were looked down on in the public schools, but which were the prerequisite of industrial invention. Their evangelical faith could be severe indeed, like that of the 'rigid Calvinist' in Birmingham whom Coleridge caricatured – 'a tall dingy man' who 'might almost have been borrowed for a foundry poker', with black stubble, black hair, black clothes, and a face 'with strong perpendicular furrows', which gave Coleridge the sense of someone 'looking at me through a *used* gridiron, all soot, grease, and iron!'[17] Coleridge here sounds wantonly hostile, in a way

6 Frederick Barnard, illustration to *Bleak House* in the Household Edition, 1871–9, wood engraving.

that perhaps indicates how the figure of the Birmingham businessman was *seen*. By the early years of the century these families were moving to London; they retained their grave style of life, but were beginning to have a confidence in their money and their numbers that could equip them to influence fashion.

Certainly, by mid-century Industry wears black. We see this most strikingly when Dickens brings into contact, in *Bleak House*, Sir Leicester Dedlock – the traditional landed aristocrat with ancestors going back to the Conquest – and the ironmaster, Mr Rouncewell. For Dickens, the industrialist represents the new aristocracy that is taking over from the Dedlocks: he shows the takeover in the constituencies, where Rouncewell backs a candidate against Sir Leicester's in a rotten borough, and is able to bring his man in. Rouncewell is no Calvinist (the plot alleges that he is the son of Sir Leicester's housekeeper), but still at the confrontation he is 'dressed in black' while Sir Leicester, grand in an older style, wears a blue coat. In Frederick Barnard's illustration (illus. 6) Rouncewell wears not only a black coat and trousers, but a full black cravat, which means, what with his whiskers also, that we only see blackness, there is no bright glimpse of shirt. A sober suit of black is what he wears in the North, black is what he wears on the grandest occasion. His wearing black shows his respect for what he is.[18]

In the mid-nineteenth century, black is the uniform both of the fashionable world and of industrial money in the spa, the metropolis and the northern town. It becomes the general fashion. The detective, Mr Bucket, wears black. The question that lay behind the dandies comes then to the fore: why did the risen middle class wear black? There were material considerations: the atmosphere of the crowded industrial towns was thick with dust, iron-dust and smoke; there were the railways. It is sometimes said black was good protective colouring; though black, in fact, is hard to keep clean. The practical consider-ations do not account for the assertiveness with which black is worn; nor do they account for the fact that in the streets, and in the railway stations, women usually wore light colours, as Victorian paintings by Frith and others show.

Nor do the factors so far mentioned explain the power the black fashion had, both for those who wore it, and also (and including) those who observed it, like Baudelaire and Dickens. I have stressed the sombreness, as commentators within the period tended to do, but another side of the question, very relevant to the dandies, is the sexual attractiveness of black. Black makes a person thinner, sets off the face, perhaps suggests intensity. The glamorous and dashing smartness of the many men in black – the charged uprightness of some, the elongated and elegant languor of others – is apparent in innumerable nineteenth-century paintings of balls or promenades. Even in the animal kingdom, Charles Darwin noted, blackness is a feature of sexual evolution:

With the common blackbird . . . and even with one of the Birds of Paradise, the males alone are black, whilst the females are brown or mottled; and there can hardly be a doubt that blackness in these cases has a sexually selected character. . . . With several birds, in which the male alone is black, and in others in which both sexes are black, the beak or skin about the head is brightly coloured, and the contrast thus afforded adds greatly to their beauty.[19]

The beauty of black, and its play in human sexual selection, was astutely observed by Charlotte Brontë. At the party given by Mr Rochester, Jane Eyre records that 'the collective appearance of the gentlemen, like that of the ladies, is very imposing: they are all costumed in black; most of them are tall, some young.' Of the ladies, she notes that 'many were dressed in white'. It is a black-and-white picture (with certain strong touches of purple or crimson), an excite-ment of contrast. The ladies are the more mobile: 'They dispersed

7 Rolinda Sharples, *The Cloak-Room, Clifton Assembly Rooms*, 1817, oil on canvas. City of Bristol Museum and Art Gallery.

about the room, reminding me, by the lightness and buoyancy of their movements, of a flock of white plumy birds.' The men are dashing but vertical, some 'soldierly', others 'gentleman-like'.[20]

Something of the look of the scene is caught in Rolinda Sharples's painting *The Cloak-Room, Clifton Assembly Rooms* (illus. 7) which dates from earlier in the century (1817), but illustrates well the direction fashion was taking. The women are mainly in white, wearing dresses of embroidered net or lace, over silk or satin under-dresses. The white-haired man to the left is dressed in the older style, with light-coloured knee-breeches and lighter stockings. The stooping man to the right is a transitional type, wearing black knee-breeches, black stockings. The man to centre-left is dressed as Brummell dressed, in skin-tight black trousers. It is the man to the right of him, in looser black trousers, who is dressed as the century was in future to dress. The men at Mr Rochester's party would all be in his style. But clearly there is not yet, quite, the strictness of colour contrast, or the erect verticality, that were so to impress Jane Eyre. Sadly, too, none of the men in Sharples's painting are as striking or as 'beautiful' as Jane's Mr Rochester, who seems, on his late entry at his own party, the very personification of the potency of black, with a play of white and jet in his physique as well as in his clothes. Jane speaks of 'my master's colourless, olive face . . . broad and jetty eyebrows, deep eyes, strong features, firm, grim mouth – all energy, decision, will'.

Mr Rochester, of course, is a figure dark in many ways: he conceals a mad – a suffering – wife; for Jane Eyre he must be mutilated in order to be married. In human sexual selection, black is not only a smart glossy coat: it is also daring and can be dangerous, and a sign of dangerous sex. It easily alludes to death and pain, and can heighten the excitement of damaging and binding. These last 'black' values are at least in part culturally derived: witness the fact that black has not always been as important for pornography as it is in our time. That is to say, part of the sexual excitement of black derives from the values black has had in society; and that these values have been dark indeed is clear from the testimony of Baudelaire and Dickens. For them – and they both were dandies who themselves also wore black (Baudelaire more systemati-cally than Dickens) – black was not only the colour of smart men at balls, and interesting blighted young men, it was the livery of their world and the sign of a kind of dark apocalypse. Dickens connected black with cruelty not merely in the case of his obvious villains, but also and more subtly in such figures as his dark and black-clad lawyer Mr Jaggers. Jaggers is a not unsympathetic figure, and possibly is cruel in order to be kind, but certainly he has cruelty in his make-up, and is notably harsh both with himself, and also with women (not that he is responsible for Molly's scars):

'I'll show you a wrist,' repeated Mr Jaggers, . . . 'Molly, let them see your wrist.'
'Master,' she again murmured. 'Please!'. . . .
[He] turned that wrist up on the table . . . that last wrist was much disfigured – deeply scarred and scarred across and across.[21]

In *Jane Eyre* black is the colour not only of the powerful, passionate and attractive Rochester, it is the colour also of another 'master', the Revd Mr Brocklehurst:

I looked up at – a black pillar! – such, at least, appeared to me, at first sight, the straight, narrow, sable-clad shape standing erect on the rug; the grim face at the top was like a carved mask.

Brocklehurst is the headmaster of a school for girls, a black policeman of the soul who is, even more, a policeman of social attitudes. 'I wish her', Jane's 'benefactress' tells him, 'to be made useful, to be kept humble', to which Brocklehurst replies:

'Your decisions are perfectly judicious, madam. Humility is a Christian grace, and one peculiarly appropriate to the pupils of Lowood; I, therefore, direct that special care shall be bestowed on its cultivation amongst them.'

We later see him in his authority, addressing the ranks of his cropped, underfed, drably dressed pupils ('We are not to conform to nature. I wish these girls to be children of Grace'). All his effort is to train poor women to be kept in their place, brainwashed – soul-washed – into self-effacement and obedience. He admonishes his pupils and staff together, with a combination of Christian severity and sadism, fastening his gaze on any plait of hair he sees and demanding that it be cut off. His own women, however, are luxuriously appointed. His daughters wear ostrich-plumes over tresses elaborately curled, his wife is trimmed with ermine and wears 'a false front of French curls'.[22]

With the figure of Mr Brocklehurst we encounter most clearly both the politics and the sexual politics of black. It is true that the presentation of Brocklehurst is *so* black, and so stark and diagrammatic in its satire, or its attack, that one might accuse Charlotte Brontë of the black-and-white of melodrama. But the passages are written with intensity and pointedness: Brocklehurst seems not just a villain, but a portentous figure for Charlotte Brontë, a reminder that, as concerns mastery, the story of the men in black is a black one indeed, and a black one often also for women. In the light of this grimmer side to the subject, there seems point in attempting a fuller account, and reviewing in a longer perspective the history of men's wearing of black.

8 Annual Feast of the Order of the Holy Spirit, held at Pentecost, Detail from the
Statuts de l'Ordre du Saint Esprit. Bibliothèque Nationale, Paris.

2 Black in History

Black is rich and has many meanings, but still its most widespread and fundamental value lies in its association with darkness and night, and with the ancient natural imagery that connects night with death. As a pigment smeared on skin, in primitive societies in several continents, it is associated with evil, death, disease; with witchcraft and misfortune. Warriors going to war may make themselves black, both to look bigger and to frighten their enemies with the sight of death. Black may, for the same societies, have positive values also, and be associated with black rain-clouds – urgently yearned for – and with black alluvial mud, promising new germination. It may be associated with desire in the night, and fertile sensual love: a woman may blacken her vulva with soot made from tree-bark; a man may decorate his body with pounded specularite (*hara*) and be 'surpassingly beautiful with the *hara*'s blackness'. But even with peoples in person lustrously and beautifully black, who value the blackness of their skin and use black pigments as an elegant and beautiful body decoration, it seems still that the dominant associations of black as an artefact, a pigment to be applied – indeed as an ethical word and idea – are the negative ones. Black is beautiful: but still, in language and in decoration, a large space is made for negative black – for the perception, that seems hard to avoid, that death, a curse, suffering, sorcery, pollution, sin, betrayal, disease, are 'black'. This in turn may mean that the association of black pigments with sexual attractiveness is not a matter only of the natural attractiveness of a lustrous glossy blackness, but may, as in the modern West, involve a sense of danger, making black exciting, daring. Similarly, the fact that black pigments may be restricted, for instance, to people over twenty may mean that a rich deep black is (and why not?) the colour of maturity. But it suggests too that black is a colour to be handled with care, it is the colour of dark matters and not safe for everyone: several levels of initiation might be required before wearing it.[1]

Black was a power colour in civilizations centuries before patricians began to wear it in Europe. Though it is beyond the scope of the present study to range far outside Europe, it is worth noting that from the eleventh century BC to the seventeenth century AD, the emperors of China regularly wore a black tunic – black being the original colour of Heaven. And when the Emperor met his ministers formally in the morning, they all would wear black (later in the day, the ministers, like lesser officials, would wear lighter colours). So already, and long before the King of Spain in black conferred with black-clad courtiers, there was the association of black with the grave impersonality of authority.[2]

In Europe, too, its oldest association is with death, with grief, and with the fear of death. As the colour worn by mourners, its use is very old. It is sometimes suggested that the use of black for mourning was a medieval development: but its use at that time was revival, not invention. Roman mourners wore black togas (though the deceased body itself was wrapped in a white toga). And funeral processions in ancient Greece wore black.

Picturing funerals, we may imagine trooping mutes, a funereal shuffling in a gloom of grief: but originally the putting on of 'black weeds' was part of a more desperate act of grieving, of an attack on oneself for still living when the light of one's world had gone. Aeschylus's *Choephori* opens with the arrival of a chorus of mourning women: 'What is it that I see?' Orestes exclaims, 'What is this concourse of women coming hither conspicuous in sable weeds?' And the cry of the Chorus is:

Marked is my cheek with bloody gashes, the furrow newly cut by my nail: for ever is my heart fed on wailings; and the rendings of tissues ruining the vesture, make a noise through my sorrows, the breast-protecting robes being torn through smileless woes.[3]

Their black is a part of their violence of grief, which is a violence of self-defacement that includes tearing their clothes, and their bodies also. Their speech is full of darkness and night, and blood, foreboding and terror: for the darkness of this play is not the darkness only of bereavement and loss, but also of a new conjuration of murder. *The Choephori*, which opens dramatically with the entry of the mourners, closes dramatically with the entry of the Furies, again clad in black:

Orestes: Ah! ah! ye handmaids, here they are in the guise of Gorgons, in sable vestments, and entwined with densely woven snakes.

The Furies are the children of the night – in the next play, their own, they cry out 'O black Night, mother, dost thou behold these things?' But they are not grieving, the black they wear is rather the colour of the fear they inspire. We cannot identify with them, we can only flee, or labour to appease them, their colour is the colour of their rage to consume us.

As presented by Aeschylus, the values of black dress are negative only: to don black is to negate one's prospering self. And worn by others, black may be fearful, the colour of a power that may negate life and soul. These two values, of the solemn cancelling of one's self, and the terror of being cancelled, killed, are two of the profound constants of black. The first is manifest in mourning dress, worn especially by women, as *The Choephori* reminds us, and as we see in Mediterranean countries today, where women must know only self-denial following the loss of their men. The second use, the fearful, has been exploited by disciplinary forces through the ages; and the Furies are an ancient police of the psyche. The Furies are, of course, black-clad women: in *The Choephori* they seem the embodiment, in Orestes's mind, of the inescapable rage of his injured, murderous, and now murdered, mother. At the level of traditional imagination, a terrifying black figure may be feminine, as in the image of the witch (who seems a nightmare version of the widow, being normally husbandless). In real terms, in history, black frighteners have been men, reaching in our century their most horrific form, in the SS of the Third Reich. In myth, too, the supreme black frightener has been male, in the person of Satan, shown in paintings dressed in black since at least the fourteenth century.[4]

Black, in other words, seems primarily to have been the colour with which one buried one's self – the colour that, having no colour, effaced and took one's self away; the colour of what is most frightening in the dark, of the chthonic deities, of a terrifying power come from the underworld. It was the former of these values that was first to be engaged in the use of black that developed within the Christian Church. Anciently, priesthoods had not worn black. The Priestess, at the start of *The Eumenides*, says of the 'black' Furies: 'Their dress is fit to wear neither at the images of gods, nor within the dwellings of men.'[5] Both Roman and Levitical priests chiefly wore white, a colour – or rather, an absence of dye, for the material used was cotton especially – thus linked with sacred office. And Christian priests, in the first millennium, chiefly wore white, associated at once with sacredness and with purity: so St Jerome in the fourth century said priests should 'with clear conscience and clean garments handle the sacraments of the Lord'. Jerome had some reservation about white – a colour that could suggest an over-fastidious delicacy – but he had reservations too about black: a colour that, when worn by the clergy, seems already to have the value it has so often carried since, being associated by Jerome with 'an ostentatious seriousness'.[6]

None the less, black, and dark colours, were worn by priests, in the Eastern Church especially: the clergy of Constantinople were wearing black by the fifth century. In the West, black made slower progress, and even the monastic orders, some of which later were clad all in black, such as the Benedictines, originally wore undyed fabric. This might be wool, and might be in the cream/grey/brown range, though anchorites in the desert had also worn haircloth, skins, and camel hair. The ascetic life was associated with coarse dark materials; as also was mourning wear, which might be black, but also might be drab and brownish, made of dark undyed cloth. As forms of monastic dress became standardized, the use of black cloth increased. One of the formal duties of a monk was to mourn. By the eleventh century the Benedictines were known as the 'nigri monachi', the black monks. Their reformed successors of the eleventh century, the Cluniac monks, also wore black.

Not to give too black a picture, one must add at once that the celebration of the Mass itself is associated, on most occasions, with light and often highly coloured clothes. There were also, of course, monastic orders in white. The reformed form of the Cluniacs, the Cistercians, chose white, as, earlier, had the Carthusian Order. In a twelfth-century correspondence between St Bernard of Clairvaux (a Cistercian) and Peter the Venerable (the abbot of Cluny), Peter argues the case for black as against white. His main contention, naturally, is that there are more important issues than colour, and a monk may be a good or a bad monk equally in black or in white. But colour has its meaning: in white is figured 'gaudium et sollempnitas', joy and festive solemnity, it is the colour of the transfigured Christ.[7] Peter calls black the 'colorem humilitati et abiectioni', the colour of humility and of cast-away wretchedness; again he calls it a 'colorem magis humilitati, magis penitentiae, magis luctui', a colour more of humility, more of penitence, more of grief and grieving. For these reasons, he thinks black a colour more fit for regular monastic wear than the joyous white. The engraving of a Benedictine monk (illus. 9) is of a later date, but the Benedictine habit has changed very little between the eleventh century and the twentieth: the Benedictine in the engraving is a column of shadow, swathed in a black that is humble, mournful, penitent.

Though Peter prefers black, he also ridicules the way in which white monks ridicule monks in black, and black monks ridicule monks in white. The practice is absurd since, as he says repeatedly, the flock of Christ includes white and black sheep together – a relevant comparison, since monastic habits would especially be made of white or black wool. As to black, that one of the duties of a monk was to mourn, it was a duty that was natural in a religion growing from a particular death.

9 'A Benedictine Monk', engraving.

And Christian asceticism more generally includes a perpetuation of the mourner's attack on himself, an unending demonstration of unworthiness to live, as in a grief that is never laid to rest. It should perhaps be mentioned here that the black worn by Muslim teachers and religious leaders, by Muslims at Ramadan, and by Shia Muslims more generally, is specifically mourning black, in perpetual commemoration of the death of the Caliph Ali.[8]

Black was also worn, liturgically, in ordinary churches, for masses for the dead and on days of penitential fasting. From roughly the beginning of the second millennium, the Christian Church was destined to use ever less white and more black. As to large-scale reasons for this change, it may be a consideration that the world was expected to end with the first millennium, when Christ would return to administer the Last Judgment; and when this did not happen, the Western Church took more black, as a sign both of grief and of guilt. This may be an aspect of the matter. What is also true is that as the second millennium progressed, the whole large loose imperial community of Western European Christendom – which had, in different forms, been a Holy and Roman Empire – was suffering increasing pressure to break up. Slowly it did break up, into the emergent nation states. And what one finds is that the black habit moves from being the dress of enclosed ascetics to being the mark of those orders that went out into the world, and made it their business to police Christendom and hold it together, detecting heresy, and founding schools and universities to instruct all in the orthodoxy that made Christendom one.

Especially there were the Black Friars, the Dominicans founded by Domingo Guzman in 1215 and known later in the Church as 'Domini canes', the watch-dogs of God. It must be supposed they were sincere and devout, and truly great preachers and teachers. St Thomas Aquinas was a Dominican. And the aim of St Dominic himself had been to persuade, not to burn, those in heretical error: the order was first licensed as the Order of Preachers. The Order was born, however, during the crusade against the Cathars, and in 1233 was entrusted by Pope Gregory IX with the task of making inquisition for heresy (Dominic had died in 1221).[9] So individual friars, with small secretariats, rode through Languedoc, questioning sometimes whole populations of villagers, and consigning the impenitent to punishment by the secular arm, which had a tradition of burning. And when the Spanish Inquisition was formally instituted, by a papal bull in 1478, again the first commissions were given to Dominicans. The most famous of the Spanish Dominican Inquisitors is perhaps Torquemada, a potent figure in Protestant demonology, though he regarded himself as a reformer. A later castigating Dominican incendiary is Savonarola. He was not himself in the Holy Office, and indeed he was later judged heretical, and burned.

With the Black Friars one encounters the great paradox of black. For black is a negative quantity, the absence of colour: considered *as* a colour, which one chooses to wear, it is the sign of denial and loss. Yet self-denial can also give power, and authority over un-denied selves. A perfection of self-denial may make one holy, a person to be heeded with reverence and awe: and black, as the colour of power over oneself, has come to be associated with impressive, intense inwardness. How much more powerful, then, is a large group of men who have chosen to unite in the severest self-denial, and to work as one for what they think good. The Dominicans espoused poverty and were harsh on themselves, and they were formidably effective. It is perhaps with the Dominicans that black becomes a colour of power. They did not themselves man the rack or the stake, they were formally commis-

10 Workshop of Giovanni Bellini, *A Dominican as St Peter Martyr*, probably 1510–16, poplar-wood panel. National Gallery, London.

sioned to persuade and save. But if one were a captured Cathar or Waldensian, submitted to recuperation by a Dominican friar, robed in self-denial but with military back-up – as the Dominicans were to be the spiritual back-up of the Spanish and Holy-Imperial military – one might well give their black its ancient value, as the colour of those powers that strike fear into the soul.

They were reinforced in dutifulness by their own martyrology, and the painting of a Dominican as St Peter Martyr, an Italian inquisitor assassinated in Lombardy in 1252, indicates how a Dominican would be seen by Dominicans (illus. 10). For the painting, from the workshop of Giovanni Bellini and probably of the 1510s, was originally a portrait of a particular friar, not impaled or cut. But it was an aspect of the aspirations and impersonality of members of the Order – expressed also in their robes – that individual friars sought to merge with, and to personate, the saints they revered. In other portraits, individual friars will hold the attributes of St Dominic and in effect *be* the Saint, for the Saint's presence in them is what matters most about them. In this case, the palm, sword and knife are later additions to the painting, equating this friar with a holy martyr, and indicating too, with almost surreal effect, the world of holy pain within which a Dominican friar lived.

The Dominicans, it should be said, were not, like the Benedictines, clad solely in black. As the portrait indicates, their black cloak and hood were worn on top of a white cloak and hood: the white symbolizing the soul to be redeemed from black sin. Doubly clad, they were strongly bonded. For in any case to wear the same clothes as other people is to assimilate to the group and enjoy its strength: any uniform has this effect. But if the uniform worn outside is one's inner soul also, at one with other souls in the spiritual chorus, then the bonding will be deep as well as apparent. And if the uniform is double, and manifests both aspects of the human soul – the sinful and potentially damned, and the saved – then the individual who wears these clothes is not only deeply bound to his brothers, the 'friars', he is also urged to be moving always from one group to the other, from the damned to the saved, to those in the truest bond of all. To the congregation the priest's clothes are a part of the sermon, drawing them in through this picture of the soul, which will be black but may be white. Something of this ancient rhetoric of dress survives in later, smart uses of black, where it is important that a white undergarment shows at breast and cuffs, and where it is important that this undergarment – it may be a dress-shirt, it may be starched – should be shining white and 'spotless' (though its meaning has presumably shifted from a statement about the soul to the statement that the wearer is the soul of honour).

The habit had the more spiritual eloquence because, unlike much priestly dress, which only gradually assumed the form it was known by, the Dominican habit was revered as directly and divinely inspired: it was, as it were, Revealed Dress. In a painting in the National Gallery, London (illus. 11), by a follower of the Dominican Fra Angelico, the Virgin is seen presenting the habit both to the Blessed Reginald of Orléans (on the left) and, on the right, to St Dominic himself – who at the same time, with medieval economy, is seen already wearing it. As much as possible the Virgin holds the garment by its white part (pulling it out from within the black), since white is the colour most fit for her

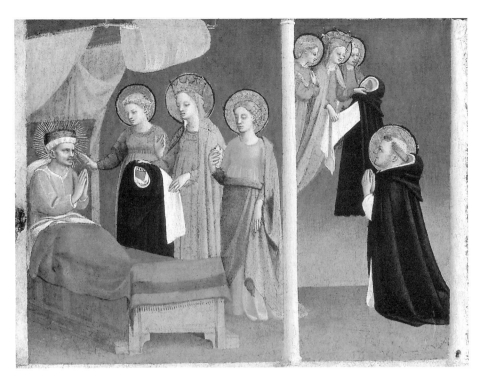

11 Follower of Fra Angelico, *The Vision of the Dominican Habit*, early 15th century. National Gallery, London.

touch. Only one thumb, on the hand that is further from us, touches the black of penance and death, though, as the kneeling figure of Dominic shows, the black cape was the dress the Dominican showed to the world. Dominicans were enjoined, in general, to practise the virtue of penance.

The Dominicans are early and formidable representatives of power reinforced by a sombre uniform. Also in black were the Augustinian Black Canons, founded in 1256, from whose numbers Luther later came. There were also the military religious orders. Black was worn, with a white cross, by the Hospitallers – the Knights of St John – and one might here more distinctly speak of black as the uniform of a strict-disciplined force, of a severely spartan holy army, since the Hospitallers, though sworn to celibacy and monastic discipline, were at the same time real soldiers, committed to redeem the Holy Land by slaughter. Specifically they wore black because they derived from the Benedictines in Jerusalem. Black was worn by the Hospitallers of St Lazarus (also founded in the twelfth century), and, more importantly, by the Spanish Order of Santiago. It must be said, however, that black was not the principal colour of the military orders, who – as perhaps befitted a crusade outside the bounds of Christendom – wore white: white with a red cross for the Templars, white with a black cross for the Teutonic Knights. And from the 1240s onwards, the Hospitallers wore red surcoats (with a white cross) when going to war.[10]

Outside the Church, few people wore black, though lepers in the fourteenth century were frequently required to wear black or grey.[11] Chaucer's pilgrims, in the 1380s or 1390s, are a many-coloured band. The knight himself is still wearing his worn crusading clothes, but his squire is embroidered like a meadow, with fresh flowers white and red. The forester wears green, the miller has a white coat with a blue hood. Many of the pilgrims wear mixed colours, the merchant is in 'mottelee', and the Sergeant of Law in a 'medlee cote'. The haberdasher, carpenter, weaver, dyer and tapister are all in the livery of 'a solempne and greet fraternitee', while the Doctor of Physic is clad in 'sangwyn', a blood-red cloth, which he wears with 'pers', Persian blue, lined with taffeta and silk. We are not told the colours worn by Chaucer's clerics, but it is unlikely that at this date they would all have worn black. Over the coming centuries, however, not only clerics but doctors of physic, sergeants of law and barristers, and indeed merchants, knights and squires, were all to take on black. One might say Chaucer's pilgrims were dressed smartly for a pilgrimage: they would have looked duller in their workaday clothes. But that is precisely the point, for it was not only work-wear, but also smart dress, that was, quite quickly, to go black.

Chaucer's own man in black is not found in the *Canterbury Tales*, but in his early poem, *The Book of the Duchess*:

> But forth they romed ryght wonder faste
> Doun the woode; so at the laste
> I was war of a man in blak,
> That sat and had yturned his bak
> To an ook, an huge tree.
> 'Lord,' thoght I, 'who may that be?
> What ayleth hym to sitten her?'[12]

What ails him is grief, he is wearing black for its oldest purpose, mourning: his lady has died. His grief is so consuming, it hardly seems right to refer to his black as dress. Rather, as Chaucer describes him, his black wear *is* his grief, the sorrow within him exposed to the world: 'to derke ys turned al my lyght'. To himself he is one whom 'deth hath mad al naked', and is not so much sorrowing, but rather has become sorrow: 'For y am sorwe, and sorwe ys y'. He is, then, different from many of the other men discussed in this book: for his black is the black

of love. Grief can only be black as night if one has loved the person who
has died.

> Our hertes wern so evene a payre,
> That never nas that oon contrayre
> To that other, for no woo. (ll. 1289–91)

Since black came to have so many un-loving meanings, it is worth
recalling its original sense, one of total desolation and loss. It is when
the love drops out of grieving that mourning becomes more show than
sorrow; then black clothes move from signifying grief to signifying the
privileges claimed by grief, and from these to signifying a broader
privilege.

As the mourners in Aeschylus are answered at the close by the black-
clad Furies, so Chaucer's man in black has with his grief, his Fury, the
figure of 'fals Fortune', who though not black-clad is dark within, 'As
fylth over-ystrawed with floures'. In a peculiar bitter twist, this Lady
Fortune is described like a mocking mime of the fair lady he has lost,
for she 'loketh faire', and he applies to her that word he used so often of
his lady: 'debonaire'. The denunciation is so vehement that one may
guess she has been appointed to embody the blacker vision of his
bereavement, the thoughts of his fair lady (who, as he describes her, is
mostly a fair body) turned to corruption, with possibly, at the back of
all, his anger with his lady for dying.

If black is the colour of grieving love, it is also the colour of the grief
of love, of the misery of a heartfelt unreturned love. When Chaucer's
man in black describes the misery he felt when his lady did not love
him, he uses just the same terms he will subsequently use for his grief
at her death. A later poem of the Middle Ages, treating the colours
worn by lovers, notes that one wears blue for fidelity, and another,
white, for purity, and another, vermilion, like blood; but:

> . . . cilz qui plus la veult avoir
> Pour son grant dueil s'en vest de noir.[13]

He who desires her most, because of his great sorrow, wears black.
And if one wants someone one loves with the same intensity one wants
back someone who has died, then the colour of mourning will be the
colour of loving too. At the same time, the fact that the beloved will still
be alive to see the lover grieving gives his black a more assertive and
aggressive character, public as it is. There is an element of performance in it, there could easily be a degree of pose. And the figure of the
lover in black – the young man melancholy with yearning love – is a type
that recurs in history, to be seen in Renaissance miniatures and heard

heaving heart-emptying sighs in the Romantic period, echoed a little later by the black dandy Pelham, contriving a negligence that will vouch for his passion.

The melancholy of the young lover in black is clear in the face of the young Knight of St John in a portrait by Franciabigio (illus. 12), a painting that may serve at the same time to illustrate the dress of the military orders. Though the Knights of St John were bound to asceticism and rigorous military exercises, this knight hardly looks either martial or spartan. His story is in the words inscribed on the parapet, 'tar vblia chi bien eima' (slowly he forgets, who loves well). The letter he holds is illegible, except for the date, 1514. Anyway, he does not look at it; he knows, all too sadly, what it says.

There was a quite different way in which, among the bright colours of the medieval world, a black-clad person might be conspicuous: when he wore black as the colour of shame. A knight who had disgraced his Order might do so. Such a figure, clad in the black of a secular penance, eats at a separate, uncovered table in the foreground of the feasting of the Order of the Holy Spirit (illus. 8). Many of black's meanings turn on its character as the colour of self-effacement: black mediates curiously between the conspicuous and that which is not to be seen. Black thus might seem the very colour of (to use Fred Davis's term) 'identity ambivalence'. In the Japanese theatre, black is worn by stage-hands, and by master-puppeteers, as a visible sign that we are not to see them; they are 'invisible' (as is perhaps the implication of the black worn by servants in the nineteenth century). The dishonoured knight, alone at the feast, is startlingly conspicuous, yet also he shrinks, and looks down as if wanting not to be noticed. And no one else does see him, no one looks his way. It is as if he were not there, though still, in his disgrace, he is centredly impossible not to see.

Black, in the early years of the fifteenth century, was little worn by princes (though black was worn for feast-days at the Polish court).[14] One may imagine the strong effect gained, in this bright-coloured world, if the monarch of a country should choose to wear black, as did Philip the Good, Duke of Burgundy (illus. 13). Philip first wore black when his father, Jean sans Peur, was murdered by the French in 1419; and his decision afterwards to wear black almost always had, certainly, an honourably menacing character: it was a signal to the French that he did not forget. He was praised by Aeneas Sylvius above all other princes for his anxiety to be avenged.[15] His black goes at the same time with his profession of Christian virtue: he offered to sponsor a crusade, and volunteered to fight the Infidel in single combat, so we may think his black clothes, and serious demeanour, contributed to his being known

12 Francesco Franciabigio, *Knight of St John*, 1514. National Gallery, London.

13 Philip the Good, Duke of Burgundy, from a dedication page of the *Chroniques de Hainault*, 1447–50. Bibliothèque Royale Albert ler, Brussels.

as 'le Bon'. In Philip's case we see the transition mentioned earlier, whereby the prerogatives of grief become with time, and by a profession of piety, the assertion of a larger grave prerogative – as if, by his great grief, Philip has seized a moral height, and by shrewd instinct stayed there, enjoying a moral fortification of his ducal eminence. All the same, his court was famous for its splendour, and his own black gowns were luxurious, often of black velvet, so his dress here is not only serious but elegant. Lean and angular, in his black, figured velvet gown, his black doublet, black hood and black hose, he is at once slightly sinister and almost dashing: we see how, as a contemporary noted, 'he walked solemnly, carrying himself well and with nobility'.[16] That he is powerful and knows it is clear not only from his face, but from that of the man kneeling to him. That he could be a grim figure too – a man to fear at a siege or on a battlefield – is perhaps suggested by the sharp edges and jagged points of his lean silhouette. His black is at once dangerous, retributive, a sentence passed on the killers of his father, and Christian, devout, judicial. He is the fifteenth century's picture of power and virtue in one, a standing, authoritative black silhouette.

That black, in Burgundy, had the gravity of authority, of power in its solemnity, is suggested by the fact that Philip's Chancellor, Nicholas Rolin – an unloved figure, not thought of as 'bon' – used also to wear black. He can be seen in the same illustration, standing to Philip's left, in a black gown more sober than Philip's, but with the chain of office round his neck. And the black gown, with its solemn impersonality, was to be the wear of many king's ministers. It was a sign of the way their selves were effaced in the ruthless enactment of the will of their lord. At the same time, and precisely through its quality of effacement, black could also be the colour of the opposite of power, of defeat, of humiliation as well as of humility. When Philip crushed the revolution of the citizens of Ghent, over 2000 Ghentish burghers processed to ask his pardon, barefoot, without their hoods, and dressed in black.[17]

Burgundy was powerful during Philip's reign, and his court and aristocracy influenced fashion through Europe. The Burgundian fashion was known for its use of black, in the clothes of men and women alike. It is clear from wardrobe accounts that black was a good deal more popular than would appear from artists' scenes alone of Burgundian life – the artists preferring, as Margaret Scott has noted, 'red, green, blue and pink, probably because black is a difficult colour to introduce into small pictures without "killing" other colours'.[18] But black clothes, or outfits including black garments, are worn in many portraits of individuals, and it is clear that in the fifteenth century black was beginning to have the value as a fashion colour that it has often had since, and indeed has now – carrying, in its smartness, the suggestions at once of importance and sophistication. The fifteenth-century author of *Le Blason des couleurs*, Jehan Courtois, a Burgundian, describes black as sad, the colour of the earth and of melancholy, and the most humble colour there is: for this reason, he explains, it is worn by mourners and by monks. None the less, Jehan observes, it is at the same time of great dignity and state, and as a result great citizens and merchants, men and women, are richly apparelled in it: 'Ceste couleur pour le présent est la plus requise en habitz qui soit, pour la simplicité qui est en elle' (This colour is at present the most popular colour in dress, because of the simplicity which it has).[19] It is, precisely, sophisticated to know how to wear, with effect, 'simplicity'. In fact, Jehan complains, black has grown so popular that everyone abuses it, turning it into curtains and drapes.

The manufacture of black cloth was still at this date arduous and expensive, making black clothing impracticable for the poor, and a mark therefore of social distinction. The process consisted, if one did not use natural black materials like black wool, in superimposing colour on colour till colour was killed: normally by boiling galls, and then overdyeing with woad and madder, to produce a colour that was still not what we would call jet-black. The process was to remain especially arduous and imperfect until the Spanish discovered Indian logwood early in the sixteenth century, at the Bay of Campeachy in Mexico. Indian logwood – 'blood-redwood from Campeachy' (*haematoxylon Campechianum*) – provided a true black: the dye was then more easily produced by boiling chips of logwood in water. But still the work was sensitive and demanding. The piles of moist chips must be left to ferment to just the right point. The material to be dyed must first be mordanted with salts of iron or tin, and the actual process of black-dyeing took five or six days. It is perhaps worth remarking that the popularity of black increases not in the years following, but in the years leading up to the discovery of a more efficient and economic dye.

Black did not lose its gravity as it became a smart colour to be used in society. In some illustrated gatherings or hunting parties, where black garments are prominent, its effect is to heighten the smartness of those present. But even to those figures it also adds weight (in comparison with the pure-colour scenes), while it is clear from many portraits that black was a colour worn, or chosen for the occasion, to show that one mattered and to show one was serious. The young man holding a ring in a Netherlandish painting of the 1450s (illus. 14) is fashionably smart (as we see also from the fur that trims his gown), but also sombre. Indeed, the background to this portrait is filled with the reduplicated design of rain falling from clouds, with the words repeated 'har las uber gan' (Lord, let [this] pass over), a motif known in other fifteenth-century paintings, and one associated also with the complaints of a lover. He is certainly a young man enduring tribulations.

To what extent the black of the ducal court, Philip's black, promoted a wider use of black, and to what extent Philip himself was conforming to a broader turning of taste towards black, is difficult to assess now; probably both factors worked together reciprocally. It may be pertinent, in the background both of Philip's black, and of black dress in Burgundy more generally, that Burgundy, in the mid-fifteenth century, was at the apogee of its power. Black, it would seem, can easily represent not just gravity but important gravity, or the gravity of importance, alike for princes and for nations: the more so if, accompanying the importance, there is an apprehension that this power cannot last. Burgundy did not last. It was an aggregate of separated territories, and by the end of the fifteenth century it was broken again in parts.

The more immediate question however is whether one should draw a connection between the gravity of the black clothes, and of the grave

56

14 Netherlandish School, *A Young Man Holding a Ring*, probably 1450–60, oil on oak. National Gallery, London.

faces of the Burgundians, and the large-scale grimness of life in those years – years of prolonged warfare (including the Hundred Years War, which began in 1338), with a recent history of famine and of hideous epidemics. One is obviously wary of connecting the taste for wearing black, which grew steadily through the fifteenth century, with the Black Death itself, which had raged in the middle years of the fourteenth century. Fourteenth-century dress was noted not for its sombreness but on the contrary for its colourfulness, and especially for its fashion for parti-coloured clothes. Often the divide had run down the centre, so a person was black on one side but red on the other, or blue on one side and white or green on the other. There had been, at the same time, a mistrust of such clothes, and in a ferocious passage in the sermon of Chaucer's parson – a passage not in its Latin source – parti-coloured dress is attacked with ascetic fury:

And if so be that they departen hire hoses in othere colours, as is whit and blak, or whit and blew, or blak and reed, and so forth, / thanne semeth it, as by variaunce of colour, that half the partie of hire privee membres were corrupt by

the fir of seint Antony, or by cancre, or by oother swich meschaunce. / Of the
hyndre part of hir buttokes, it is ful horrible for to see. (ll. 426–8)

(And if they divide their hose in different colours, like white and black, or white
and blue, or black and red, and so on, then it seems half their genitals are
erupting with ergotism, or are cancerous, of have some other catastrophe. The
rear view of their buttocks is hideous to see.)

Evidently such scathing criticism told, or answered to a change in
popular mood, for dress certainly grew more sober and sombre at the
turn of the century. In particular, the white or red halves of clothes
departed, while the black halves grew to engross whole garments.

It is also true that latterly through the fourteenth century, and even
more through the fifteenth, a cult of death developed, a taste for
decorating tombs with a realism of decay – melting flesh, skulls, rib-
bones, worms. From 1400 on, the Dance of Death is elaborated, in
which three dead men dance with three living men. They are to be seen
now in paintings and carvings, but the Dance was also performed, for
instance by the order of Philip the Good at his mansion in Bruges in
1449. Towards the end of the century, the dancing corpses are
replaced by a single dancing skeleton: Death come in person to partner
each of us in turn. It is in the context of these practices, in which the
hideous over-familiar facts are accommodated by means of morbid
play, that one may understand the extraordinary funeral procession
that Philip the Good had mounted for his father. Not only did Philip
and his retinue wear black, they also carried black standards seven
yards long, and the procession as a whole held two thousand black
vanes. Philip, on another occasion, wore a mantle of black velvet that
hung from his horse to the ground. It is not surprising, in this society, to
see the colour of mourning distributed through the clothes of the
fashionable.

As the serious faces in portraits show, life was a grave matter. A new
wave of piety, the 'devotio moderna', had for its ideal the austere and
pure-hearted imitation of Christ's life. Many of the portraits of the
time are of the donors of altarpieces (illus. 15), seen kneeling at the
edge of a scene of the Nativity – joining, in effect, the shepherds and
the Magi – but wearing, as the other figures do not, black gowns that
are fashionable and rich, and which also suggest gravity, humility,
piety. Their faces, in deep prayer, are solemn indeed, as they
contemplate their fate should intercession fail. If one wants to see a
connection between the surrounding conditions of life and the
developing habit of wearing black, one is perhaps on the safest ground
in suggesting that the way in which recurrent evils (war, famine,

15 Simon Marmion, *St Clement and a Donor*, probably 1480s. National Gallery, London.

plague) were taken to heart was as punitive visitations, just scythings by God, enforcing a conviction of human sinfulness. Death is thought of in terms of sin, and sin in terms of death; and the tonalities of an anxious penitential piety are repeated in the clothes people often wear, which, however rich, smart and important, still carry in their colour a precautionary humility, and can serve, *sotto voce*, as 'sinne's black memory'.[20]

Such figures at prayer, gravely dignified in black, with preoccupied, unillusioned, unoptimistic faces, recur in the paintings of the Flemish artist Hugo van der Goes. He evidently had within him what he painted so often in others, for he himself succumbed to religious melancholia. He represents uneasy and troubled souls, in an art that itself is eerie and troubled, one disturbing to look at with its odd shifts of scale. By the end of the fifteenth century, when black had become the most popular colour in dress, Burgundian culture both wanted, and was equipped, to gaze directly at its fears. It is no surprise that it is at this date, in northern Brabant, that Hieronymus Bosch appears. In his pictures, fears, demons, lusts and horrors are brought clearly into the light, and colour is sometimes poisonously important; but still he makes a large and glistening use of black. His demons, who are at once fallen angels and human sins, shine against black backgrounds, or teem through black buildings on fire or in ruins, or clamber from black wells and cracks in the ground, or wear black hoods, black bucklers, black capes, or have black beaks, black claws, black tails, or *are* black toads, or black birds, or black thin slithering snake-lizard creatures close-twined round bare human legs. Brutal-imbecilic faces float in black space, mocking Christ in thorns. When he paints the ascent to the Empyrean, Bosch invites us to look up a long illuminated tunnel, which turns the black night it is cut through into a solid like coal. The whole Bosch vision, which is one vision of the inner world of the Burgundians, was greatly admired by at least one later black-clad monarch, Philip II of Spain.

In the central panel of Bosch's *Temptation of St Antony* (illus. 16), not only is the Saint mocked, but the penitential black robes he wears are in effect mocked by the black cowls and hoods worn by several of the monsters. One, just above him, with a snout that turns into a trumpet puffing smoke, wears a hood like a monk's. A garrulous head to the right of the Saint wears a black cowl and white wimple like that of a nun (the bodiless head next to it wears a well-to-do lay form of black hat, like a black turban, similar to that worn by the young man in illus. 14). Just behind Antony, a boar-snouted bravo in black swaggers alcoholically, with a knife by his purse, a lute under his arm, an owl on his head;

16 Hieronymus Bosch, *The Temptation of St Anthony*, central panel from a triptych, 1510, oil on panel. Museu Nacional de Arte Antiga, Lisbon.

while below the Saint, leaning on the wall, a small lounging figure wears an intriguing anticipation of the nineteenth century's top-hat. Out of this cauldron of follies and appetites the Saint himself looks directly to us, with a weary, guarded but steady look that offers a measure of reassurance: while his right hand, raised in blessing, also points into the inner chapel, in which we see a small crucifix, brightly lit in the deep darkness.

There had been a tradition in Christian iconography of sometimes representing Christ – especially the transfigured and dazzling Christ – at the centre not so much of radiant light, as of a deepening, intensifying darkness. This tradition was based on Jewish belief, according to which God dwelt in ineffable darkness, but had been Christianized by such authorities as Dionysius the Areopagite. Dionysius said 'the divine darkness is that "unapproachable light" where God is said to live', and spoke of the 'intangible and invisible darkness of that Light which is unapproachable because it so far exceeds the visible light.'[21] This unimaginably deep darkness, burning as it were with holy fire, gives a benign character to the religious use of blackness. It is a different black from that of the monk's habit, which is penitential and mournful. We may recognize something of this dark-blazing character in the darkness in which Bosch's crucifix hangs, when we see that beside the crucifix there stands the figure of Christ himself – the risen Christ, who, here, is wearing black: intensely deep black, deeper, for instance, than that of the Saint.

With the risen Christ as a man in black, we come to that use of black that embodies Christian mystery. This figure does not occur frequently in art, but may be seen in Holbein's painting on the theme of 'Noli Me Tangere' (illus. 17), in which a melancholy, pale-faced Jesus has cast back a blood-red cape to show a black gown, which, with its leather girdle and full sleeves, resembles the habit of a monk. The Magdalene also has a black gown, presumably in mourning for Christ; and Christ's black may represent human sin and death, still worn by him since he has not yet ascended. Christ may be shown in black at earlier points of the Passion. Bosch gives him a black robe in the *Carrying of the Cross*: and it is not inappropriate that Christ should wear, during his humiliation in the Passion, dress that in the Middle Ages was proper to penance (though penitential dress might also be white). At an earlier

17 Hans Holbein, *Noli Me Tangere*, 1524, oil on wood. Royal Collection, Hampton Court Palace, London.

point still in the narrative, and presumably in anticipation, Christ is shown wearing black in Van Dyck's painting of the arrest in Gethsemane. The Christ in Bosch's *Temptation* has, however, both risen and ascended, so while his black robe may allude to the human death he has shared with us, it may also represent – merged as it is with the surrounding darkness – the divine darkness in which God dwells. Nor might one be surprised to find that the God of Bosch was a God discovered in deepest night.

There is reason to relate the black fashion of the fifteenth century to the special grief and disturbance of the time – a period that has been called 'the most psychically disturbed era in European history', and of which Johan Huizinga has said 'no other epoch has laid so much stress on the thought of death'.[22] At the same time, there is a further, urban complication to the argument. Burgundy was a ducal, chivalric society: but still its power was based on its wealth, and its wealth was not so much based on the aristocratic estates, as on the wealth of its merchant cities in Brabant and Flanders. And it is in the fifteenth century that it becomes a regular practice for merchants to wear black.

Chaucer's merchant did not wear black, nor did his shipman, and some successful merchants in Burgundy dressed richly and colourfully and behaved like small princes. This was adventurous behaviour, since burghers, however rich, were still seen by the court as commoners and 'villeins': while a black gown could be at once rich, modest and serious, and therefore was eminently prudent wear. Because it is colourless, black can seem to a degree classless, and can therefore serve as a good protective colour for an ascendant or would-be élite. The merchants were hardly yet an élite; but the merchant's black gown could acknowledge his importance and dignity without violating the prerogatives of a sumptuary society. In *Le Blason des couleurs* Jehan Courtois says that black, worn by a merchant, signifies 'loyaulté', a word that, in the present context, one must take to mean trustworthiness, fair dealing. Black is serious and means business, in more senses than one: black will not let you down, or default on its word (its word is its bond). And in the late-medieval period, long black gowns, with their associations of penitential piety, might also have served as a form of talisman to protect their rich wearers from the taint of usury.

The thinking of the merchants on the subject of colour is possibly reflected in the decision of certain Jewish communities, early in the fifteenth century, to wear black. Though both the Hasidim, and rabbis generally, are now associated with black clothes, black had not anciently been important in Jewish dress, which in the biblical period had been especially of white linen (stitched, for richness, with violet, purple and scarlet yarn). Under Greek and Roman influence, Jewish dress was chiefly white, the natural colour of its material, which was mainly linen and wool. Under the Muslims, Jews often wore yellow; in the West they wore the fashions of the country they lived in – with, after 1215, the obligatory coloured badge (often yellow, but sometimes blue, red or red-and-white). More than from their clothes' colours, they were known by the hats they wore, which were round, wide-brimmed, with a pinnacle in the centre, and, again, most often yellow. It is fair, therefore, to conclude that when Jewish communities opted to wear black, they were responding not to meanings of black in their own tradition (though black had long been the Jewish colour of mourning), but rather to the perceived values of black in Western Christendom. These values are made explicit in the agreement on a self-infliction of sumptuary laws reached at Forli in Italy in 1416:

In order that we may carry ourselves modestly and humbly before the Lord, our God, and to avoid arousing the envy of the Gentiles, we decree that until the end of the above-mentioned term [the ten years from 1416 to 1426] no Jew or Jewess shall be permitted to make a *foderato-cinto* [a form of cloak], unless it be black. . . . No man shall be permitted to wear a silk or velvet *giubetta* [again, a cloak] except in such manner that it is completely concealed. . . .[23]

There is an inner and an outer garb. The inner garb may be luxurious and coloured, as outer garbs normally are, but if so it must be hidden totally: so one wears, like a knowledge, an *invisible* show of wealth. The visible outer wear proclaims: Don't see me, except in so far as you see that I am humble and pious. Especially, it is the role of black to deflect the resentment growing wealth could provoke.

It is clear that merchants, whether Jewish or Christian, both kept their place and knew their value. The pale, grave dignity of the successful merchant, dark-clad supplier to the richly dressed quality, is to be seen most famously in the Arnolfini marriage portrait of 1434 (illus. 18). Giovanni Arnolfini, an Italian living in Bruges, supplied the ducal court of Burgundy with silk and cloth of gold (for not all the court wore black): he supplied the court, in other words, with its richest colours and damasks, and was himself of great wealth, but still, in his marriage portrait, he wears an over-garment of low-toned purple-brown material, while his hat, doublet, hose and shoes are black. His shrewd, grave face is almost priestly.

It may seem a contradiction, having suggested that Duke Philip's black became the black of power, to suggest that the merchant's black was in any sense classless. But black is a paradoxical colour, ostentatious through the show it makes of renouncing ostentation. The man in

64

18 Jan van Eyck, *The Marriage of Giovanni Arnolfini and Giovanna Cenami*, 1434, panel. National Gallery, London.

black can sidestep the social staircase because he seems to take his stand on a moral stair instead, and indeed to take the high ground precisely through humility. And if merchants wore black to be grand without offence, so too might princes wear black to show that, though princes, they also had humility. Black was certainly a moral colour, signifying (according to Jehan Courtois) justice in judges, simple honesty ('simplesse') in women, penitence in sinners, as well as trustworthiness in merchants. Of course, the moral appearance needed the support of actual, visible, audible devotions, from merchant and monarch alike. Philip the Good did not neglect these, and Jehan's own liege lord, Alfonso, King of Aragon, Sicily and Naples, who 'mostly wore black clothes' – and plain black too, he was 'seldom seen clad in silk or brocade' – might pray on his knees before an invited ambassador many hours of the night.[24] Alfonso, it would seem, was a truly pious man with a true humility: every Holy Thursday he would wash the feet of as many poor men as he had years of life, 'washing them in proper fashion: drying them afterwards'. It is true, too, that piety was power in the late Middle Ages, and humility had authority. As to the new bourgeoisie, it is hardly likely that rich merchants washed the feet of poor men: you perhaps needed to be a king for such an act to 'tell'. But merchants made sure they were seen to be devout, as is clear from the many representations of them already mentioned, on their knees at the edges of the sumptuous alterpieces they had donated.

With the arrival, in Philip's court, of the successful solemn merchant in black, one has something like the basic cast of black power-dressing in European history: priest, prince and merchant, each gravely authoritative, and reinforcing by their co-presence their shared right to respect and reverence in a disturbed grim world. Indeed, black-gowned merchants were emerging as important figures in many European states: and in one above all, which could be said to be, more purely than Burgundy or any northern state, the merchant state *par excellence*, Venice.

Venice, that opulent, congested imperial capital, was chiefly a black-clad city. Like other Italian city-states, it liked to see itself as a New Rome, and the long gown worn by the well-placed Venetian was called a toga: but it was a black toga. The black was mercantile, for the patricians of Venice differed from the nobility of other states precisely in having been, from time immemorial, 'in trade'. The noblest were those who had the longest investment in transit shipping to and from the Lagoon. From the age of twenty-five, both patricians and the secondary class of citizens were expected to wear, both winter and summer, and both when out and at home, the black 'toga' or 'vesta'. They wore a *bareta*, or cap, that was normally black; and they carried over their shoulders a strip of black material, the *becho*, a long-tailed hood that, over the years, had become a kind of stole to be carried by the privileged. Underneath these garments the Venetians wore black hose. In 1498 a visitor from Milan noted that 'nobody stirs abroad in any other costume; it is a style certainly very suited to grave persons. They all look like Doctors of Laws.'[25]

A group of patricians, proud but unassertive, close, stand on the left side of Titian's *Presentation of the Virgin* (illus. 19). Though the others wear black, the patrician in the foreground wears the red senatorial toga, against which the black *becho*, which they all would be carrying, shows clearly. Evidently he leads the patrician delegation to this sacred event. Venetians did not wear black on every occasion: at processions and feast-days they were encouraged to wear red, or cloth of gold, or another colour, *paonazzo*, the hue of which is not now certain, but which was within the blue–violet–crimson range. Processing in their damasks and silks, the patricians were figures of opulent colour. It is clear, however, that, luxuriously rich though Venetian life became, the

19 Titian, Detail from *The Presentation of the Virgin in the Temple*, 1539, oil on canvas. Galleria dell'Accademia, Venice.

Venetians did not easily give up their black – to judge at least from the occasions when notable grandees, even a Vice-Doge, were fined 100 ducats for wearing black where they should not have done (for instance at the Gran Conseio).[26] Black and red are the dominant colours in Venetian paintings, which usually show formal and festive occasions, when more red than normal would have been worn. Black was also worn by Venetian women, and by the many nuns Venetian marriage customs produced.

The Venetians themselves attributed their traditional colour to their piety and virtue. So Sansovino records that 'the Fathers, being strongly attached to religion . . . had recourse to a species of costume suitable to their gravity, and such as might indicate modesty and respect'.[27] Whether or not the Fathers – the *padri* – were, as Sansovino claims, 'filled by a solicitude to do no wrong to any man', Venice certainly was noted for its evidences of piety: its many religious processions and festivals, the patriarchates and many bishoprics within its gift, the many pieces and bits it had of the True Cross and saints (in addition to the alleged remains of Mark), and its many priests and nuns. It was observed that Venetian piety was far from disinterested, and perhaps

existed mainly as the invocation of blessings on, as even the conse-
cration of, the Venetian trading interest. Pope Pius II complained of
the Venetians, 'except for the state, which they regard as a deity, they
hold nothing sacred, nothing holy. To a Venetian . . . that is pious
which increases the empire.'[28]

Presumably there is truth in this. Faiths sustain societies, and
Venetian Christianity gave divine sanction and providential destiny to a
corporation of conquering merchants who at intervals had wars to fight
with the Ottoman, the Holy Roman, the papal and the French empires,
and who faced all the time, individually, the particular anxieties of
seaborne trade:

> *Bassanio:* But is it true, Salerio?
> Have all his ventures failed? What, not one hit?
> From Tripolis, from Mexico, and England,
> From Lisbon, Barbary, and India?
> And not one vessel 'scape the dreadful touch
> Of merchant-marring rocks?
> *Salerio:* Not one, my lord.[29]

We might see Venice as a disparate, tumultuous, wary community
which used not only its laws but its strict emphatic faith to nerve and
confirm itself in sober aggrandizement, a form of social church (to
borrow Durkheim's term) in which, like certain later Protestant states,
emphatic dutifulness to God and virtue was closely combined with
devotion to business, trade and profit and devotion to international
power. In other words, we see in Venice an early form of the
conformation – to recur in seventeenth-century Holland and nineteenth-century England – of the Christian-commercial empire in
black. The black materials may be rich, the finest velvets, but still the
black is devout as well as mercantile: it shows restraint, gravity and
seriousness about one's business, which *is* above all business, but
which, one trusts, is the Lord's business too. One would need to be
serious – one would need to pray – if one believed one had, in a
dangerous world, a commercial–imperial destiny.

The Venetians had worn black before kings or courts wore black,
and it may be that this serious colour gave dignity to a nobility that
lacked imperial or papal patents. An element of the grave pride of the
serious merchant, grown rich through industry and careful risk, owing
allegiance to no higher caste and no hereditary king but proudly
administering his own republic, shows in the long straight folds of the
'toga' – which at this point one might think of not only as Christian and
Mercantile, but also as Republican Black. Venice was not, of course, an
egalitarian republic, any more than the Dutch republic was later to be,

and within the republic, black, though widely worn, and worn by women as well as by men, was worn as something like a prescribed uniform only by men of wealth, of standing, of power in the society. Its gravity is again the gravity of authority, of office, of the magistracy of a class, enacted in the innumerable actual magistracies which composed a Venetian patrician career.

One must be careful and continent in attaching meanings to colours, so it is only lightly and warily that I note how one might align the civic appearances of Florence and Venice – the relative colour and brightness of the Florentines and the sombre dark of the Venetians – with the contrast pointed to by Jacob Burckhardt when he spoke of 'Florence, the city of incessant movement, . . . and Venice, the city of apparent stagnation and of political secrecy'.[30] It would be simplistic to identify the wearing of black clothes with an inclination to secretiveness (one might more aptly, regarding the Venetians, cite the prudent guardedness of a merchant aristocracy). Still, the Venetians had a great deal more of a reputation for keeping matters 'dark', including transactions on their overlapping and interlocking committees, than did their chosen imperial predecessors, speaking out with echoing rhetoric, in senate and forum, in togas that were white.

20 Agnolo Bronzino, *Portrait of a Young Man*, probably 1550–60, oil on wood. On loan to the National Gallery, London.

3 From Black in Spain to Black in Shakespeare

By the beginning of the sixteenth century, black was definitely seemly, and could be more or less smart and stately, or more or less reserved, at the wearer's initiative. It was popular in other city-states than Venice. So when Castiglione, in *The Courtier* (1528), addresses the question of what 'the raiment of our courtier' should be, he observes, in Hoby's translation:

> Moreover I will holde alwaies with it, if it bee rather somewhat grave and auncient [sober], than garish. Therfore me thinke a blacke colour hath a better grace in garments than any other, and though not throughly blacke, yet somewhat darke, and this I meane for his ordinarie apparrell.[1]

The courtier defers in his dress, as in other matters: his black or dark clothes have a respectful and self-respectful seriousness in dutifulness, which makes the 'grace' of his courtly loyalty. Black is for his daily wear; over armour, the courtier should have 'sightly and merrie colours', and his garments for pleasure should be 'pompous and rich' (*pomposi e superbi*). But black might be worn by all at court, and by princes as well as by courtiers. The identity of the young man in Bronzino's portrait of the 1550s (illus. 20) is not certain: the sitter may be one of the elder sons of Bronzino's main patron, Cosimo de' Medici, Grand Duke of Tuscany. What is certain is that he has distinguished rank, and though his self-possessed gaze is cool, what especially he shows, in person and dress together, is the 'better grace' of black, which could be worn by young men without needing to imply grief, and could be attractive as well as serious.

Interestingly, at the point where he comments on the courtier's clothing, Castiglione notes the power aspect of dress. He regrets that Italians dress after the French, or Spanish, or Dutch styles, rather than having a style of their own; and he reads this imitativeness as a sign of national weakness, even as 'a prognosticate of bondage'. He cites the case of Darius, who, 'the yeare before hee fought with Alexander, had altered his sword he wore by his side, which was a Persian blade, into the fashion of Macedonie'. When Castiglione speaks of black, it is less clear whom he thinks the Italians are imitating, since he thinks black is intrinsically graceful for courtiers (though few would have worn it 100 years earlier). The principle inspiration is indicated, however, when he says of the clothes Italians wear that, excepting 'triumphes, games, maskeries', 'I coulde wish they should declare the solemnitie that the Spanish nation much observeth, for outwarde matters many times are a token of the inwarde.'

It was Spain, more than any other nation, that was to be responsible for the major propagation of solemn black both throughout Europe, and in the New World. Spanish black was fed by a grave native tradition, and also, very directly, by the black of Burgundy. For the Emperor Charles V (King Charles I of Spain) had originally been the Burgundian Charles of Luxembourg. He was descended from Philip the Good as well as from the Habsburgs, and when he inherited the Spanish throne in 1516 he brought with him to Spain the black-dominated style of the Burgundian court. In Titian's portrait of 1548 (illus. 21) we see the ageing Charles dressed wholly in black: indeed, he seems almost to have no shadow, as though, in his black, he himself is shadow. And he has dressed, for this portrait, very much as Philip the Good had dressed, since the sole decoration he wears, over the black gown, is the Order of the Golden Fleece that Philip had founded. The Golden Fleece was to develop a talismanic character. Charles's father had made him a member before he reached the age of one; and the wearing of black clothes with the Golden Fleece was to become almost the uniform of the Burgundian/Habsburg monarchy. There is an identity in colour spanning two centuries between the clothing Philip the Good wore in the 1450s; the clothing Charles V wears in Titian's portrait; the clothing Philip II wears in almost all the portraits of him; and the clothing worn by Philip IV in portraits by Velázquez.

It is Philip II, however, the son of Charles V, who is something like the pivotal man in black in Europe's history. He ruled Spain from 1556 to 1598 and could seem the archetypal sinister monarch, brooding in plain chambers in the bleak Escorial, procuring murders and patronizing the Inquisition, himself in black and transmitting his will through a secretariat of Black Friars. This was the austere monarch whose taste in art was for the demonology of Hieronymus Bosch. It may, therefore, give some recuperating touch of reality to recall that he struck his contemporaries as a man 'who looked very ordinary, dressed in black just like the citizens'.[2] The citizens were known as the *gente de capa negra*, and had their own tradition of dignified solemnity, preoccupied as they were with the special honour of each native and Christian

21 Titian, *Charles V*, 1548, oil on canvas. Bayerische Staatsgemälde-sammlungen, Munich.

Spaniard. Philip is modestly dressed even in the sharp-lit apocalyptic vision of El Greco's *Dream of Philip II* of *c.* 1580 (illus. 22). The picture shows Philip's political and religious universes. He kneels with the monarchs and prelates of Europe, while above him, through a break in the stone-grey clouds, the souls of the blest hymn the Holy Name, in a tender light: rose with pale gold. Immediately at Philip's back (he kneels, on his cushions, on the very brink of it), a ravenous, black-dog Hell Mouth yawns, within which the green-grey bodies of the damned writhe in a kind of white ice-fire. And between Heaven and Hell Mouth, in the company of monarchs wearing cloth of gold and ermine, Philip kneels seriously in sober, plain black clothes.

If Philip dressed like a citizen – that is, like a merchant – this is

22 El Greco (Domenikos Theotocopoulos), *The Dream of Philip II, c.* 1580, oil and tempera on pine. National Gallery, London.

perhaps not surprising, since he also was much preoccupied with money, worrying (necessarily) about the costs of court life as well as of the Armada, and about the servicing of the loans he had raised, which threatened bankruptcy on an imperial scale. Since Spanish society was notoriously divided between the courtly feudal world and the mercantile world of the cities, it perhaps shows good instinct on Philip's part to wear a style of black that associated him – the supreme aristocrat – with his somewhat menaced urban citizenry. But the black clothes that Philip was noted for wearing were not in origin mercantile or citizenly. He was extendedly in mourning for his second wife, Elizabeth de Valois, whose death, it is clear, afflicted him with real grief (for two weeks he was wholly shut away, refusing to see even pressing state documents). And there were other deaths, in particular that of his daughter Catalina in 1597, at which he wept, raged and howled in a way that made his courtiers worry for his life. But, as had Philip the Good earlier, he continued to wear black beyond the natural term of mourning, and clearly the colour was congenial to him for more reasons than grief.

Why, in later life, Philip wore black so consistently, it is not possible to know for certain, since he never himself explained his dress. He was interested in astrology, and Geoffrey Parker notes that

he may, for example, have preferred to wear black because this was a colour associated with the planet Saturn, with which the king felt special sympathy; certainly the treatise on magic known as the *Picatrix*, of which he possessed a copy, claimed that dressing in black clothes was an effective means of drawing down on the wearer the beneficent influences of Saturn.[3]

There is no proof that this was Philip's motive, but it is a relevant consideration: if any human practice is 'overdetermined', it is clothing. Whatever Philip's particular reasons for wearing black, he would hardly have done so without having some support from a larger tendency of fashion. This, it is clear, there abundantly was. And plain black, with its impersonality, was appropriate wear for a serious governor, who wished to show his strict power was disinterested and just. Philip, working in close conjunction with his secretary, the Dominican priest Diego de Espinosa, replicated the 'picture' of a century before, when Philip the Good, wearing the colour of mourning beyond the period of mourning, governed Burgundy with the black-gowned Nicholas Rolin at his side.

One must not, then, make Philip II too sinister a figure, as is done when he is characterized as a cold spider at the heart of a black web of schemings. He liked gardens and Dutch tiles, and Titian as well as

Bosch, and in his later years he worked not only with Black Friars at his beck and call, but also with his daughter Isabella beside him, drying ink and passing him papers. He still was harsh, and given to harsh pleasures. The hunting he relished as exercise consisted of watching from a hide while a herd of deer was netted in front of him, to be torn to pieces by the royal dogs. Even the work of the Inquisition, of which he was a zealous patron, afforded him a serious spectatorial pleasure. Perhaps he did not say the words that Tennyson gives him in his play *Queen Mary*:

> The blood and sweat of heretics at the stake
> Is God's best dew upon the barren field,
> Burn more! (v. i. 46–8)

But Philip liked to preside at *autos-da-fé*, and mused to his secretary about them: 'It is something really worth seeing for those who have not seen one. If there is to be an *auto* during the time I am [in Toledo], it would be good to see it.'[4]

Philip's patronage of the Inquisition included a zeal, informed with a genuine but merciless piety, to see its work extended. The Inquisition tried 'social crimes' such as bigamy, homosexuality and fornication as well as heresy: it was, in effect, both the thought police and social police throughout Philip's possessions. If Philip, in wearing black continuously, was in part taking to himself the colour of the Church, he was specifically adopting the colour of (as it were) the Church Disciplinary, of the Dominican Inquisitors. With the utmost sincerity he used religious faith for social control, in effect making himself not only the supreme magistrate, but the supreme priest-policeman of his strict Christian state. If, then, his black dress had a citizen-like modesty, in keeping with his desire to be addressed simply as 'Sir' ('Señor'), and not as 'Your Sacred Catholic Majesty', this modesty was of the colder kind. It went with his willingness (unlike his widely journeying father) to be a nearly invisible, though most potent, monarch. Philip preferred to stay in Spain, by choice in his simple chambers in the Escorial, governing through intermediaries, and doing as much business as possible on paper rather than in person. His almost permanent black dress fits his desire to recede, to be inconspicuous, a monarch who might be mistaken, as he sometimes was, for a citizen or minor official or priest, but who could still, unseen, assert a power as frightening as that of his God.

Because Philip wore black constantly, his courtiers did also. Perhaps they had not all his severity; black was certainly a good foil for the rich jewellery the gold of the New World made fashionable. Black became the uniform of officials and men of power throughout Philip's possessions – in New Spain as well as Spain, and Naples as well as the Netherlands. The already part-black Burgundian style was in effect both eclipsed and consummated in the new black of Philip's extended administration. Spain was the most powerful nation in the world, and therefore not surprisingly it set international fashion. Nor is it remarkable that the wearing of black should have spread in a period of political change that saw the increasing utilization of a cruel state religion to regiment a resistant empire. Black often has been the colour of asceticism, and asceticism is discipline whether it is inflicted by a hermit on himself, or by an overlord on a nation. One may note here that Philip's great fear was that the Spanish dominions would break apart, as earlier there was fear of Christendom fragmenting. Actually, thanks to Philip's exertions, the Spanish Empire (as it was later called) had still a certain lease of life. Even so, if one is thinking of black and power, it seems one may associate black not so much with power securely enjoyed as with a resolute assertion of power within a period of political anxiety. And one should perhaps see all the features of Philip so far mentioned – the harshness, the religious zeal, the mistrust of his ministers, the procured murders, the empowerment of the Inquisition, the resort to astrology, the desire to withdraw in shadow and to withdraw from view, and indeed the desire to wear black clothes – as the many reflections of a dominating and lifelong anxiety. And Philip and his government had real enemies, including the Turks, the Dutch, the French and the English, while they also believed they had enemies within the gates: the Spanish Moors, Spanish Jews and Protestants. They had reasons for anxiety.

This is not to suggest that black-clad officials and men of power must necessarily be anxious. Once a black-clad hierarchy has become established, black seems rather the expression, by all concerned, of their acceptance of authority's bonds; an acknowledgement, both by those in command and by those subdued to them, of a scale of obligations in the power-relation. But Philip, it is clear, was a workaholic monarch who worried all his life, and was famous too for mistrusting everyone. And if one looks back to the portraits of Philip's predecessor Charles V, and considers Charles's subtle face, with its weight of grave care, one may associate his black too with the anxiety as well as the momentousness of empire. Indeed, the cares of empire contributed greatly to the decision of Charles V, at the age of 55, to abdicate the entirety of his monarchies, dukedoms, principalities and Empire, and retire to a monastery. The principal ceremony of his retirement had been his abdication as ruler of the Netherlands on 25

October 1555, in the great hall of the castle of Brussels: Charles attending all in black, with the Order of the Golden Fleece round his neck.

It is perhaps at this point, having in mind black's association at once with power and with care, that one may note a further association, formed in these years, which has since kept a strong (not universal) hold, one visible more recently in some aspects of both Russian and American dress – in, for instance, the dark suits and black coats and attendant dark uniforms of the presidential entourage. This is the association of black not only with power, but with centralized power and with the power of the state. My purpose in mentioning Russia, however, is, at this moment, to digress. Muscovy had its own historic associations of autocracy and black, which I cite for comparison with those of Spain. For in the years (the 1560s) in which Philip was encouraging the Dominicans in their inquisitorial vigilance, Ivan IV, the Terrible, was in the process of establishing his own distinct regal domain, the enormous Oprichnina, and his personal guard, the black-clad 'men apart' or Oprichniki. Ivan swore the Oprichniki to absolute loyalty, a loyalty that must take precedence over friends, parents, family, and rewarded them with estates and immunity from the law. They wore all-black uniforms and rode black horses, bearing on their saddles the emblem of a dog's head and broom, signifying that they would hound traitors and sweep them away. At Ivan's command they burned, raped and killed.[5]

Scourging Ivan's enemies, and with a licence to wreak havoc on their own account, the Oprichniki must have appeared a sinister troop. There can be no doubt, however, that Ivan's first purpose in making them wear black was to institute them as a kind of secular priesthood. The Orthodox clergy had worn black since the fifth century, and in Russia a man in black was first and foremost a man of God. Ivan swore on the Cross the Oprichniki to loyalty, and intended them to serve him with the absolute devotion with which an ascetic serves the Lord. Indeed, within the dense forests of the Oprichnina, within the fortified town he had built at Alexandrovsk, within its palace surrounded by moats, walls and ramparts, Ivan lived with an inner core of 300 Oprichniki whom he called the Brotherhood: he gave them monastic offices, and governed them as 'Abbot'. The arrangement sounds like a parody of the Orthodox vocation, but the Oprichniki were commanded to attend real matins, and were imprisoned if they did not, while Ivan himself prayed in the morning for two or three hours. Later the Oprichniki feasted and drank, while Ivan stood at a lectern reading from sacred books. When he himself dined afterwards, he argued theology; following dinner he might visit the torture-chambers to witness an interrogation. At ten he retired, and blind men told him stories till he slept; at midnight he was woken, for divine service. The whole schedule seems in part an exaggerated mockery of Philip's rule, commanding his Dominicans and praying and confiding with them, withdrawn in his vast Escorial. On Ivan's part it was an extraordinary combination of religious parody and piety, of carnival and autocracy, of holiness and savagery. From this distance in time it looks like cruel madness; but at all events it shows, precisely by the extreme it presents, how the long association of black dress with the Church could be augmented and enlisted for secular duties, and could work in the interest of ruthless absolutism, turning the disciplines of piety into totalitarian rigour.

The Oprichniki were perceived by their victims as dark in the sense of terrifying and evil. Prince Kurbsky, in his denunciatory biography of Ivan, consistently calls them 'the children of darkness' – men who wear the black livery of the evil they do. And it must be supposed that, with his odd double perspective on the Church, which meant he could simultaneously mock and yet imitate monastic life, Ivan intended his private priesthood, black-mounted and black-clad, to have the authority of priests and yet be feared as devils: an intention that would show a grisly, but shrewd, power-psychology on Ivan's part, perhaps not wholly out of place in a religion where an omnipotent God has assigned to merciless demons a policing and punitive role in his Universe. The Oprichniki demonstrate, in the starkest combination so far seen, the opposite aspects of black. Black is the sign of their selflessness in devotion to their work, yet the nature of that work, the persecution of the Tsar's enemies, makes them for their victims (which included whole classes of the population) a black terror, Death riding not on a pale horse but on black horses to catch you.

This is perhaps the most horrific aspect of black: when the man in black has effaced, with his own self, his common humanity, in order to be the utensil of a power. The Oprichniki were, however, men apart. Ivan himself is never represented in black, and black does not seem, at this date, to have been fashionable in Muscovy to the degree it was in Western Europe. That fashion – to return from my digression – was a European usage that was frequently thought of as being, and to a good extent was, the Spanish fashion. It was the fashion of the most powerful nation in the world, that nation being at the same time, famously, a 'closed society'. Enforcing that closure, the native Christian population, and its aristocracy and monarchy especially, had increasingly employed the Church, in the form of the Holy Office, to subdue, discipline, terrorize and execute Spanish Jews and Spanish Moors, whether or not they converted to Christianity, and, more recently, Spanish Protestants or supposititious Protestants; and to suppress Protestant books and many humanist books, and indeed many forms of study and science. One should perhaps not too hastily identify the large-scale black fashion with the anxious repressiveness of a closed and ferociously conservative society; but the manner of Spanish dress does suggest such a link, for the Spanish black fashion was at the same time a fashion for rigid, constricting, encasing clothing, which costume historians universally call 'severe'. It tended to adopt forms 'imitating the protective and hostile forms of armour'.[6] A particular feature was the high tubular collar, topped by a starched ruff, which gave the Spanish gentleman no option but to be literally, rigidly, erectly stiff-necked. Philip is wearing such a collar in *The Dream of Philip II* (illus. 22). And this style embodied in the most literal way the Spanish conservatism and opposition to change: that is, it did not change, or changed hardly at all, while the fashions of other nations evolved, so that by the later seventeenth century, Spanish gentlemen in portraits, in their traditional capes and breeches, and high-collared black jerkins, were living costume history museums. Foreign visitors to Spain registered as remarkable the constancy and ubiquity of black. The Frenchman Antoine de Brunel, travelling in Spain in 1655, found it a land of black, the women wearing black lace or black veils, even pages wearing black, not coloured liveries as in France; while foreign envoys visiting the Spanish court were advised that they must put on black clothes before they could see the King.[7] The monarch at that date was Philip IV, who loved the arts and yet also loved the black style. It was he who, in 1623, had formally made black official and obligatory for Spanish court dress. In Velázquez's portrait (illus. 23), made at about the time of Antoine de Brunel's visit, Philip is in black, and black surrounds him. He gazes coolly, with distinct hauteur and a Habsburg thrust, as it were from a tank of blackness. We know his body is there from scattered decorative glimmerings, and of course from the gold chain that carries the badge of the Golden Fleece.

Spanish black is, then, clearly the colour chosen by Spanish society. Peter the Venerable had, 400 years earlier, commented on the special enthusiasm of the Spanish for the use of black in mourning: he was struck by the fact that they not only all wore black at a funeral, but that they even blackened their cattle.[8] One should neither exaggerate nor underestimate the exacerbating effect of the particular initiatives of Philip II. And Philip himself, as noted earlier, had chosen to dress in a style that chimed with, but did not initiate, the style of his citizens. The

23 Diego Velázquez, *Philip IV of Spain c.* 1656, oil on canvas. National Gallery, London.

black capes of the citizens could not, however, have influenced international fashion, while the style of the Spanish Court, and above all of Philip and his clerical and aristocratic administration, did have Europe-wide repercussions. Perhaps what is most striking is that this fashion was transmitted especially to those states most in conflict with Spain – England and the Netherlands: so that from having been the uniform of Spanish Catholicism, black was to become, complementarily, the uniform of anti-Spanish Protestantism. The black-clad combatants look back at us still, from portraits of the Spanish by Velázquez, of the English by Van Dyck, of the Dutch by Hals and Rembrandt. This colour-sharing by enemies should not surprise us, if we consider the bitterness of those wars, and the extent also to which at that time political and national conflict expressed itself in rival forms of sacrificial religion. A wartime religion will be ascetic, and asceticism itself has perhaps always been as much a military as a religious virtue: an operational necessity for an army, or a community, or an individual fighting for life in terrible straits. One must be willing to die to hope to win. Military discipline itself, as against an armed rampage, became obligatory in this period.

Soldiers themselves deal in real death; they have hardly needed to wear black, and often have been far from doing so. When, in the ancient world, soldiers fought hand to hand, there was little purpose in being camouflaged; and perhaps some advantage, for heroes at all events, in being dauntingly splendid and gorgeous. So Caesar had been pleased to lead an army of dandies. And at all times colour is courage, it makes a brave show, and furthermore it identifies your side – and also, of course, deserters: if you saw your colour running the wrong way, you shot at it. The colour red may suggest courage and heart, the roused blood keen to act. It may also, like black, play on fear: your own blood is vulnerable to a man made of blood. But soldiers, too, might wear black: often black lacquer was laid on dress armour, as in Robert Peake's portrait of 1593 (illus. 24). It had, in fact, been the practice, since the Middle Ages, for suits of full armour to be painted, and often they were treated with black paint, which protected the metal, and presumably also gave them now the menace, now the protective 'invisibility', of the man in black. The Black Prince was so-named, in some accounts, because his armour was black.[9] The soldier in Peake's portrait exploits the values both of black and of the colours red and gold. The gold edging to each plate and scale of the armour suggests this soldier's splendour and martial nobility; the red scarf tied in a bow on his arm is perhaps his courage, and his willingness, too, to shed his own or his opponent's blood. His black is his discipline and severity, also his intensity, as he threatens death to others and also has made of death an armour.

The wars in which Spain was increasingly involved were the inevitable breaking out, in savage secessionist and supressive violence, of developing divisions, national, ethnic and economic, which were manifest also in the opening of the greatest rift in Christendom, the separation of the Reformed from the Catholic Church. The war that was fought on the ground with cannons and pikes, at the cost throughout Europe of acreages of corpses, was fought also in the mind, in language, in Heaven. It was fought by churches and church organizations that increasingly, in the stress of conflict, resolved

24 Robert Peake the Elder, *Portrait of an Unknown Military Commander*, 1593, oil on panel. Paul Mellon Collection. Yale Centre for British Art, New Haven.

themselves into institutional machines, indeed into 'institutions' in something like the modern sense, with economies and rigidities of command-structure, and a new impersonality of organization. It is hardly surprising, then, that both sides, Reformation and Counter-Reformation, came to use the same livery of disciplined, death-ready, ascetic self-effacement – that they came to wear black. On the Catholic side, the main warrior institution had been specifically founded on the military model, in that Ignatius of Loyola, with his soldiering past, wanted the Society of Jesus both to be, and to be organized as, the army of the Church (though the General of the Society was an administrator-general, and was not meant to carry, as he has subsequently been presented as carrying, a military title).[10]

Though the Jesuits now are famous for their black, and though their 'General' came to be known as the Black Pope, it had not been the intention of Ignatius for them to wear black, or any assertively priestly garb. He was as strongly opposed to monastic uniform, as to choirs, chanting and the use of the organ, 'for these things which adorn the divine worship of the other orders, we have found by experience to be no small hindrance to us; since we devote a great part of the day and night to the bodily and spiritual care of the sick'. Ignatius had, in other words, his own un-aesthetic, practical-minded, generous form of puritanism, which included his dismissing as spiritual luxury the customary observances of priestly asceticism, such as 'fasts, scourgings, going bare-footed'. Among these addictive priestly distractions he included 'fixed colours of dress'.[11] The Vatican was less willing for the Jesuits to be so individual, and though the Society avoided a rigid specification of dress – and allowed different wear in different countries, so that Jesuits in China dressed as mandarins – it soon became the practice for Jesuits in Rome to wear black, with a distinctive black cape having a high 'Roman' collar. The strong connection of the Society with Spain meant that Spanish black – clerical style – had a strong influence also; and the fact that the Jesuits were so potent in education, with an extraordinary record of achievement in the founding of schools and universities, meant that many were known by the black gowns they wore as tutors and doctors. These considerations led in due course to the general wearing of black by Jesuits, making them, with the Jansenists, the two main forms of 'noir' in Stendhal's *Le Rouge et le noir*. Given their dress and their militancy together, their willingness to use worldly tactics in dealing with the world, and indeed their willingness, in spite of their constitution, for political intervention, it is not surprising they came to be seen by their opponents as a kind of insidious half-secret army, 'black' in something like the modern, distinctly sinister sense. In the Protestant perspective, they are the fanatic praetorian élite of Romanism, a private papal army and police at once – for they were placed directly at the Pope's command – wearing (when not insidiously disguised) the black of the assassin. It is necessary, then, to remind oneself of the difference between the ministering and educating Society of Jesus and the Church's earlier black-caped disciplinarians, such as the Dominican Inquisitors, and the Knights of St John, who were a good deal more prompt with the rack, sword and stake. The Jesuits, too, practised formidable severities, but they are also represented by the wonderful figure of Francis Xavier, moving on from country to country through the Far East, evangelizing and healing: skipping barefoot through snow with a Siamese hat at a jaunty angle, while throwing an apple up and down; or, very shortly before his death from exhaustion, presenting himself, arrayed in silks, before the Japanese *daimyō* Hirado, and upbraiding him to his face for his sodomy while at the same time placating him with the gifts of a grandfather clock, a music-box, a musket with three barrels, and a cask of port wine.

If it was true of Ignatius, it was true too of the other great reforming individuals, that it was not their purpose to enjoin their followers to wear black, or any set vestment or uniform. Though the Reformation, like the Counter-Reformation, came to wear black, it was rather because several strains of blackness, running through European history, converged irresistibly in the new urgencies. Martin Luther – who saw the Church itself as a form of spiritual clothing – wore a black habit originally because he was an Augustinian Canon. The theology of that Order had a pessimistic cast, reflected in their penitential robes; and an element of Augustinian pessimism, tied with a melancholy personal to Luther, runs through his later thought on human depravity.[12] And, as virtually every portrait shows, he continued throughout his life to wear black. He did so when preaching, as in the portrait by

25 Lucas Cranach the Elder, *Martin Luther*, 1547, oil on panel. Stadtkirche, Lutherhalle, Wittenberg.

Lucas Cranach the Elder (illus. 25). It is the black of the inner human sinfulness, of depravity, worn without in honest contrition; and worn no longer with ritual intention, but rather as the avowal of a personal grim inwardness with human failing.

Calvin, for his part, wore a black gown because he had trained in law: so it chanced that he and Luther wore the differing liveries of the two kinds of 'clerk'. If Ignatius had sought a military discipline, Calvin imposed the strictest legal rigour on the fate of souls, on the government of churches, indeed on the will of God, who seems turned by predestination from being the light of Heaven into a great fixed-term contract with an infinity of non-negotiable clauses. But it was not the practice of either Calvin or his lieutenants to ordain specific vestments for their ministers. Their ordinances were rather negative, a discouragement of clothing that suggested priestliness, of garments 'defiled with infinite superstition'.[13] There was no prohibition on the black gown itself, which many people wore, but rather on white priestly overgarments, such as the surplice. So when, in the 1560s, the Bishop of Winchester, Robert Horn, sent the Swiss Protestant Heinrich Bullinger the Order of Administration of the Church of England, Bullinger replied:

I do not approve of the linen surplice, as they call it, in the ministry of the Gospel, inasmuch as those robes copied from Judaism, savour of popery, and are introduced and established with injury to Christian liberty. . . . I wish, however, that the habit in which the minister performs Divine service should be decent, according to the fashion of the country, and have nothing light or fantastic about it.[14]

As a result the Reformed minister, while not wearing a black habit, would wear in the pulpit the black gown of the educated clerk or doctor. Though this practice had originally the shock of a man preaching in ordinary clothes – so Bullinger himself was praised because he mounted to the pulpit 'in seiner burgerlichen kleidung' (in his citizen's clothing) – the black gown and white ruff did become associated with the office of the wearer. In time they became the new priestly uniform, a new black form of sartorial authoritarianism, as the dress of citizens and even doctors changed. More generally, it seems in the nature of the self-effacement of black that it easily suggests an office as much as the office-holder, and thus has something like an inherent tendency to move from being a fashion to being a uniform (as happened also with the dress of lawyers). Moreover, the privileged position of the preacher in a Reformed church meant that his dress, however sober and 'ordinary', was likely with time to become privileged dress. The 'position' of the minister was literally a matter of being in

26 Anon., *The Temple at Charenton*, 1648, watercolour on vellum. Det kongelige Bibliotek, Copenhagen.

the centre (since there was no altar), and of being set often at a great height in the air. In a watercolour of 1648 of the 'temple' at Charenton (illus. 26), the tiny pastor in black, preaching very much from on high, repeats in his clothing the background black of the prodigious tablets of the Old Testament Commandments set in the roof above him. Doubtless he echoes in his sermon Calvin's own words from the pulpit: 'We are never so guiltless in the eyes of God that he does not have good reason to punish us'; he will, perhaps, conclude with a prayer (like Calvin's) that 'it pleaseth Thee to make our labour prosper'.[15]

It became Protestant practice so consistently to wear black in the pulpit, and so frequently to wear black outside it too, that it would not be wrong to consider the consonance between the black dress of 'Puritans' and their cast of spirituality. And what may be true of Luther seems very likely true of many Lutherans and Calvinists, of Dutch regents and English Roundheads – that their austere black style does

27 Wolfgang Heimbach, *Portrait of a Young Man*, 1662, oil on oak. National Gallery, London.

reflect the intuitions of Protestantism, and in particular the conviction of depravity. The soul is deep-dyed in sin, and has no option but to wait for a Deliverance no human act can hasten. All one may do is live devoutly, according to the attitude that Max Weber was to call 'intramundane asceticism'. While one must be wary, in trying to read faces in portraits from the past, one can I think see, in the 'expression' of this period, the changing timbre and tone of European inner life. If one looks from Bronzino's Italian young Catholic of the 1550s (illus. 20) to Heimbach's young Danish Lutheran of 100 years later (illus. 27), one sees a quietly lively sensuousness, perhaps something sweet, in the first young face that seems quite extinct in the later, which has by contrast a cold mistrustful guardedness, not amiable and not happy. Indeed, the Lutheran's mouth shows more displeasure, is more downturned, than that of the middle-aged Philip IV (illus. 23). One can, of course, find diverse moods in portraits, and there are laughing Calvinists painted by Frans Hals, but still one can see, taking many pictures together, the changed temper of the life of northern Europe, with a gain perhaps in introspection, and a loss of supple vivacity.

Theological and introspective issues apart, one might suppose, as to lay fashion, that a severe style will be in part a response to harsh circumstances: it is the style that will survive a prolonged period of pain, and bitter struggle, and constricted and endangered living. That was certainly the situation of the Dutch Republic in its first 100 years, surrounded by enemies, at war with Spain, and under constant guard also against the sea, which periodically reinvaded the land. Its political system was a challenge to monarchies, its Protestant faith a challenge to Catholicism, and its growing wealth a challenge both to enemies and to allies alike. In its isolation it maintained its morale through the incessant reaffirmation, by its pastors and regents, of its privilege and righteousness as the new chosen people of the Lord. It was a society united by recurring anxiety, and it is hardly surprising that many people, both men and women, and at all levels of society, wore the same colours, the black with white ruff, worn also by the preachers of the Reformed church. That the Dutch Golden Age was mainly a black-clad age we see in its paintings, from portraits to genre scenes.

The four officers of a guild in Van den Eeckhout's painting of 1657 (illus. 28) are not severe like Heimbach's young merchant. They are less solemn indeed than many of the gathered regents in group portraits by Rembrandt, and it may be that their geniality is related to their being officers of the Coopers' and Wine-rackers' Guild. St Matthias, the patron saint of coopers, is depicted in a frame behind them holding his axe. The picture reflects at the same time their serious importance, and their importance as members of a tradesmen's guild, rather than as aspirants to noble station: especially it shows their serious solidarity, their desire to dress identically, with seriousness and propriety (though the younger men wear the collar that was in process of superseding the older man's ruff). This is the first illustration in *Men in Black* to show such standardization.

Black in the United Provinces seems different in character from the power-black of the Spanish Empire. One might, as Simon Schama has suggested, think rather, on Durkheimian lines, of a society united in a kind of social church.[16] It was a society marked by extremes of wealth, and a rich Amsterdam merchant might display his prosperity, and his enjoyment of it, in the materials of which his clothes were made, in velvet, satin, silk. But even the rich wore, predominantly, the same colour that most people wore – and the poor wore black fustian. The Dutch clung to their black through the remainder of the seventeenth century, even while the brighter fashions of France percolated through the countries round them. They seem a nation for whom black was important, not as the robe of hierarchic power, and not simply as a

tribute to Calvinist morality, but rather as the broad, defining cloak of the whole threatened and thriving, beleaguered and warring, anxious and thrusting new republican bourgeois nation.

England by contrast seems at this date a country containing within itself the wars that raged through Europe, with its successive regimes of Protestant, Catholic and Protestant again, its alternating waves of religious persecution, its swings between Catholic monarchism and Calvinistic republicanism. In England, too, the different black fashions of Europe converge. English puritans, within the Church of England but of Calvinist allegiance, refused to wear the surplice and would wear only the black cassock. Black was fashionable at court, where it was a Spanish fashion (and Mary I had been for a time, though hardly more than technically, the wife of Philip II). It is true that in Elizabeth's court there was a good deal of white-with-black, the black then taken to symbolize constancy, the white the virginity of the Virgin Queen. But chief ministers of the Crown wore black – as did William Cecil, 1st Baron Burghley, and as had Thomas Cromwell, 1st Earl of Essex. Theirs is the black of dedication, of the man made over wholly to the enactment of the princely will he serves. The portrait, after Holbein, of

28 Gerbrand van den Eeckhout, *Four Officers of the Amsterdam Coopers' and Wine-rackers' Guild*, 1657, oil on canvas. National Gallery, London.

29 After Hans Holbein, *Thomas Cromwell, 1st Earl of Essex*, 1533–4, oil on panel. National Portrait Gallery, London.

EARL OF ESSEX.

Cromwell (illus. 29) suggests the narrow shrewd ruthlessness of a man more than glad to sink his self in that enactment. Black was also the fashion among Protestant merchants, for Calvinism took strong root in the London business community. English parliamentarians would wear, when sitting, the black gowns they also wore for serious occasions in general (as, it should be said, did councillors and senators elsewhere in Europe, notably in Genoa). Parliamentary black was apt, for the parliamentarians too were on serious business, and on God's business also they believed, which was later to include cutting off the King's head.

Officers and gentlemen might wear colours other than black, so of course might tradesmen, farmers and sailors: black never became universal for men in the way that it virtually did in the nineteenth century. Even the most zealously puritan communities, for instance those who had crossed the ocean to Massachusetts, did not necessarily wear black. They wore 'sadd' colours, which could include low-toned greens and greys as well as black (though they did wear the black felt steeple hats tradition has always placed on them).[17] It is still true that many kinds of black coincided in late sixteenth- and early seventeenth-century England. That even the smarter wearing of black was the smart surface of an anxious life, where no head was guaranteed safe on its shoulders, may be suggested by the wary sad-eyed faces in many portraits of those years. Charles I had in his wardrobe, in 1634, ten suits of black satin (to seven of cinnamon, six of fawn, four of green), which doubtless were smart, in the richly lustrous style we know from Van Dyck's portraits of many nobles of those years, but which also were fit wear for a monarchy fallen on serious times.[18]

A black prince

To move from history to literary history, there appeared at the beginning of the seventeenth century England's symbolic man in black – Prince Hamlet. Shakespeare's own faith, if he determined on one, is opaque to us, but there is reason to think that his father was Catholic, while his mother came from a notable Puritan family. So in Shakespeare the opposed severe extremes of Christianity, which had both recently been persecuted as the political tides changed, met. There is in his work a strain of ascetic severity and revulsion; and Hamlet can seem to mourn a larger evil than his father's death:

> Tis not alone my inky cloak, good mother,
> Nor customary suits of solemn black . . .
> That can denote me truly. . . .
> . . . I have that within which passeth show,
> These but the trappings and the suits of woe.[19]

In his appearance and stage-presence, Hamlet draws on several currents, for in his black he must have some resemblance to a young prince of the Spanish court, and of many courts; and equally to a young notable in the Calvinist and Lutheran states. I should like at this point to draw closer to *Hamlet*, since it is, I think, still a living text we all half-know by heart, and one in which many elements of the black tradition converge, so that in knowing Hamlet we may glimpse the dark side of his time.

Hamlet's decision, for instance, to continue wearing mourning, when the court has abandoned its weeds for a wedding, is at once perceived, both by the court and by the audience, as dramatic and ominous, and involving more than grief. It is certainly disconcerting to Claudius, who takes him to task for persevering in obstinate condolement, calling him impious, unmanly, and incorrect to Heaven. As the killer of Hamlet's father, Claudius is right to be uneasy, for the natural way to read Hamlet's black clothes would be as contemporaries read the weeds of Philip the Good, another princely son of a murdered father: that is, as evidence that Prince Hamlet did not forget his father's death, did not forgive it, and would avenge it when he could. In modern criticism Hamlet – or Shakespeare – is sometimes reproached for being un-Christianly vengeful. But it is clear that in the late Renaissance, at least for princes, the avenging of a father's murder was a duty and a virtue. Philip the Good was praised in his lifetime for sustaining a war for sixteen years in order to avenge the outrage done to John the Fearless.[20]

At the same time, Hamlet's black is of grief, and in prolonging his wearing of it, he follows not only Philip the Good but also Philip II, the latter mourning both his father and, even more, Elizabeth de Valois. Hamlet, too, extends his mourning in such a way that the prerogative of grief becomes a moral prerogative also, as if by virtue of his bereavement he is more righteous than colourful worldlings. And Hamlet is full of moral contempt for ordinary people – drinking and hollering and whoring. It is as if grief can make a person a righteous black-clad priest. Hamlet is not, of course, pious, as were Philip II and the black-clad Alfonso, King of Aragon, Sicily and Naples; but Hamlet's nihilistic account of life in this world, and of his own depravity, conforms to that which an ascetic might give (black also was penitential):

I am myself indifferent honest, but yet I could accuse me of such things that it were better my mother had not borne me. I am very proud, revengeful, ambitious, with more offences at my beck than I have thoughts to put them in, imagination to give them shape, or time to act them in. What should such fellows as I do crawling between earth and heaven? We are arrant knaves all, believe none of us. (III. i. 122–30)

Black was humble – the colour of humility and self-effacement – and Hamlet uses his black wear in a way that both Philip and Alfonso did: as a form of dressing by which the aristocrat or prince could achieve an emancipation from social hierarchy, without materially disowning its advantages. It was a way of escaping censure for possessing the highest of worldly baubles, royalty, which of course worked more successfully, the more genuine the prince was in his humility. It seems that Philip II had a real humility, and also, for all his recessiveness, something of the common touch: he could dress like his citizens, pray with his citizens, and at intervals he enjoyed being mistaken for one of them. Alfonso, a considerably more attractive monarch, certainly had humility. It does appear that the princes who wore black tended to be, whatever melancholy features went also with their black, princes good at conversing with their subjects. Hamlet can enjoy joking with gravediggers, not saying who he is – so that black, the colour of invisibility, is the colour of incognito too, as it also was for Philip II. Most famously, Hamlet will talk with the players, in a humane, humorous, attractive way, while still telling them what to do, and even how to act.

A notable feature Hamlet shares with Philip II and Alfonso is his amused contempt precisely for elaborate courtly dress. So Osric, when he appears, is for Hamlet a 'waterfly' and 'lapwing', and his flourishes with his hat both amuse and irritate the Prince. Hamlet can laugh at Osric's display, because wearing black is dressing down, not up. In the same spirit he mocks Osric's jargon of courtliness:

Osric: The King, sir, hath wagered with him six Barbary horses, against the which he has impawned, as I take it, six French rapiers and poniards, with their assigns, as girdle, hanger, and so. Three of the carriages, in faith, are very dear to fancy, very responsive to the hilts, most delicate carriages, and of very liberal conceit.
Hamlet: What call you the carriages?
Osric: The carriages, sir, are the hangers. (v. ii. 144–54)

The humour of these exchanges, where the Prince mocks the courtier from the standpoint of common humanity, is in the same spirit as the many anecdotes in which Alfonso exposes the vanities of the rich-living and the affected. Given Hamlet's whole situation, it is not surprising that his remarks belong especially to Death's jest-book: many of Hamlet's jokes are as black as his clothes, and not only in the graveyard scene. For instance, he says of a wholly innocent man whom he has himself killed in a rash mistake:

King: Now, Hamlet, where's Polonius?
Hamlet: At supper.
King: At supper? Where?
Hamlet: Not where he eats, but where a'is eaten. A certain convocation of politic worms are e'en at him . . . (iv. iii. 16–21)

Hamlet's humour shades into the caprices of his 'antic disposition' – itself, it has been suggested, not only a disguise but a needed relief. Alfonso, King of Aragon, did not put on an antic disposition; he simply was famous, at one and the same time, for wearing black and for making jokes, so that even jokes he had not made were attributed to him in jest-books.[21] This figure, of the jesting prince in black, joining humanity at once through his humble clothes and through his humour (even when grieving), is one of the more attractive aspects of black.

Perhaps the salient characteristic of Hamlet's dress of humility, and its cooperation with his self-image, is that, at key points, he really seems not to think of himself as a prince, but rather to be imaginatively identified not only with citizens but with people of lesser degree, and in less happy situations:

> For who would bear the whips and scorns of time,
> Th'oppressors wrong, the proud man's contumely,
> The pangs of dispriz'd love, the law's delay,
> The insolence of office, and the spurns
> That patient merit of th'unworthy takes,
> When he himself might his quietus make
> With a bare bodkin?   (III. i. 70–76)

How much experience would a late medieval or Renaissance prince have of whips and scorns, oppressors, proud men, delaying lawyers, rude officials, ignored merit? These lines would seem to show a generous largeness of feeling in Hamlet – supposing, that is, that Shakespeare is himself remembering, not forgetting, that it is a prince who is supposed to be speaking (for a poet-actor trying to live mainly by the pen would have his knowledge of whips, scorns, oppression, pride, rude officials, ignored merit).

None the less, there is an element of game-playing, and perhaps of falsity, when a prince chats more or less incognito with subjects, as there is in any modern politician saying warmly 'Hello how are you?' to people he does not know. For all his friendliness, Hamlet is a prince, and knows it and shows it, putting Horatio in his place when he needs to, and revealing quite a different and un-humble perspective when he is unexpectedly challenged by Horatio, after he has related his clever joke-murder of two former companions:

> *Horatio:* So Guildenstern and Rosencrantz go to't.
> *Hamlet:* Why, man, they did make love to this employment.
>   They are not near my conscience, their defeat
>   Does by their own insinuation grow.
>   'Tis dangerous when the baser nature comes
>   Between the pass and fell incensed points
>   Of mighty opposites.   (v. ii. 56–62)

This brings us to the darker aspect of Hamlet himself, for these are two more corpses to be put to Hamlet's account, as it comes to seem, by this stage of the play, that his black clothes are the sign not only that he mourns the death of his father, but that he is himself a Death, and will bring death to numerous others, as well as to the murderer of his father. In this he resembles Philip the Good, who killed many others while he delayed confronting his enemy. The humble princes in black were not self-effacing to the point of passivity: they were active, each stands before a mound of corpses. Philip II killed very many; Alfonso of Aragon was also a warrior. Hamlet cannot approach their score – he never mounts the throne – but certainly he is dangerous to know, killing indirectly, or directly but by mistake, in what proves to be a grisly

30 Eugène Delacroix, *The Murder of Polonius*, 1834–43, lithograph. British Museum, London.

black-comedy of errors, not only Ophelia but her whole surviving family, and not only sentencing old schoolfriends to death, but seeing his mother die too before, at very long last, he manages to kill his father's killer. As Horatio says to Fortinbras: 'So shall you hear of . . . casual slaughters'.

There are no contemporary illustrations to *Hamlet*, and indeed no illustrations at all of the play for more than 100 years after it was first performed, so I have taken the liberty of sidestepping history and enlisting Shakespeare's best-of-all illustrator, Delacroix. *The Murder of*

Polonius (illus. 30) catches the tragi-comic spirit of the play, with its elements of grotesque, the feet of Polonius just showing beneath the arras. The young mother holds back her son, who, in this illustration, turns from being what in previous scenes he was, the 'sweet prince' (Delacroix had a woman model for him), and begins to show an aspect of the demonic: caught on the edge of becoming a killer, a person who has conjured death and, maybe, invited damnation. His mouth and face harden, as one hardens before hitting. His eye is strange, almost a fish-eye, both large and with something dead about it: an eye faced with a problem like a cliff, intractable, unsurmountable.

One might say that Hamlet was unfortunate, no killer by nature: the black inside him is grieving not murderous. But he is willing to accept the role of a Death, taking it as an appointment on the highest authority:

> . . . For this same lord
> I do repent; but heaven hath pleas'd it so,
> To punish me with this and this with me,
> That I must be their scourge and minister.   (III. iv. 174–7)

Being a scourge was almost a vocation, just as Tamburlaine was 'the scourge of God'. 'Black' matters are not clear-cut. Black – blackness – is a negative quantity that makes a positive impression, and consequently, almost inevitably, black has tended, in matters both of value and of dress, to be paradoxical. In particular there is a recurring irony, where black may be shown to be not so black – as in dashing, stylish, attractive black, or respectable black, 'decent black', or pious, humble, godly black – and yet does prove, after all, to have sinister elements. As humble, penitential self-punishing black becomes stern judicial black that will tie people to pieces of wood and burn them. In Hamlet's case we see a person suffering evil and bereavement, and precisely through taking these things so to heart, becoming infected by death and death-dealing. So, on the moral level, the Hamlet who suffers such grief for his father – and who, in his grief, is tolerant of his father's sins – becomes Hamlet the preacher, standing in moral tyranny over his mother:

> Nay, but to live
> In the rank sweat of an enseamed bed,
> Stew'd in corruption, honeying and making love
> Over the nasty sty!   (III. iv. 91–4)

For criticism Hamlet has proved paradoxical: for Goethe he was 'a lovely, pure, noble and most moral nature', while August von Schlegel concluded that he 'is not solely impelled by necessity to artifice and dissimulation, he has a natural inclination for crooked ways; he is a hypocrite towards himself.' D. H. Lawrence wrote:

I had always felt an aversion from Hamlet: a creeping, unclean thing he seems, on the stage, whether he is Forbes Robertson or anybody else. His nasty poking and sniffing at his mother, his setting traps for the King, his conceited perversion with Ophelia make him always intolerable. The character is repulsive in its conception, based on self-dislike and the spirit of disintegration.'[22]

Lawrence's reflections were suggested by a provincial Italian performance, in which the itinerant Hamlet 'was absorbed in his own self-important self-consciousness':

His legs, in their black knee breeches, had a crawling, slinking look; he always carried the black rag of a cloak, something for him to twist about as he twisted in his own soul overwhelmed by a sort of inverted perversity.

Lawrence connects this dislike and self dislike with a sense of corruption in the flesh, nourished in the preceding hundreds of years. It does seem a deep feature of the sensibility out of which the play comes, that its sense of the body's corruption by death is united with its sense of corruption by sin. Hamlet's fascination with death and the rotting body is moralized in a disgust with the fleshy, sweating, coupling human animal, and he feeds on such thoughts and invites them to possess him, wrapping himself in them as in his black cloak. The whole development of the black fashion, in priests, princes, merchants, courtiers, pious citizens – black never shedding altogether its penitential character – occurred in a culture in which a preoccupation with sin and depravity was merged with a preoccupation with death. The vocation of the monk was a vocation of mourning; Philip the Good was cloaked always, however richly, in his father's death; Philip II made his own cult of death, not only prolonging his mourning for Elizabeth, but making his Palace of the Escorial a grand sarcophagus, where he could sit, in a small chapel beneath his living-quarters, surrounded by the gathered corpses of his ancestors. The black-clad merchants commissioned paintings of themselves, kneeling in prayer for what was to happen to them at death. The painting of Christ that Holbein executed with most conviction is not the 'Noli Me Tangere', but his painting of Christ as a sacred corpse. Hamlet – both the prince and the play – shows Shakespeare as the spokesman, or poet, of a culture's 200 years fascination with death and sin in one:

That skull had a tongue in it, and could sing once. How the knave jowls it to th'ground, as if 'twere Cain's jawbone, that did the first murder. This might be the pate of a politician. . . . Or of a courtier . . . and now my Lady Worm's, chopless, and knocked about the mazard with a sexton's spade. . . . Here's another. Why, may not that be the skull of a lawyer? Where be his quiddities now? . . . . Alas, poor Yorick. . . . He hath bore me on his back a thousand times, and now – how abhorred in my imagination it is. My gorge rises at it. Here hung those lips that I have kissed I know not how oft. Where be your gibes now? . . . not one now to mock your own grinning? Quite chop-fallen? Now get you to my lady's chamber and tell her, let her paint an inch thick, to this favour she must come. Make her laugh at that. . . . But soft, but soft awhile. Here comes the King. . . . Who is this they follow? And with such maiméd rites? . . . . What, the fair Ophelia! . . . . I lov'd Ophelia. . . . Dost come here to whine, to outface me with leaping in her grave? Be buried quick with her, and so will I. (v. i. 74–274)

It was at once as the black-clad high-life hero, and as the embodiment of the cult of death, that Hamlet left a mark on the stage of his own day – in, for instance, the figure of Vindice in *The Revenger's Tragedy*, who first appears holding the skull of his dead love. It is as if Tourneur had wanted to elide into a single dramatic tableau the moment when Hamlet, holding a skull, talks about his lady's favour, and the subsequent moment when he turns to behold the dead Ophelia carried before him.

Hamlet is not darkened solely by grief and death, he is in addition, famously, a representation of the Humour of Melancholy. 'Melancholy' means literally 'black bile': of the various human types or Humours, Melancholy was the one most frequently discussed (notably in Burton's *Anatomy of Melancholy*). There was a traditional representation of the melancholy man, both in popular verse and in stage performance, precisely as the man in black – as a man half-hidden by a long black cloak and a large black hat (who then sounds like an English perception of the man of Spanish fashion, complete with solemn style). John Davies, writing of 'yonder melancholy gentleman', cited 'his long cloak . . . his great black feather'.[23] By stage tradition, Hamlet is bareheaded, but equally he traditionally employs a black cloak, and certainly he is dressed in black. This is not to make Hamlet a stereotype of Melancholy. He seems rather to represent Shakespeare's offer, in relation to that stereotype, to present the sensation of the deeper melancholia. Death loses its sting for Hamlet, and becomes like a dream, because life is become lifeless and all its roads dead ends. The universe, and man, are dust. As you take arms against your troubles they become a sea not an army, the sword turns back on you as in suicide, but already you are drowned in a death like troubled sleep. An observant psychologist, Shakespeare gives Hamlet symptoms of depressive illness: he can contemplate, and inflict, pain and death without affect. The play's power in this presentment has penetrated subsequent literature deeply, doubtless because the play speaks from a melancholia nurtured by the culture – one cultivated in precisely those places this study has visited, in Europe's many enclosures of dying thoughts, and especially in its high-walled gardens of mourning monks and mourning kings, and its many manses where pastors have pondered depravity.

This is not the place to attempt an aetiology of melancholy: though one may also note, apropos both of Hamlet and of other literary Hamlets to be discussed below, that in Shakespeare's presentation the melancholic's vision goes with a damage to his ability to love, and with a tendency to see – in his particular dark glass – a blank, or fear, or death, when he looks at women. His blackness includes a derogation of the feminine ('Frailty, thy name is woman!'), though the feminine in himself is uncertainly negated. He knows he is no Fortinbras: one might call him Shakespeare's most feminine hero. This is not to say that he is without a princely manliness: rather that he is – as he has always been found – not only the darkest, but also the most sensitive, most whole, the richest and most fascinating personality and persona of all the lead roles in Shakespeare. It was not without reason that Delacroix had a woman model for him. He is the male role in Shakespeare that has, most often, been played by women – most famously by Sarah Bernhardt.

There is something that seems deliberately indeterminate about Hamlet. It does appear that Shakespeare had a generalizing intention for him. When we laugh at the exchange –

Gravedigger: . . . young Hamlet . . . he that is mad and sent into England.
Hamlet: Ay, marry. Why was he sent into England?
Gravedigger: Why, because he was mad. He shall recover his wits there, or if he do not, 'tis no great matter there.
Hamlet: Why?
Gravedigger: 'Twill not be seen in him there. There the men are as mad as he.

(v. i. 143–50)

– it may be that for Shakespeare this was so good a joke just because at the same time he was not joking. For there were more Jacobean young Englishmen than John Donne, who shared Hamlet's fascination with death-jokes and sin, with wit and with winding-sheets. But beyond any, as it were, English connection, Hamlet has been identified with the shadow-side of the Renaissance, and not only with its fashion of melancholy, but with its whole sceptical interrogation of an ungoverned universe. His speech is fed by streams of Erasmian and Montaigne-minded thought, attacking the confidences of the late Renaissance world. He lives in a restlessness of suspicion and fear, in a mistrust of courts and kings and elders, and of soldiers and wars as well as of women and the body. If he says at one point, contemplating death stoically, 'The readiness is all', it is only to add a few lines later 'Thou wouldst not think how ill all's here about my heart'. Shakespeare himself seems not to want to tie him down, and makes it impossible, I think, to say where the lines should be drawn between his philosophical pessimism and his sickness of soul. He does seem to personate a final turn of the European ascetic tradition, a rejection of the world and its snares not so much in deference to Heaven as in a facing of the fact that the universe is dark, together with the resolution, ironic and with some humour, to live in it so. It is not surprising that every age since Shakespeare's has found him up to date, or that he has been of such interest to later dark writers like Melville and Beckett. He will remain current, a man whose black clothes, finally, are the dress of his dark ontology.

A black general

The move to Othello, in the next tragedy Shakespeare wrote, is a move to a different and deeper black: not adoptive black – dressed black – but natural black, the black of black skin, which is wholly of life not death. On the English stage, this black is still in a sense adoptive, since the actors playing Othello have usually been white: but Othello's dark presence on stage has no association of penitence, asceticism, melancholy. Rather, he is a figure of energetic dignity, almost – in his language – of majesty. As the drama accelerates one is likely to associate his blackness with his big intensity, his force of passion, opaque blood. He seems visibly to be, when loving, the dark-night intensity that passion has; later he seems to be, in person, the darker darkness inside passion. It is notable then that he in his jealousy, and Hamlet in his disgusted puritanism, may use the same language about sex.

It was already clear that Hamlet's language of asceticism, whether he was castigating Ophelia or his mother, was as much the language of jealousy as of morality: all he can see in any woman is Gertrude's frailty, and even his own father has to intervene (spectrally) to make him desist when he attacks Gertrude with language more apt coming from her husband than from her son. Jealousy was a part of Hamlet's blackness, and in this sense it is perhaps as though, in Hamlet's black clothes, the looming vague presence of the waiting Othello was starting to show through the earlier protagonist; or as if Hamlet's 'suits of woe' have in the next tragedy passed into the black being of the hero.

This is a fancy, but one that may serve to raise, for proper consideration, the sensitive, vital issue I have not so far touched on in this study of blackness – the issue of race (there is no suggestion, in the play, that Othello wears black clothes). For it is undoubtedly a fact that the whole negative ethical imagery, whereby blackness and darkness mean 'dead', 'bad', 'not there', made its contribution, over the centuries, to the European disparagement of Africans. Apart from the rapacity and cruelty frequently, and the blithe blind trust in an intrinsic superiority always, with which West Europeans treated the 'salvages' they encountered in their voyages, the fact that the African 'salvages' had black skins meant that they incurred a reduplicated stigma. As Malcolm X has observed, it is clear from a perusal of the *Oxford English Dictionary* that the 'dark' and 'bad' values of 'black' regularly attached to Africans, both in popular and in literary discourse. The *OED* is a useful selection of testimony precisely because its avowed purpose was simply to exemplify neutrally the different words applied to Africans – without prejudice, as it were. And whether or not an element of unconscious bias was present in the minds of the selectors of citations, the various words used for Africans have their own built-in bias, which wanted to find the blackness of Africans distinctly 'other' and ugly: 'Ther was no grace in the visage. . . . Sche loketh forth as doth a More' (Gower, 1390); 'The uggly Maurians . . .' (Barclay, 1509); 'Out there flew, ryght blacke and tedyous, A foule Ethyope' (Hawes, 1509).

Of course, not all the references are as insulting as these; the sense of racial 'difference' perhaps shows especially in the recurring proverbial saw, to the effect that the blackness of the African cannot be washed off: 'I wash a Negro, Loosing both paines and cost' (Middleton, 1611); 'As sure to miss, As they, that wash an Ethiope's Face' (Villiers, 1688); 'In the most elegant language, she labours to wash the Aethiop white' (Wesley, Sermon lxviii, 1791). Of course, it never occurs to the European natives that their whiteness, or pinkness, or faded blotchy sallowness, might be a pigment applied to their surface, which could be washed off. But the proverbs about washing or not washing off the Africans' blackness all imply that, first, one would naturally think such blackness *had* been painted on, because it isn't naturally or rightly human to be so black, and second, the realization – no it can't come off, they really are as black as that. Perhaps the crowning injustice for Africans was that devils were regularly represented as black, facilitating many casually obnoxious equations: 'A kind of fish called Negroes or Sea-Devils' (J. Davies, 1666); 'He's dead long since, or gone to the Blackamores below' (Cowley, 1663). Moreover, not only devils, but The Devil is often black, or manifest as 'a black man'. 'The Devil in the shape of a black man lay with her in the bed' (Glanvill, 1681). The last, and cruellest, twist comes in the other, complimentary, proverb: 'Divels are not so blacke as they be painted' (Lodge, 1596); 'For the Devill is not so black as he is painted' (Howell, 1642). In other words, the Devil's black could be washed off, whereas the African really is as black as he appears to be painted.

There are some neutral references. But what are harder to find in the *OED* are references unqualified in their admiration of Africans. Popular debate about negroes was prejudicial, and was liable, even up to the eighteenth century, to be detained by such issues as 'Whether Negroes shall rise in the last day'. The answer, given by one popular almanac, was 'He shall not arise with that Complexion, but leave it behind him in the Darkness of the Grave, exchanging it for a brighter and a better.' Individual intelligent commentators had recognized the relativism of the human sense of beauty, among them Sir Thomas Browne:

Whereas men affirm this colour was a Curse, I cannot make out the propriety of that name, it neither seemingly so to them, nor reasonably unto us; for they take so much content therein, that they esteem deformity by other colours, describing the Devil, and terrible objects, white.

He quotes pertinently from the Song of Songs, 'I am black but comely'. And Ben Jonson wrote, for performance at court in 1605, the *Masque of Blacknesse*, 'because it was her Majesty's will'. On a shore peopled with tritons and sea-maids, Oceanus ('the colour of his flesh, blue') greets Niger ('in forme and colour of an Æthiope'), welcoming to Britain 'the Masquers, which were twelve Nymphs, Negros, and the daughters of Niger'. Niger, in the principal speech, celebrates the beauty of black women: 'in their black, the perfect'st beauty grows . . . their beauties conquer in great beauty's war'. In particular he celebrates 'the fix'd colour of their curled hair (Which is the highest grace of dames most faire)'. None the less, it is the argument of the masque that the African women will be better accommodated in England, where 'their beauty shall be scorch'd no more'. And near the close Jonson takes away much of what he has given by introducing a white Æthiopia ('her garments white and silver'). Æthiopia personifies the moon, which, Jonson claims, the Æthiopians worshipped by this name. Æthiopia then celebrates Britain, its weather, and especially its sun (and King),

> Whose beams shine day, and night, and are of force
> To blanch an Æthiope, and revive a Corse.
> His light scientiall is, and (past mere nature)
> Can salve the rude defects of every creature.

The black nymphs, it seems, must be white nymphs at last, and so not problematic in this Britain of Jonson's, on which, it appears, the sun never sets. The value of black, in the masque, is its value as spectacle.[24]

It is dangerous, nevertheless, to generalize about a culture on the evidence of words alone. The European visual tradition has a more attractive emphasis. The assumption, for instance, that one of the Magi who attended Christ's nativity was an African meant that in the pictures that truly had pride of place in the culture – altarpieces – there was the recurring representation of a noble and wise African monarch. Such a monarch, handsome, young and dignified, clad both majestically and elegantly in black robes, may be seen in the centre panel of Geertgen tot Sint Jans's *Adoration* of *c.* 1465 (illus. 31). Maybe it is apt that it is a Burgundian artist who realizes the beauty of a black man in black. And this king's black gown is not itself African: it is a black gown, lined with brown fur, such as a Duke of Burgundy might have worn. The elegance of this Christian African king is heightened by his erect stance (though his head is slightly tilted towards Christ), and by the long steep diagonal of the hem of his gown. The lines that make his figure are the most decisive of any figure in the picture, while at the same time his conspicuous blackness draws attention to him. In the picture's composition he balances, also, the figure of Mary on the other side, whose own robes, as is frequently the case in Burgundian nativities, are so deeply dark-blue they are nearly black (blue and black, it may be noted, had been ecclesiastically identical).

Yet even so, and in this context, and with all this said, the nobility of the African Magus is not unqualified. For if it is part of the visual tradition that one of the Magi was African, it is also part of the tradition that the other two were European or European-looking, and that they took precedence over the African Magus. Often the African Magus is behind the other two, both in the sense that he is the third or last of them to enter the stable, and in the sense that they are nearer the foreground of the picture than he is. Often again, as in this painting, the African is standing while the other two Magi kneel – standing as if he must wait his turn to kneel: their turn comes first. At the same time, the fact that he is standing makes him appear to be in attendance on the other two. It is true that often the African Magus is the youngest, so he may cede place to the others for reasons of youth, not race; and then his relative youth allows the painter to make him the most handsome of the Magi. On the other hand, the fact that he is younger gives the European-looking Magi the advantage in authority. Furthermore, it would seem part of the tradition that it is the African Magus who brings the myrrh, the bitter herb, as against the purely attractive gold and

frankincense. The features I mention are standard: they may be seen in this painting, and in most Adorations (consider, for instance, the Adorations of Rubens). A further feature of Geertgen's work is that the upright beam at the corner of the stable comes down in such a way as both to frame, and mark off, the African Magus, while the steep perspective of the roof-beam, cooperating with the diagonals of the African's gown, seem almost to displace him to a wing of the altarpiece. Yet, none of these considerations qualify the main impression given, that, at any rate in Burgundy in these years, black could be seen not only as a beautiful and elegant colour to wear, but as a beautiful and elegant colour to be.

Fine-looking Africans may be found in other paintings, and not only in Adorations. The few Africans in Bosch's *Garden of Earthly Delights*

32 Master of the Mornauer Portrait, *Portrait of Alexander Mornauer, c.* 1470–85, oil on softwood. National Gallery, London.

are handsome and slim-limbed. It is also true that one can find in visual art more or less disparaging visualizations of Africans, corresponding to the linguistic clichés. There is, furthermore, the neutral but hardly honorific use of Africans for visual punning – a use that enrols the African as an unusual creature, maybe fabulous, like a griffin – which we find especially in heraldry, but also in painting. In the portrait of Alexander Mornauer (illus. 32), town clerk of Landshut in Bavaria in the 1470s, the object nearest to us in the picture's foreground is the small ring on Mornauer's thumb, with the device of a moor's head. Presumably Mornauer wore that ring, and both he and the painter are glad to see it foregrounded, because both enjoy the pun on the first syllable of Mornauer's name. Of course, the pun only has its charge because Mornauer is not a moor, and it is unthinkable that he should be one. At the same time, the fact that Mornauer is dressed almost entirely in black – both out of civic *gravitas* and out of perfect fashionableness of the 1470s – gives the pun a further, not malign, twist. If Mornauer has the moor's head on his hand, he has also clothed his own body so as to match the moor's.

In this context, one might ask more distinctly how the author of *Othello* presents Africa and Africans, not only in that play but in his *œuvre* at large. On this question, as on most, Shakespeare is multiple-minded. Racial contempt for black Africans can certainly be found: 'Sylvia . . . shewes Iulia but a swarthy Ethiope' (*Two Gentlemen of Verona*, II. vi. 26). Such a reference is hardly substantial, however. A fuller indication of the range and sway of attitudes available to a Renaissance intellectual is given in the early play *Titus Andronicus*, in the presentation of Aaron the Moor, the lover of Titus's captive, Tamora, Queen of the Goths. For the Romans, Aaron's blackness is ugly, abhorrent, and bad, to be spoken about with vehement sarcasm:

Bassanius: Believe me, queen, your swarth Cimmerian
 Doth make your honour of his body's hue,
 Spotted, detested, and abominable. (II. 3. 72–4)

Even the sympathetic Lavinia is contemptuous:

 . . . I pray you, let us hence,
 And let her joy her raven-coloured love. (II. 3. 82–3)

Given these voicings of traditional attitude, it is worth noting that the young Shakespeare gives Tamora herself – no African – a long and beautiful love-speech to Aaron, which shows that (unlike the noble Romans) neither she, nor Shakespeare writing her part, have any problem:

 My lovely Aaron, wherefore look'st thou sad,
 When everything doth make a gleeful boast?
 The birds chant melody on every bush,
 The snake lies rolled in the cheerful sun,
 The green leaves quiver . . .
 Under their sweet shade, Aaron, let us sit . . .
 We may, each wreathed in the other's arms,
 Our pastimes done, possess a golden slumber . . . (II. 3. 10–26)

Aaron, none the less, is the villain of the play, and when the inevitable equation is made between his black skin and evil, the words are put by Shakespeare into his own mouth:

> . . . O, how this villainy
> Doth fat me with the very thoughts of it!
> Let fools do good, and fair men call for grace,
> Aaron will have his soul black like his face.   (III. i. 202–5)

With his own sarcasm, he acknowledges that the Grace of God is a product reserved for fair-skinned fair-thinkers, while the alliteration makes these 'fair' men foolish, good grace to them. In other words, as one might expect of an African villain on the Elizabethan stage, he is presented as wanting, zestfully, to be a black devil. He is then confronted with just these clichés, when the nurse, bringing his own baby on stage, describes it with popular prejudiced superstitious idiocy:

> *Aaron:* . . . What hath he sent her?
> *Nurse:* A devil.
> . . . A joyless, dismal, black, and sorrowful issue!
> Here is the babe, as loathsome as a toad
> Amongst the fair-faced breeders of our clime.   (IV. 2. 61–8)

To which Aaron very sympathetically rejoins:

> Zounds, ye whore! is black so base a hue?
> Sweet blowse, you are a beauteous blossom, sure.   (IV. 2. 71–2)

And presently he defends his son and his colour with a grandeur of heroic diction that prefigures Othello himself – with, also, at last and justly, a defiance of the white race for its limey colour, pallid or painted:

> I tell you, younglings, not Enceladus,
> With all his threat'ning band of Typhon's brood,
> Nor great Alcides, nor the god of war,
> Shall seize this prey out of his father's hands.
> What, what, ye sanguine, shallow-hearted boys!
> Ye white-lim'd walls! ye alehouse painted signs!
> Coal-black is better than another hue,
> In that it scorns to bear another hue; . . .   (IV. 2. 93–100)

Still, for the action of the play, increasingly he is a black devil. Lucius calls the child, to Aaron, 'this growing image of thy fiend-like face' (V. i. 45). And, like a fiend, Aaron not only commits evil but makes sick-black jokes about the evil others do, saying of the mutilated Lavinia 'Why, she was washed, and cut, and trimmed!' At the end he is arraigned as the black source of black evil in the play, 'Chief architect and plotter of these woes' (V. iii. 122), though actually the most hideous acts have been performed by others. He is sentenced to be buried 'breast-deep in earth' and starved to death. In a late medieval or Renaissance perspective, this was an apt punishment, since black was the colour of earth: according to Jehan Courtois, black represented earth, and humbled us by teaching us that we come from earth, that we are made of earth, and that we will return to earth. ('La couleur noire', Jehan says in his final reference to it, 'nous enseigne comment nous debvons penser que nous sommes venuz de terre en nous humiliant, que nous sommes faictz de terre et que nous retournerons en terre'.)

Shakespeare's revelations of an emancipated view are then momentary: the main tendency of his play conforms safely to the European assumption that a black African is likely to be a black devil, an assumption that was also a stage convention – witness Muly Hamet, the 'foul ambitious Moor' in George Peele's *Battle of Alcazar* (1594). There is no suggestion of devilry in Shakespeare's later play *The Merchant of Venice*, where a prince of Morocco appears briefly as one of Portia's suitors. He could indeed seem a preliminary sketch for Othello, since he has a solemnly high notion of his own worth, is not brilliant, and speaks with a grand, picturesque, elevated diction (in other words, he conforms to a stereotype subtler than the black-devil, but still a patronizing one):

> The Hyrcanian deserts and the vasty wilds
> Of wide Arabia are as thoroughfares now
> For princes to come view fair Portia.   (II. vii. 41–3)

He leaves with the same dignity: so there is a shock for us in the brusque couplet with which Portia, our heroine, sums up the scene we have seen:

> A gentle riddance. Draw the curtains, go.
> Let all of his complexion choose me so.   (II. vii. 78–9)

The change, emancipation, brave blow struck, is then momentous when we come to *Othello*, in which another lady of Venice is wooed by an African, and loves him and marries him, with no suggestion from the playwright of her having any difficulty, or anything mischievous or unnatural in her attraction, or anything other in her than the finest and most admirable whole-hearted love. Others in the play make those insinuations, showing a fair range of the inflections of racist malice, but the effect of all such comments is only to make clearer the pure-heartedness, and courageous persistence, in Desdemona's love. Whether in the presentation of Othello himself there is any element of racial condescension is a more delicate question; we can easily say if we want to that it is an element of his 'character' that he is simple-hearted (though big-hearted), extremely credulous, and solemnly and grandly egoistic, both in general and in his love as well – which has a different accent from Desdemona's:

> She loved me for the dangers I had passed,
> And I loved her that she did pity them.   (I. iii. 167–8)

Though his character has a magnificently noble outline, and a noble as well as a jealous-violent intensity, it is not subtle, and it would be hard to argue that Shakespeare enters into Othello's psychology with the same intricate inwardness with which he realizes Hamlet or Macbeth. More so than the other tragic heroes, Othello can seem a case of The Other as Tragic Hero. Critics have felt that even Othello himself, in his soliloquies, does not quite fully enter his own experience, but rather 'is cheering himself up' (T. S. Eliot), or, 'contemplating the spectacle of himself . . . is overcome with the pathos of it' (F. R. Leavis).[25]

Certainly the play seems, at least as much as *Hamlet*, to rely much on the 'spectacle' of its hero. And the blackness of Othello's skin contributes to theatrical effects that can hardly help being, in performance after performance, magnificently and more-than-magnificently beautiful. In a wonderful critical jump, Emrys Jones, in *The Origins of Shakespeare*, finds an affinity between an entrance of Othello, and the torch-lit scene of Christ's arrest at Gethsemane: the tall dignified hero arraigned but refusing flight or evasion, restraining his supporters' ardour and quietly stilling their swords. 'The scene', Jones writes, 'is usually (in my experience) the most brilliant visual moment in the play . . . its swords and torches and chiaroscuro effects ("Dusk faces with white silken turbans wreath'd") make it, despite its brevity and rapidity, intensely memorable and beautiful.'[26] But though the Othello of these scenes is so different from Aaron, the 'black devil' is not wholly forgotten. It is, of course, one of the black–white ironies of the play that even though Othello succumbs to jealousy and vengeful murderousness, still the truly black soul in the play is not his but that of his white lieutenant Iago: he is the profoundly jealous-evil 'demi-devil' and 'hellish villain'. There is in the play a structure of references to angels and devils that expand its love-jealousy-and-murder drama into dimensions of religious grace, damnation and evil. A nineteenth-century illustration by Sir John Gilbert (illus. 33) attempts to convey this quality, bathing the vulnerable Desdemona, who lies asleep in bed, with a more than natural light and brightness, and representing Othello, who looks not like an African but like a European in black make-up, as a man at once black, and, as it were, in the darkest shadow.

33 Sir John Gilbert, illustration to *Othello* from Staunton's edition of Shakespeare's works, London, 1858–60, wood engraving.

And it is a part of the structure of heaven/hell references that the figure of the black devil should prove, at the crucial moment, to be Othello himself:

> *Othello:* 'Twas I that killed her.
> *Emilia:*   O, the more angel she,
>   And you the blacker devil. (v. ii. 131–2)

She says again, 'Thou art a devil.' He has earlier associated his colour with the 'bad' forms of blackness, seeing his reputation (a prominent issue in this play) specifically as blackened:

> . . . My name, that was as fresh
> As Dian's visage, is now begrim'd, and black
> As mine own face . . .   (III. iii. 392–4)

'*My* name' is the Folio reading; the second Quarto has '*Her* name', and Othello can think of Desdemona, unfaithful, as blackened or black. He calls her, for instance, a 'fair devil' – that is, a white version of a black being. At that key stage in a Shakespeare tragedy, when the hero abdicates his soul, Othello is shown, in a posture of prayer, consecrating himself to the black evil he invites to possess him:

> Arise, black vengeance, from thy hollow cell,
> Yield up, O love, thy crown, and hearted throne,
> To tyrannous hate, swell, bosom, with thy fraught,
> For 'tis of aspics' tongues!   (III. iii. 454–6)

When Othello learns the hideous mistake he has made, he knows fiends will snatch him, he commands devils to whip him, he belongs with them in hell.

Nor is the issue so metaphysical as I have perhaps made it appear. In the Elizabethan period, the blackness of the black man was popularly associated not only with devilry, but with animality, sexuality, bestiality. There is an endlessness of abusive citations, to the effect that negroes 'are beastly in their living' (Andrew Battell), 'are very greedy eaters . . . and very lecherous . . . and much addicted to uncleanenesse' (Samuel Purchas), that they have 'large Propagators' (Ogilby), that 'in Ethiopia . . . the race of men is very keen and lustful' (Jean Bodin).[27] Iago plays at once on the animal and on the diabolic prejudices in his attempts to madden Desdemona's father: 'Even now, very now, an old black ram / Is tupping your white ewe . . . the devil will make a grandsire of you . . . you'll have your daughter cover'd with a Barbary horse' (I. i. 88–111). It seems Iago believes his description, since he later announces (somewhat suddenly) 'I do suspect the lusty Moor hath leaped into my seat'. Shakespeare's position is not Iago's: Othello has a generous fineness that moves Iago to hatred. But it does seem also to be in Shakespeare's mind that Othello, being an African, does have strongly in him, for all his nobility, the sexual and animal part of man, which, in jealousy, becomes murderous savagery: '. . . if there be cords, or knives, poison, or fire . . . I'll tear her all to pieces. . . . Pish! Noses, ears and lips . . . I see that nose of yours, but not that dog I shall throw't to . . . I will chop her into messes. . . . Goats and monkeys!' Shakespeare's major tragedies turn on the rising, or raising, of evil, and the horror and thrill of *Othello* is in watching the obscene, tortured, rapt cooperation of Othello and Iago in releasing, conjuring, raising, as one would raise the Devil, the jealous-murderous savage animal in man, hovering in wait below the noblest love. There are manifold ironies in the play: we see an evil white man, who feeds on others' pain, goad a noble black man to murder his white wife. The ironies do not, however, emancipate Othello wholly from the conventional expectation that one would find in a black man both a black devilry and a black animality.

The equivocal residue of colour-mythology in a masterpiece so much about a noble love transcending race and colour barriers – a masterpiece that none the less has by the end affirmed the extreme difficulties of mixed-race marriages – may be taken as an index of how deeply the symbolism of black and blackness was embedded in European sensibility. It must then be with many provisos that one returns to the observation that the different forms of visible blackness in the consecutive heroes Hamlet and Othello do have a symbolic relation (whatever else is involved of mourning and of race) to the 'darkness' that comes to fill the interior of each of them, and which in each case has a large element of sexual hatred tending to murder.

Shakespeare certainly uses all the resources of theatre to make it clear that both Ophelia and Desdemona are wholly innocent victims of the sombre men who cause their deaths: a reminder again that the black and dark figures I have been discussing have often been figures more of darkness than of light for the women who have stood in their path. A reminder, too, that however self-denying and grave and philosophical the associations of black may be, there is also a recurring connection not only between black and death but more particularly between black and violence. The black of mourning may originate in a violence of grieving, and a violence against the self is part of the whole story of asceticism; but it is violence not only against the self, but against others, including the innocent, that is associated with the black of the Dominicans, and the black of Philip II's court (let alone that of Ivan IV). It is not hard, of course, to associate black with biding anger, with violence stifled, but the violence does not for ever stay stifled. Othello kills Desdemona; and even Prince Hamlet, who can seem the saddest and noblest, and in some ways the most sympathetic, of the many black-clad figures so far mentioned, even he, in those moments when he wakens from his sick sad sombre lassitude of soul, does so usually in order to attack, damage or kill.

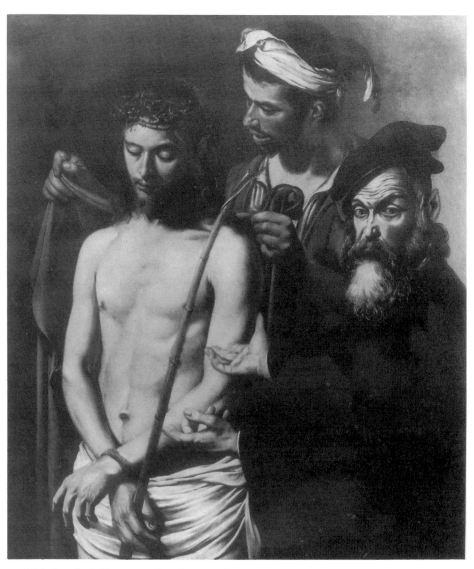

34 Michelangelo di Caravaggio, *Ecce Homo, c.* 1604–5, oil on canvas. Palazzo Rosso, Genoa.

4 From Black in Art to Dickens's Black

It was in the years of the Reformation and the movements counter to it that black became prominent in the palette of artists: in the work, most notably, of Caravaggio, whose style was influential both in Spain and in the Netherlands. Caravaggio was not the first artist to illuminate his pictures as with a spotlight, within an encompassing expanse of black. Two Burgundian artists already mentioned in this study, Geertgen tot Sint Jans and Hugo van der Goes, had each painted a Nativity nightpiece, in which a tiny bare Christ-child radiates brilliant light, picking out and modelling the Virgin's face against the dense black dark. In both pictures the darkness seems protective, not bleak, as it were the dark within a secure shelter, and perhaps the darkness within which God dwells. But though these pictures are further instances of fifteenth-century Burgundian black, each was exceptional in the *œuvre* of its artist, while Caravaggio made it his life's work to investigate and repeat the effect of a single concentrated light-source on bodies from which every other source of light is cut off. The result is a dramatic, even theatrical, art, often harsh in its contrasts in a way that fits the violence of Caravaggio's own life. For the light in his pictures has normally a sharp edge, and though that edge may be the border of a shadow, often it may be the lip of a gash or the brink of a severed neck, while the blackness behind is insistent in its blankness.

Caravaggio might use black clothing to constitute some of the black areas he wanted, for instance the robes of Dominican Friars. Most notably, though, in his *Ecce Homo* of *c.* 1604–5 (illus. 34), a picture that I have to say seems far from his best, he places in the foreground the figure of Pontius Pilate dressed solidly in black. Pilate's face especially seems crudely worked, but at all events is harshly vigorous, staring starkly from the painting towards us. He is dressed in the style of the early sixteenth century, a period used by seventeenth-century artists to indicate past time: he could be a merchant or scholar as well as an official. It is difficult not to think that the artist has some form of accusatory intention: challenging the well-placed men in black in the world as to whether they affirm, or betray and sell, the good. In any case black, in its official and self-effacing capacity, suits Pontius Pilate, who chose not to choose, and to be the utensil of a mob.

Another artist might use black with the deepest gentleness: the black in Georges de la Tour is a still depth of shadow attending his finely graded lights, with their tranquil and often humble source, a child's face, a candle. The Spanish painter Ribera, by contrast, seems almost to have rejoiced in the potentiality of art-black to conjure the harshest Christian severities: in his saintly ascetics, with their denied bodies barely clad, still in piety in cellars of shadow; and in his writhing martyrs, spotlit twisting in pain in the dark.

A complementary factor, encouraging the new black art of *chiaroscuro*, was the black clothing that sitters, from end to end of Europe, would wear when their portraits were painted. Black-clad infantás pose for Velázquez, black-clad nobles for Rubens and Van Dyck, black-clad burghers for Rembrandt and Hals. There was perhaps a convention involved: you might well wear black when sitting for a portrait, it gave you dignity and stressed your face. But sitters frequently wore their own clothes for portraits; and since the conventions of the day allowed black both for formal and for daily wear, it is hard to argue from the colour that sitters dressed either up or down for their portraits.

A further consideration again is that artists themselves, when they painted themselves, tended to paint themselves in black. It may be that sometimes they wore black when painting, as the artist does in Vermeer's picture (from the rear) of an artist at work: for black was, as it were, a white-collar work-colour, worn also by musicians, instrument makers and important people's secretaries. But the fur-lined black robes that the old Titian wears are grander than that: they are heavy, imposing, senatorial. Poussin (illus. 35) seems to carry the black drapery of art, arranged in loose folds up and over his shoulder, rather than a practicable garment. Velázquez, painting *Las Meninas*, seems to be wearing the costume of the Knights of St Iago (Philip IV made him one), but the red cross was, in fact, added afterwards, so presumably his black dress is what he would normally have worn at once as a courtier and as an artist. Clearly different considerations counted with different painters: the black Rembrandt wears in some of his self-portraits is more like the everyday dress of his time. While it was not a rule, for Rubens painted himself both all in black, and not all in black, it does seem to have been the dominant practice for artists, in paintings, to be seen wearing black, however strong their commitment to light and clear colour. So Signorelli paints himself in black, beside a black-clad monk, in a picture that otherwise shows all his hues, in a flying-

35 Nicolas Poussin, *Self-portrait*, 1650, oil on canvas. Musée du Louvre, Paris.

writhing arabesque of aerial bodies and trailing drapes.

Since all these artists both loved rich colour and painted it beautifully, their donning of black is a point of interest. An aspect of it, perhaps, is black's self-effacement and invisibility: we are seeing the artist now, but he normally is the person we do not see. He is himself unseen because he is the seer, he is the invisible part of his paintings. One may especially think this, looking at Van Dyck's portrait of himself with Endymion Porter (illus. 36). Porter is brightly dressed, the principal subject, and Van Dyck beside him is – his head apart – almost hard to make out, his lustrous black-satin cape so recedes into shadow. His black, at the same time, has formality, importance: and of course the likely main value of the black clothes artists painted themselves wearing was precisely the serious impersonality of black, signalling their subservience to the high impersonal demands of an art. They were at once priests and doctors of art.

Aside from his portraits of himself, Rembrandt – it is clear from his biblical scenes – liked rich deep colour in clothing. But his sitters did not, and in order to paint people in colour he had to get them into fancy

dress, paint them as Belshazzar or Claudius Civilis. At the same time, he did relish dark clothes too, and the intensity they suggested, especially when they set off a pensive face. He is glad to place his people against that recent innovation, the densely dark background (a feature now associated with Christian story: pagan subjects preferred colourful backgrounds, as in Rubens's scenes from Ovid). So Rembrandt sets his people against serious black, then raises to them a strong but not harsh light: a light very different from Caravaggio's torch, for instead of making the lights and shadows fight, it brings the face forward in a tenderly patient interrogation. The light respects the dark, and often it is in the verges of shadow that his faces most live, in the hints of several expressions at once, in which you feel the play of the nature of the person.

Rembrandt is poised between the old coloured world, and the new solemn world of black-and-white, in a way that fostered richness and depth in his art. But history was going the way of the black-clothed Protestant burghers, those grave strict businessmen who were, in Max Weber's account, the fathers of capitalism. In Rembrandt's paintings one can see their strength: the black clothes merge so the man is one dark shape, triangular and rising like a mountain (illus. 37). There is a strong sense of power reserved; nor, in Rembrandt (and even less in Hals), is their Calvinism invariably joyless. They do, though, look serious about what it is that they do; and as if they believe that in being prosperous, as in anything else, they are certain to be in the right.

Studying their faces, one may think in terms of a qualified Weberism: for 'asceticism', the word Weber uses, seems not always the word for them. But their sombre clothes and thoughtful faces do suggest people on whom duty weighs – the duties of their calling, industry, probity, patience in the management of long-term investments. They seem confident, too, that the faith whose dark colour they wear will be watching over them in their work. And evidently it did, since it is essentially their uniform, modified in cut but not in colour, that the nineteenth century was later to wear.

The nineteenth century was not the first time when the middle class wore black. In the seventeenth century also, when Christian business-

37 Rembrandt van Rijn, *Portrait of a Man in a Tall Hat*, c. 1662, oil on canvas. National Gallery of Art, Washington, DC.

38 Gerard Ter Borch, *Portrait of a Young Man*, probably 1660–65, oil on canvas. National Gallery, London.

men were in the ascendant, they wore black. It is true their severity was later qualified. As the seventeenth century proceeded, Spain declined, and with it its fashion; and at the same time the Dutch republic became less threatened and anxious and ambitious, and less distinct in its style. One can see the relaxation in Ter Borch's portrait of a young Dutch fashionable of the 1660s (illus. 38). His Netherlandish black carapace is splitting, loosening to drapes like curtains over aprons and skirts; he has his black trimmings, but they are ribbons and bows. His white collar is lacily elaborated, and there are puffed white sleeves to his corpulent shirt, which itself thrusts forward into view as no regent's shirt ever would have done. He seems more ready for a minuet, than either for prayers or for a day at the counting-house.

He is Dutch-coloured (that is, antecedently, Spanish-coloured), but the shape he makes is French. In the latter years of the seventeenth century, both severity and the colour black lost some of their purchase on the dress of the powerful: a change throughout Europe that was affected especially by the fact that as Spain declined, France rose. While nations follow international fashions, it is also true (as Castiglione observed) that nations, especially ascendant nations, assert their ascendancy through style and dress. A rising nation needs to look distinctive: and France not only wanted, but must have felt it needed, to look different from Spain, whose black fashion, by the end of the seventeenth century, had come to strike foreigners as distinctly oppressive and grim. France was strong – the Bourbons indeed took over the Spanish throne from the Habsburgs; and France, and its monarchy, made a large use of white. They had done so since the fifteenth century, for the use of white had developed in France as the use of black developed in Burgundy: the colour-coding of nations was not a new development.[1] And France was the land of the lily, the fleur-de-lis. White had been the background colour of the French royal standard, and when the French army put on uniform in the late seventeenth century, their coats were principally white or grey-white. The tendency of the French court, first at Paris, then at Versailles, was to lighter tones and increasing colour. The change of hue is visible in England, where the monarch who returned at the Restoration was returning specifically from France, with a bevy of French-bred courtiers.

One should not, of course, simplify the usages of France, where both the learned and many of the citizens wore black, and where both the Jesuits and Jansenists were influential black priesthoods. The Jesuits, indeed, arranged the decor and lighting for a feast at Versailles at which everything and everything edible was black (a feast imitated, in the nineteenth century's dandy mode, by J.-K. Huysmans's protagonist Des Esseintes in *À Rebours*).[2] Black in this case was not ecclesiastical: the feast, held in the Grotte de Thétis, imitated a banquet in the Underworld, with Louis XIV presiding as Pluto, King of Hades. The Jesuits thus turned to a luxurious game the colour which in all piety they wore every day: it may be, too, that the feast had its own mystery, that in some sense those present were eating death. The black feast was, however, an exception: the other entertainments the Jesuits arranged were more colourful. The increased use of colour is not surprising in a classicizing court, less Church-bound than the Spanish court, which liked to feel itself as much at home on Olympus as in Gethsemane.

There is an increase in colour, and variety of colour, in the appearance of the late seventeenth century in Europe. But though led by the French, this change is too general to be attributed solely to the yet higher rise of France, and the lighter Parisian tone, or *ton*. For it is also true that the whole long period of increasing, then continuing, black fashion in Europe had been coterminous with a period of intensifying religious disturbance, religious dissension, then religious war. And it is noticeable that as international warfare in Europe ceases to appear so importantly a matter of Catholic armies fighting Protestant armies (not, of course, that either war, or religious prejudice, ceased), so the black fashion wanes. It does, therefore, seem reasonable to suggest that the presence, in an increasingly war-torn and corpse-strewn continent, of profound spiritual disturbance and indeed of warring spiritualities (led on both sides by black-clad priests) had provided a reinforcement, from deep sources, of what had showed on society's surface as black fashion.

Nor had black died. It is true that by the early eighteenth century male dignity had become less cumbersome. The sombre long gown had shortened to a coat, which became, when worn with matching knee-breeches, the ancestor of the modern gents' suit (though in many countries the gown, in a lighter and looser style, was still much worn, as a form of more casual and unbuttoned wear, a usage that survives in the dressing-gown still). All men of standing now also wore that curious concession to a theoretical bare-headedness, the wig: initially it was high-built, a soft tower above one, replacing the tall hat as the sign of a more pliant dignity on high.[3] The suit itself might be red or blue, the waistcoat golden. But many professional men and scholars, some men of business, and the great majority of clerics, wore serious, to-be-respected black. Black continued to be much worn in Protestant countries, in Germany, Switzerland and Denmark, for instance, in addition to (of course) the Dutch republic. It is also true that those Catholic countries that had been pre-eminent in the time of black fashion continued a substantial use of black: Spain was still dark in the eighteenth century, and an English visitor, as late as 1787, could still comment on the tendency of Spanish men to wear black. Stately black of Spanish derivation survived at the Swedish court as well as in Vienna.[4] And in Venice, which had also grown brighter (as the paintings of Canaletto and Francesco Guardi show), still the patricians wore black. A mid-century visitor to Venice, Giuseppe Baretti, noted that, 'the winter-dress of a Venetian noble consists of a long woolen black gown . . . his summer-dress is likewise black, open, loose, and shorter than that of the winter . . . the peculiar dress of his lady is also old-fashioned, and made of black velvet'. Over the black clothes the Venetians wore large cloaks, grey in summer and black in winter, though Baretti notes too 'the cloaks of the lower sort are stuffs of any colour': a confirmation of the association of Venetian black with rank. Of another city Baretti notes: 'The nobleman of Genoa dresses also in black, but after the modern manner, with a narrow silk cloak hanging down his back . . . his lady dresses often in colours; but her dress of ceremony is black silk or black velvet, according to the season' – as if the man were always on ceremony, in which sometimes his lady joined him.[5]

The black of Venice made an impression on travellers. And the long black gown of a Venetian patrician could have a somewhat sinister effect, as in the painting by Pietro Longhi of *c.* 1746 (illus. 39) of a black-gowned Venetian nobleman, stooped so low to kiss the hand of a not greatly moved lady that he looks almost as if he is wondering whether to eat it. Especially remarkable, to some visitors, was the dark tone of the Venetian Carnival. For the Carnival at Venice was the most elaborate of the European masquerades and *fêtes galantes*, which in general reached their apogee during the eighteenth century: and the Carnival of Venice was, above all, black. In this festive period, from late December to Lent, every man or woman could wear the ample black silk *domino*, with a black scarf and black hat. They wore either a black velvet mask, or a grotesque white mask, with a further piece of black silk or lace across the mouth and chin. A late eighteenth-century observer recorded that 'men and women wear the same sort of clokes, hoods and hats, all black with white masks; so that, when they lie down in their black gondolas, as they frequently do, you may guess what sort of appearance they have'. It is possible that the black *domino*, which became the masquerade dress of Europe, and which in Venice too was worn at other times than Carnival, had an ecclesiastical origin. In any event, the Venetian Carnival, a period that made intrigue easier in the tight-packed island city of alleys and eyes, is almost the most remarkable turn in the practice of wearing black in Europe. In the dead season of declining Venice the colour of its Church, of its aristocracy, of death, is translated to the over-colour of liberty, in the prolonged flare-up of pleasure in the dark depth of winter before the bleak abstentions of Lent. It was a prescribed period of de-prescription, with an anti-uniform that concealed difference, which in masking the person freed the person, and which under the don't-see-me colour of

39 Pietro Longhi, *A Nobleman Kissing a Lady's Hand, c.* 1746, oil on canvas. National Gallery, London.

black allowed what was not to be seen to be at once visible and disguised. The *domino* was a play shroud for love to play in, making a warmth under folds of silk in black boats in chilly canals. Not every Venetian had silk of course: the less well-off would use a large black cloak of other material, or – both men and women – a large dark or black man's coat. But those wearing masks were admitted everywhere, for instance to the patrician gaming-house, the Ridotto. It was a period of gaming – and of gaming with death, and with decay, age and ugliness, as the deformed white masks made clear.[6]

In France, too, black still loomed large in the wardrobes of Parisians, and even in the wardrobes of the silk-clad aristocracy. Thanks to the researches of Daniel Roche, it is possible to say just what proportion of clothing was black for the several different classes that made up Paris.[7] Thus, in 1700, a third of the clothes of the nobility were black. Black was not however, in Paris, reserved for the nobility, for a third of the clothes of wage-earners were black. The figure is only a little lower for domestic servants and for artisans and shopkeepers. And for the professions the proportion is even higher: close on a half of their clothes were black. Parisians owned coloured clothes and wore them socially, but black was much used for ordinary wear. Thus, late in the century, an English visitor could conclude that 'all persons of small or moderate fortune are forced to dress in black'. The 'forcing' factor was the mud in the streets, and this visitor seems given to exaggeration. It is clear, none the less, that black kept its currency through the century.[8]

France is, notwithstanding, the country of colour. Though dark in the streets, its civility had taken the tonalities of Watteau, of Fragonard, of dancers in rose and azure satin. The figures of Daniel Roche show black waning and colour warming as the century develops. Indeed, the use of bright colours (red, yellow, blue) rises in the nobility from eight to thirty-eight per cent of their clothing. This figure, in this context, may seem politically suggestive: were the aristocrats, in becoming polychromatic peacocks of conspicuous consumption, whetting the edge of the guillotine? Perhaps they were, but one must record that the use of bright colour by those in waged labour also increased to a third of their clothing. Most of French society became brighter-coloured through the century: a change that should probably be related not so much to directly political issues, as to the fact that it was in this period that the fashion industry, in something like its modern sense, developed – a division of the 'industrial revolution' that was at least as vital in France as in England. There was a quicker changing of clothes, and a more individual attention to what one wore, going with the century's rising attention to the individual person *as* an individual. And it would seem that France's aristocrats contributed to *sartorial* individualism at least as much as did the tardily rising bourgeoisie.

None the less, the aristocrats fell, and if their dress was not directly provocative, it still reflected the great provocation, that the total wealth of the Paris aristocracy, valued in *livres*, increased between 1700 and 1789 by over 700 per cent, a figure more than seven times that of most groups. It is beyond the capacity of the present study to address the causes of the Revolution. But since the changes in men's dress, and in particular the development of the black fashion, have frequently been connected, especially by Flügel, with the strippings and guillotinings of the French Revolution, something should be said of the colour changes of the Revolutionary period. For the most notable use of black in these years was not in the Revolution or in its aftermath, but rather in its preliminaries. Something like the role of black in this society – and in the other, blacker, societies that preceded it – is indicated in the orders of dress issued, when at very long last the French monarchy, that is Louis XVI, finally felt compelled, in 1788, to convene a meeting of the Estates General, the representative body of France, which had not met since 1614. After such a delay, some direction was needed, as to apparel that would be seemly, and the Grand-Master of Ceremonies, the Marquis de Brezé, issued instructions. The First Estate, the clergy, were to wear ecclesiastical dress, which was red in the case of Cardinals, and of white lawn for bishops, but otherwise in general was black. The Second Estate, the nobility, were to wear a black coat, waistcoat and breeches (silk or cloth as to season), trimmed with gold braid; and white stockings, a lace cravat, a sword and a hat with feathers. And the not-noble Third Estate, one half of the deputies, was to wear suits of black cloth, black stockings, and short black cloaks like those of lawyers; they were to wear plain muslin cravats, no sword, and a plain three-cornered hat.[9]

The ancient French parliament was re-conceived, then, as a grand conclave of men in black. Black, in this context, can hardly be thought (as Baudelaire thought it) democratic. On the other hand, black here does not mark rank: rather, it is the common denominator, the sign of a unity in the gathering, while rank is marked by accessories to the black. So the 'noblesse' in black could be 'very beautiful' and the 'Tiers-Etats' in black 'very ordinary'.[10] Black marks those who, in this many-coloured and hierarchic society, are met together with a serious sense of being co-governors of one nation: of a Christian nation, one must add, for it is the colour of the Church that is worn by all, and the majesty of red is reserved for the Church. Black here unites, but it unites those who revere the duties of rank, which include a duty to the fact of rank. The black of the Estates is impersonal, serious, social and devout: it includes a recognition of the *solemnity* of class, of those united in not only a Christian, but a social Church, and a social Church under serious threat. And though the prescriptions of the Marquis de Brezé did not 'take', but distinctly the reverse, they do, I believe, foreshadow one of the roles of men's black in later, English, Victorian society, revolutionless but anxious about revolution, where both those commanding and those serving wear black.

The prescriptions did not take: in particular, the Third Estate was not willing to have black imposed on it, and a rural deputy was cheered when he ascended the Tiers agriculturally garbed. And one of the first acts of the new National Assembly in October 1789 was to reject the prescription of dress for the Estates. Nevertheless, as Aileen Ribeiro has recorded, black continued to serve as a symbolic colour for those on both sides of the widening divide. The natives of the Tuileries were in mourning, both for their fortunes (in a literal sense, 'many of the young people of the first fashion and rank wear mourning always for economy') and for a chance succession of royal deaths, such as those of the Dauphin in 1789 and of the brother of Marie-Antoinette, the Emperor Joseph II, in 1790. Black was worn by some aristocrats on the principle of *morituri te saluant*: a band of aristocrats attempted to see Louis XVI, all dressed in black 'pour mourir, disoient-ils, en défendant le roi'. Louis refused to see them, and the practice of some aristocrats, of wearing mourning as a sign of loyal grief for the death of royalty, was perhaps a doubtful tribute, since it anticipated the death it mourned. And all the while a black coat and black breeches, of cloth not silk, and worn not by aristocrats and not by decree, was a sign of commitment to the dissentient Third Estate. In 1790, according to the *Journal de la Mode et du Goût*, a citizen might wear 'un habit de drap noir à la Révolution'. Black in the early 1790s was a signal of political conviction on both sides, while difference was marked by the materials chosen. Young gentlemen sitting prudently on the fence might wear black casamir (a cognate of 'cashmere'), a distinctly fine but woollen cloth.[11]

At the trial of Louis XVI, in December 1792, there was no standard dress. Barrère, the president of the court, wore a scarlet waistcoat, lead-coloured kerseymere breeches and white silk stockings – a variant on the tricolour. The King himself wore an olive silk suit. But Pétion, the deputy for Chartres who (with Robespierre) had been 'chaired' by the Paris crowd in 1791, wore black, and so did his party; and so, too, did Robespierre himself. Given the context, one might associate their black with executioner's black. They did not, however, wear black on all judicial occasions, and their solemn black is rather perhaps appropriate, on this momentous occasion, to the execution at once of a king and of a principle, the principle of monarchy.[12]

For the main tendency of the Revolution was to colour. The dominant motif was the tricolour, in which the red and blue of Paris joined the white of France, and red, white and blue became important colours in new clothes, including women's fashions, and in the many new designs of uniform then worn, in which clothing marked groups coexisting (allegedly) on the same social level, rather than stacked vertically in a class-hierarchy. In particular these colours flared in the new designs for Republican dress, prepared in the mid-1790s by the painter David and others, in which black was used virtually not at all. The new-style citizen might wear a short blue jacket with skin-tight blue trousers; a short sleeveless coat, white, with a scarlet cape; a belt with both pistols and a sword attached (the sword being now available for all to wear); and a hat with plumes. If elected a deputy, he was intended to wear a tricolour cloak, blue with a red and white border. When the Directory came to power, in 1795, the five Directors, who were the executive, dressed more richly but still in colours. A Director wore a short open coat of red embroidered in gold over a white double-breasted tunic, again embroidered in gold, with white silk pantaloons tied by a blue silk sash with gold tassels; his round hat had a tricolour panache. His *grand costume* for formal occasions had, by contrast, a coat of blue, with a red silk cloak embroidered in gold.

It does not, perhaps, need saying that the designs of David were not much adopted, and the legislators of the Directory, who were given long robes and mantles, were not admired for dressing 'en Romains ou en prêtres'. The everyday dress of the 1790s was more sober, and might still include, with lighter-coloured pantaloons, a coat or frock-coat of black: a style that, given a sharper cut, became that of the *élégants* of the late 1790s, who wore their black coats with metal buttons. Similarly, in women's dress, the lavish use of the colours of the tricolour was subdued to a larger use of black and white. It remains the case that the Revolutionary years, for all their upheavals, were years of colour in dress: even those who committed suicide, throwing them-selves in the Seine (both affluent and poor, and old and young) were frequently dressed in bright colours, as Richard Cobb records. The principal exception, in sombre *demi-teintes*, is a retired servant of the old regime.[13]

The plain style of menswear, which came to the fore through these years, was, as recorded in earlier pages, much influenced by that of the English gentry, who had economized and simplified their jackets and legwear for ease of riding on their country properties. *L'Anglomanie* continued through the Revolutionary period, so that as Philippe, duc d'Orléans, had worn an English frock-coat and greatcoat in the 1780s, so in the 1790s Marat wore a 'pepper and salt coat in the English fashion', and by the late 1790s the principal form of hat that survived was the English round hat. Not all elements of the coming plain style were English, and the working-class trousers of the *sans-culottes* were to evolve into the legwear of the whole male gender (and, in the twentieth century, into the legwear of both genders).

England itself had, through the eighteenth century, been pursuing a

40 William Hogarth, *Marriage A-la-Mode – II*, 1743, oil on canvas. National Gallery, London.

plain programme, for all the influence of French colours and lace. London was thought of in the eighteenth century as a sober-clad city. Its professional men wore dark or black clothes, and its dissenting and Quaker businessmen preserved a signal sobriety of style, deliberately drab or dark. The same styles were worn in America, and when, with Independence, Washington was inaugurated in 1789 as President of the United States, he wore a suit of dark-brown woollen cloth (of American manufacture). He did, however, at his second inauguration in 1793, wear the more aristocratic 'full suit of black velvet' with 'his hair powdered and in a bag; diamond knee-buckles and a light sword with grey scabbard'.[14]

For black had remained a smart colour, especially if trimmed with gold lace or embroidery, and had been as stylish, in the mid-century, for an English rake as for a French marquis. In the second painting in Hogarth's *Marriage À-la-Mode* series (illus. 40), the dissolute young husband, having returned home in the early hours with another woman's bonnet in his pocket (which his wife's lap-dog is rooting out), sits splay-legged, jaded, white-faced from partying, still wearing the smart coat-and-breeches of jet velvet that evidently he had put on the previous day. The young couple's steward, walking out of the picture in despair to the left, wears a dark-coloured coat – a coat that presumably *had* been black – but if so, this is a different black, the old self-effacing black of the serious diligent clerk, clerks having become by this time something less than learned men, moving rather in the book-keeping direction. He waves the bills that the couple have incurred and will evidently have difficulty meeting.

The rakes and beaux, however, were the froth. If the eighteenth century in England was a show of wigs and ribbons, and large, and black, beauty-spots on powdered male faces,[15] discerned between the thin window-curtains of rocking sedan chairs, still, below the leisured levels of the chocolate-drinking classes, the businessmen and scholars, and the mechanical inventors and investors in inventions, were rational, industrious and distinctly sober. Many of them wore drab, and not a few of them wore black. Revolutions and wars could not end their prosperity, and while monarchies and republics were upset, profits accrued in the counting-houses of Europe. It must, therefore, seem as though the businessmen of Europe were only, at long last, coming into their inheritance when the early years of the following century saw the wearing of men's black expand again and become *à la mode*. This development was heralded by dandies and sanctioned by Romantics: but the new style was worn most sustainedly and sedately by the captains and the beneficiaries of industry and trade.

Returning, then, to the European merchant class, with its readiness for black, manifest in earlier periods and reinforced in the nineteenth century, we come to the great connection between black and power – which is the connection between black and money. Money, of course, may wear different uniforms, both luxuriously ostentatious and spare and money-hiding. And black can work to both these effects, depending on the material and cut of clothing. But the dress of wealth has often not been black, and the renewed dominance of black in a supremely wealthy age needs explanation. If the earlier black fashion had been influenced, as it were from below, by deep issues of spirituality in a war-torn continent, it is hard to find such factors mattering so extremely in the mid-nineteenth century. The connection with spirituality would seem rather to lie in such a collocation of an anxious, urgent making of money with an ascetic spirituality taken deeply to heart as Max Weber, most signally, has elaborated. And though Weber's hypothesis has been much challenged, and is not now accepted as a reliable account of cause and effect, it is a powerful picture he gives – of the anxious Puritan committing all his unresting diligence to the husbandry of money, and, forbidden to squander, reinvesting his profits so as to become, if his work is blessed by the Lord, a decidedly prosperous ascetic. It is an account that fits in

England the rise of the Quaker business families, and inventors and projectors of the Industrial Revolution, trained in the dissenting academies and exhorted in chapel.

In his *History of Men's Fashion*, Farid Chenoune mentions 'Weber's equation, puritanism + capitalism = austere nineteenth-century male dress', but also cites Daniel Roche's cautionary observation, that 'in the absence of more detailed studies, prudence requires that we regard this picture, almost too neat to be true, only as a hypothesis.'[16] And for himself, Chenoune notes (perhaps rather airily: it is all he has to say on the whole large question) that 'making too much of the "puritanical" aspect of the phenomenon, seeing it in terms of renunciation, impoverishment, and loss (indeed mourning), probably overstates one aspect of a revolution that also heralded a sturdy, strong masculine ideal stemming from rites and roots more complex and less one-sided than is generally acknowledged'.[17]

If we now confront face to face the black-clad nineteenth-century citizen, we see the point of these cautions, for it is manifest that, even apart from the dandy fashion discussed earlier, many men who were not of dissenting, or Reformed, or Huguenot background, and who were not classifiable as ascetic capitalists, wore black. Again, we see in portraits many faces rising from black suits that scarcely suggest a Weberian history. Ingres's portrait of *Monsieur de Norvins* (illus. 41) has hardly the look of the puritan ascetic: though the post he held at the time – he was Napoleon's Chief of Police in Rome – might suggest an association with disciplinary black. But Jacques Marquet de Montbreton de Norvins was also a poet, he was to be a biographer of Napoleon, and his black might as easily be read as Romantic, and as exemplifying, or prefiguring, the dandy fashion. Returning to England, one may cite George Eliot, who seems to see English severity as more apparent than profound:

The correct Englishman, drawing himself up from his bow into rigidity, assenting severely, and seeming to be in a state of internal drill, suggests a suppressed vivacity, and may be suspected of letting go with some violence when he is released from parade.[18]

She wrote this, however, late in the century, in her own last novel, and her earlier fiction, with its various emphases on the depths of English moralism, suggests that there was less tension earlier in the century between the severe style and the inner person.

One may note, too, that if French commentators have been cautious with the Weberian argument, there would after all have been a difference between Catholic and Protestant businessmen: even though

41 Jean-Auguste-Dominique Ingres, *Monsieur de Norvins*, probably 1811, oil on canvas. National Gallery, London.

both religions have their severe pieties, the inner self-policing would seem to have gone further, with more damage to sensuousness and the capacity for pleasure, in the Protestant cultures. If the French adopted the black fashion, knowing it to be the English fashion, it might have been, in France, a degree more at variance with the disposition of the wearer. (So one might argue that Michel Foucault's reading of the nineteenth century's professed asceticism as an oblique index of the middle class's adjustment to its bodily and sexual well-being, though accurate for Catholic France, still understates the deeper-damaging ascetic strains in Protestant England.[19]) At the same time, it was not an English critic, or a commentator with a Weberian axe to grind, who then read the black fashion most emphatically in terms of (to quote Chenoune) 'renunciation, impoverishment, and loss' – it was Baudelaire. And it was not only later critics, or only English Victorian critics, who saw the age as funereal, or who saw, even in the smart styles of high life, the appearance of an ever-perpetuated mourning: Baudelaire saw it, Gautier saw it, Musset and Maupassant saw it; as in England Dickens saw it, and John Ruskin, and, later, Oscar Wilde.[20] It is not a matter either of writers merely choosing to see or 'read in' a mournfulness, for the nineteenth century did have its own cult of

42 Jean-Auguste-Dominique Ingres, *Monsieur Bertin*, 1832, oil on canvas. Musée du Louvre, Paris.

death, a cult of grieving much and long, of decking funerals elaborately in many black stuffs, and of wearing mourning black for an extended period of time. The 'funereal' connection cannot be set aside as easily as Farid Chenoune with his 'indeed mourning' implies. As to the connections that Weber drew, one would have to allow that the association of a pious asceticism with capital may be found in French practice also. And in portraits one may find, if one looks, severely mercantile faces, accompanying black suits, showing a grim prosperity that would equip them to have sat with Rembrandt's regents. As, for instance, in another Ingres portrait, *Monsieur Bertin* (illus. 42).

Since dress is always both over-determined and polysemic, it is not easy to establish which considerations dominated the determination of nineteenth-century fashion. And a real quantification of case histories is obviously beyond the scope of the present study. Faced with the need still to try to see the nineteenth century with some sort of wholeness, I shall present more fully the literary testimony. The case for doing this is that the nineteenth century was also the great century of the novel – of the novel as the record of social life. The novel recorded unceasingly manners and appearances, and endlessly 'read' the meaning of manners: and, as we have seen, the 'blackness' of the age – of both the age as a whole, and of its dress – was perceived, quite explicitly, as a large enigma which also went deep. In America, Melville praised Hawthorne for his 'blackness', seeing it as an ability to register the blackness of moral destructiveness, as well as that of New England dress, and connecting this ability with Hawthorne's puritan ancestry.[21] In France, *Le Rouge et le noir* comes early, before the large-scale black fashion, and Julien's black suit is distinctly clerical and tutorial, a suit for a seminarian (and certainly it is read as the suit of a learned asceticism, though Julien has his 'suppressed vivacity'). In *Madame Bovary* we see that not only husbands and bourgeois wear black, but that even the lovers we dream of must do so: so Emma, turning from her physician-husband in his professional frock-coat, desires first a preferable imaginary 'husband in a black velvet coat' and later a lover who will 'dress all in black and grow a little pointed beard, to look like the portraits of Louis XIII'.[22]

As to English fiction, I have mentioned Charlotte Brontë's collocation of the severely disciplinary black of Mr Brocklehurst with the romantic black of Mr Rochester. With Brocklehurst we return to the Calvinist connection; and George Eliot, who describes various men in black, gives the greatest prominence, and her minutest attention, to the Calvinist banker Bulstrode. His nightmare of criminal equivocation with his conscience is made the dramatic climax of *Middlemarch*, her novel of broadest social scope. Above all there is the testimony of Dickens, who was at once the most distinctly detailed, and yet also the most imaginative, delineator of the daily life of his age. He registered together both the many inflections of black dress in his time, and the many kinds of blackness that seemed to characterize his world, and he did so, as his fiction developed, with an ever more urgent sense of the depths of this dark.

Since Dickens sees black in several aspects, it may be most helpful to begin with those places where, *pace* M. Chenoune, Dickens does see matters as Weber himself was later to see them (which is not, of course, to suggest that one can rest, finally, on a Weberian explanation). There is the passage, for instance, in chapter Three of *Little Dorrit* where the hero, Arthur Clennam, returning from many years abroad, perceives with a fresh depression the black deadliness of a London Sunday:

Melancholy streets in a penitential garb of soot, steeped the souls of the people who were condemned to look at them out of windows, in dire despondency. In every thoroughfare, up almost every alley, and down almost every turning, some doleful bell was throbbing, jerking, tolling, as if the Plague were in the city and the deadcarts going round.

He proceeds through the old business heart of the city, 'passing now the mouldy hall of some obsolete Worshipful Company, now the illuminated windows of a Congregationless Church', until he arrives, among silent warehouses and wharves, at the near-defunct business premises of Clennam. The house is 'all but black', even the frames of the mirrors have 'black figurines carrying black garlands'. Clennam visits the present head of the House:

On a black bier-like sofa . . . propped up behind with one great angular black bolster, like the block at a state execution in the good old times, sat his mother in a widow's dress.

In James Mahoney's aptly dark illustration to the Household Edition (illus. 44) Mrs Clennam emerges firm-faced from a blackness textured like her widow's weeds, from which also emerges, in a contrary curve, the dark-suited body of her smart-dressed son, leaning towards the light but gazing back with a face echoing hers into the shadow. Mrs Clennam has been a formidable businesswoman, of the puritanical and Old Testament school: she reads to her son from the Bible 'sternly, fiercely, wrathfully – praying that her enemies (she made them by her tone and manner expressly hers) might be put to the edge of the sword, consumed by fire, smitten by plagues and leprosy'. Her Calvinistic capitalism is, perhaps, the more horrifying in its cruel frigidity because she *is* a woman, 'beyond the reach of all seasons', 'beyond the reach of all changing emotions'.[23]

Little Dorrit was published in the 1850s, and one could wonder, since Weber associated Calvinism especially with the formative nurturing of capitalism, whether Mrs Clennam has come in late in the day. But the novel is set in the 1820s, and even then Dickens emphasizes that the House has done no real business for decades. Mrs Clennam is represented as an immobile survivor. She belongs, that is to say, to the late eighteenth century, and should be seen as a contemporary of that Birmingham businessman who so appalled Coleridge.

In the full process, as seen by Weber, once the work ethic, and the business, were working successfully, the Calvinistic theology would wither away, leaving a secular form of puritan ethic: indefatigable, joyless, a terrible self-perpetuating mechanism. To see this later stage in Dickens, one must turn to a novel written and set in the 1840s, *Dombey and Son*. This is an early novel, and Dickens had perhaps not then made the proto-Weberian connections he makes in *Little Dorrit*: in the official scheme of the book, Dombey is mainly an exemplar of the Sin of Pride. Even so, Dickens emphasizes what a cold and unhappy pride this is, and he makes it poignantly clear that Dombey, though a leading London magnate, is also the victim of ancient severities:

From the glimpses [the nurse] caught of Mr Dombey at these times, sitting in the dark distance, looking out towards the infant from among the dark heavy furniture – the house had been inhabited for years by his father, and in many of its appointments was old-fashioned and grim – she began to entertain ideas of him in his solitary state, as if he were a prisoner in a cell.[24]

This character is caught in the original illustrations to the novel, by Dickens's regular artist, 'Phiz' (Hablôt Knight Browne). In *The Dombey Family* (illus. 43), Mr Dombey, though at home with his children, wears still both his formal black suit and the cold formality itself he might wear at a business meeting. He looks indeed like a man not able to be at home, who seems visibly, in his rigid though seated verticality, to want to shrink inwards from both his children. He faces away from them, pinched-faced and tiny-mouthed, though his eyes are unhappily drawn to the daughter poised unhappily at the threshold of the room.

What Dickens does eerily well in this novel is to bring home how the work ethic is transmitted. The essential work is done terribly early: the child comes to in a joyless and almost loveless gloom, which it gradually understands to be made of morality – a morality that has scant place for pleasure or imagination, and where the only thing with magic and power is the mysterious agency of money. So little Paul Dombey learns, when he asks, 'how that money caused us to be honoured, feared, respected, courted, and admired, and made us powerful and glorious in the eyes of all men'.[25] The motive for any action is duty. Into the cold vacuum of the child's deprived nature, the ethic steadily insinuates itself; it is at home there, and the pattern is set. It is a harsh process, and Paul Dombey does not survive it.

Mr Dombey does not always wear black: at the start of the novel he has a 'trim blue coat', an early version of the blue business suit. We may still picture him as wearing black because for so many of the strongest pages of the novel he is in mourning. He has to mourn his first wife, and later he mourns Paul, but we scarcely notice the difference because in a marvellous, but also macabre, way the evocation of the funeral, and the deathliness of the house following the death of the first Mrs Dombey, turn by gradations into a kind of pre-funeral for Paul, before he dies. When away from home, Paul is housed in black academies, first that of Mrs Pipchin, and then Dr Blimber's. Black, in *Dombey and Son*, is the mourning for what is killed in Dombey himself, in Mrs Dombey, in Paul – heart, enjoyment, imagination, 'changing emotions'. It is the colour of the drive that survives these absent others, an obscure, unappeasable busy anxiety, with a twist in its heart of

43 Hablôt K. Browne ('Phiz'), *The Dombey Family*, 1846, etching for *Dombey and Son*.

jealous malice. In Paul himself there is the stirring of sly calculation, a precocious counting of advantages and costs, that emancipates him from Dickens's sentimental children.

In Dickens's work black is the emblem of ascetic strains, puritanical or specifically Calvinistic, which he found running through English life, and especially through mercantile and middle-class life. This applies whether or not the actual clothes are black. Mr Murdstone, in *David Copperfield*, who derives his money from the wine trade, is pious, puritanical and ruthless. We are not told very much about his clothes, though in Frederick Barnard's illustration to the Household Edition

44 James Mahoney, illustration to *Little Dorrit* in the Household Edition, 1871–9, wood engraving.

45 Frederick Barnard, illustration to *David Copperfield* in the Household Edition, 1871–9, wood engraving.

(illus. 45) he is certainly wearing a black frock-coat, waistcoat and cravat. What Dickens stresses in his text, with the typically poetic play of his realism, is that the blackness has passed into the man. 'He had [a] shallow black eye. . . . His hair and whiskers were blacker and thicker . . . than I had given them credit for being.' There is 'the dotted indication of the strong black beard he shaved close every day. . . . This, his regular eyebrows, and the rich white, and black, and brown, of his complexion . . . made me think him, in spite of my misgivings, a very handsome man.'[26]

The blackness of Murdstone has two aspects: it is the darkness of his cruel trade religion, but also his blackness is glossy, dark-eyed, sexually attractive. He is tall, *dark* and handsome, and silly fragile Mrs Copperfield is fascinated and falls for him. She is the complement to him. For it is a subtlety of Dickens's art that he does not show only how a Calvinistic business severity may lead to the withering of heart and sex, with the consequent liability to be fascinated by proud cold stony women – Mr Dombey's second marriage, to Edith Granger, has that basic rightness, whatever melodrama sings around it. He shows also how the severity may lead instead to a harsh, secretive desire, with sadism in it, for a frail fair flower one may love, and torment, and suffocate slowly. His blackness is given in his name, Murdstone; it is such a case as may have moved Blake to write of sick roses and invisible worms and love gone dark and secret, cherishing in the night its crimson joy.

I will mention, parenthetically, that Murdstone's warehouse, where David Copperfield is put to work, is based on the blacking factory where Dickens was briefly placed by his parents. The traumatic effect of that episode on his young life has been often discussed, and, possibly, exaggerated. One may still note passingly that this bad industrial experience with 'blacking' – the black paint that men used to put on their boots – may have played its part in sensitizing Dickens's imagination to the many shades of black that met him in his world.

Certainly his imagination fastens on the black. I mentioned earlier the industrialist in *Bleak House*, Mr Rouncewell, though the dark figures in that novel who make the strongest impression are of course not the businessmen, but the lawyers: Conversation Kenge ('dressed all in black'); the Lord Chancellor, without his robes ('plainly dressed in black'); and, above all, the *éminence noire* of the novel, Mr Tulkinghorn ('one peculiarity of his black clothes . . . is, that they never shine'). The lawyers are presented as being in mourning – as mourning, in anticipation, their clients, to whom they and their legalism may prove fatal. Dickens conveys this idea with a wonderful–

horrible poetry in the figure of Mr Vholes, taking off 'his close black gloves as if he were skinning his hands'.[27]

The blackness of lawyers does not, of course, derive directly from the work ethic. Both lawyers, and others in the 'learned professions' (physicians, teachers, the clergy) had, throughout Europe, a habit of wearing black since at least the sixteenth century. Dickens was no lover of the learned professions, but I should say something of professional black, since the professions were important in the nineteenth century, and more so with the development of the 'new professions', such as engineering. As to the law, not all its professionals were as sombrely rook-like as Mr Tulkinghorn. Judges throughout Europe had dressed richly, often in red, since judges were the deputies of the sovereigns and lords who anciently gave judgement (though there were judges in black in, for example, Portugal, Lombardy, Genoa). In the fifteenth century, many advocates had worn coloured clothes (in England the 'serjeants' were parti-coloured, blue on one side and green on the other), but in the sixteenth century advocates blackened, influenced both by the black gown of learned dignity in general, and more particularly by the black university gown. From the turn of the seventeenth century, English law students, Kings Counsel and barristers all wore black gowns.[28] By the eighteenth century the gown, in black cloth or black silk, had become a uniform over-garment, worn on top of the black coat, black waistcoat and black knee-breeches, which now were the frequent daily wear of the learned, and which, by the following century had in turn become a uniform. So Dickens's Mr Tulkinghorn, in the middle of the nineteenth century – in the middle of the age that inaugurated the trouser – 'is of what is called the old school . . . and wears knee breeches tied with ribbons, and gaiters or stockings'. The black of Mr Tulkinghorn is lustreless as mourning: his clothes, as noted, 'never shine. Mute, close, irresponsive to any glancing light, his dress is like himself.' It is the black not only of serious, but of self-effacing dutifulness: 'He never converses, when not professionally consulted. He is found sometimes, speechless but quite at home, at corners of dinner-tables in great country houses, and near doors of drawing-rooms . . .'. It is, above all, the black of service – of service at once to his clients, who mainly are the wealthy and the great, and of service to the intricated permanences of the Law. Sir Leicester Dedlock 'likes Mr Tulkinghorn's dress; there is a kind of tribute in that too. It is eminently respectable, and likewise, in a general way, retainerlike. It expresses, as it were, the steward of the legal mysteries, the butler of the legal cellar of the Dedlocks.' Mr Tulkinghorn's black is the black of a retained guardian of the guarantees of power.[29]

In many countries, the black gowns of advocates were the black gowns of those who studied law at university. In the universities themselves, Rectors and the high-ranking full Doctors might wear, on formal and festive occasions, a lordly and senatorial red; as judges, frequently, wore red; as Cardinals, the princes of the Church, wore red; and as in general civic worthies, and in England mayors and aldermen, came to wear red. But the undress wear of Doctors, and both the dress and undress wear of Masters, Bachelors and non-aristocratic students was normally black, and in many cases had been so since the fourteenth century.[30] Schoolteachers wore black gowns, as did university teachers; and if later the gown was worn less often, still the teacher, the learned man, wore a black suit. The schoolmasters in Dickens wear black: even Wackford Squeers, the proprietor of a 'Yorkshire School' where the illegitimate and the unwanted may be cheaply abandoned, wears 'a suit of scholastic black'. And the truly learned among Dickens's teachers wear the 'old school' dress of Mr Tulkinghorn – they wear, that is, black breeches. Dr Blimber, in *Dombey and Son*, is 'a portly gentleman in a suit of black, with strings at his knees, and stockings below them', and Dr Strong in *David Copperfield* is similarly clad. Though Dickens is in general critical of pedagogues, as transmitters of a sterile if prestigious pedantry, he has a reverence for Dr Strong's true passion for learning, as also for his unworldly kindness to the poor. Dr Strong in his black is seen as an innocent devout priest of learning, disastrous as a husband but none the less a saint. Walking in the courtyard, abstracted in etymology, he is contrasted with 'the stray rooks and jackdaws looking after him with their heads cocked slyly, as if they knew how much more knowing they were in worldly affairs than he'. His black has the dignity not of legal or medical learning specifically, but rather of learning as such.[31]

Physicians likewise wore black gowns in the sixteenth and seventeenth centuries, and by the eighteenth century favoured dark or black suits. In the nineteenth century they still wore black: one of George Eliot's doctors is 'not to be distinguished from a mild clergyman in appearance'. Less confined to professional premises than lawyers and teachers, they were less loyal to 'old school' breeches, and their black, if they were prosperous, was fashionable black. It was, none the less, the black of learned gravity. Even Tertius Lydgate, the young doctor-hero of George Eliot's *Middlemarch*, who is of the gentry and somewhat easy in his manner, still 'had the medical accomplishment of looking perfectly grave whatever nonsense was talked to him, and his dark steady eyes gave him impressiveness as a listener'. Gravity is the common note of Dickens's doctors: if they are doctors who minister to the great, they have a grave important taciturnity, like Doctor Parker Peps in the first chapter of *Dombey and Son*, who has a 'round, deep, sonorous voice, muffled for the occasion, like the knocker'. If they are family doctors, they are all mildness and nervous deferral, like the unnamed 'family practitioner' who also attends the first chapter of *Dombey and Son*, or like Mr Chillip in the first chapter of *David Copperfield* (another doctor attending, simultaneously, the birth of a principal, and of a novel – Victorian novels begin at the beginning). Of Mr Chillip we are told

He was the meekest of his sex, the mildest of little men. He sidled in and out of a room, to take up the less space. He walked as softly as the Ghost in Hamlet, and more slowly. He carried his head on one side, partly in modest depreciation of himself, partly in modest propitiation of everybody else.

Doctors in Dickens may be minimally characterized, though offering, still, brief good signals of medical qualification ('The doctor came too. The Doctor shook his head. It was all he could do, under the circumstances, and he did it well': *Martin Chuzzlewit*). They may be no more than brief uncharacterized bleedings, if they are of the humbler calling of surgeons. In the smaller doctors, it would appear, the black of a dutiful self-effacement may amount to the black of pretended invisibility. Their black is still the livery of an impersonal expertise, and, at the higher and more expensive social levels, one would doubtless say their black reflects the high dignity of medical learning. At all levels their manner, like their dress, is solemn, as appropriate to men who daily faced diseases they could not be sure of curing, and whose ministrations even in childbirth could end in accident, infection and death. While the black of physicians is not undertaker's black, it is the black of those who have made a profession and a 'mystery' of engaging, in earnest, in the contest with death.[32]

The most profound mystery, now become a profession, was that of the clergy. While Anglican bishops were known by their white full-sleeved rochet, and priests in general wore the white surplice in service, clergy outside the church wore a black cassock or black gown or both. In the eighteenth century they might wear the black suit – or, still, the black cassock. For daily wear, during his trip to London, Henry Fielding's Parson Adams wears his black cassock, with a short greatcoat over it that only half-covers it, making him, as Fielding says, 'a Figure likely to attract the Eyes of those who were not over-given to Observation'. In the nineteenth century, a clergyman is likely, outside church, to wear a black suit, which may include black trousers but may – again if he is of 'the old school' – include black breeches worn with black gaiters. Thus Mr Harding, Trollope's decent and truly Christian old clergyman in *The Warden*, 'always wears a black frock coat, black knee-breeches, and black gaiters, and somewhat scandalises some of his more hyper-clerical brethren by a black neck-handkerchief'. Harding's neckwear is simply old-fashioned: the 'hyper-clerical brethren' would by this date (1855) be favouring the Roman collar, while a low-church clergyman would wear a white bow-tie. Mr Harding is too true a Christian to be precisely a learned professional: that estate, in the grandeur of its professionalism, is personated in this novel by the archdeacon, Dr Grantly:

As the archdeacon stood up to make his speech, erect in the middle of that little square, he looked like an ecclesiastical statue placed there, as a fitting impersonation of the church militant here on earth; his shovel hat, large, new, and well-pronounced, a churchman's hat in every inch, declared the profession as plainly as does the Quaker's broad brim; his heavy eyebrows, large open eyes, and full mouth and chin expressed the solidity of his order; the broad chest, amply covered with fine cloth, told how well to do was its estate; one hand ensconced within his pocket, evinced the practical hold which our mother church keeps on her temporal possessions; and the other, loose for action, was ready to fight if need be in her defence; and, below these, the decorous breeches, and neat black gaiters showing so admirably that well-turned leg, betokened the decency, the outward beauty and grace of our church establishment.

It is a wonderful picture of professional Church power in the pink. That the dress of a dean, like mourning dress, might be very little different from professional dress generally is indicated in Dickens's *The Mystery of Edwin Drood*, where Mr Sapsea the auctioneer – as it were, a semi-professional figure – 'dresses at' the Dean:

he has been bowed to for the Dean, in mistake; has even been spoken to in the street as My Lord, under the impression that he was the Bishop come down unexpectedly, without his chaplain. Mr Sapsea is very proud of this, and of his voice, and of his style. He has even (in selling landed property), tried the experiment of slightly intoning in his pulpit, to make himself more like what he takes to be the genuine ecclesiastical article.

Both the dress of auctioneers, and the range of clerical dress generally in the 1860s – including the long coat of 'clerical' cut – may be seen in the illustrations to *Edwin Drood*: in which also the peculiar closed world of the more cloistered clergy is described with a mild, whimsical poetry: as with muscularly Christian Mr Crisparkle, sparring before breakfast, 'soft-hearted benevolence beamed from his boxing-gloves'. The Victorians cared for their bodies, inside their black clothes.[33]

It must, then, be a further factor, consolidating the dark fashion of the nineteenth century, that not only its ironmasters were coming to the fore, but also its professional men maintained their standing, as British society, and its economy, themselves became more 'professional'. They were able, with increasing confidence and dignity, to assert their importance *as* professionals, wearing smart dark clothes which showed their respect for what they were. In *Bleak House* we have not only Mr Rouncewell, winning his point against Sir Leicester, we have also Mr Tulkinghorn acquiring control of his aristocratic clients.

And actually the learned professions and the lawyers – who, as Dickens brings out, had their own grim professional asceticism – do belong in one broad family with the Calvinistic businessmen. Weber did not argue that Calvinism unaided was the origin of capitalism, and among the preconditions he emphasized was the development of an elaborate legal code, accompanying a rationalization of human behaviour. The lawyers in black are not irrelevant: Calvin himself – and this shows in the whole articulation of his theology – was a lawyer.

There were, further, the new professions, engineers, chemists, members of the new professional associations. They took their colour from the older professions, and it was professionally important that they should. Mr Pecksniff in *Martin Chuzzlewit*, who is a professional as well as a puritan, wears black. He is a widower, it is true, but his black also echoes both his pulpit tone and his 'professings' as an adept of architectural art. He is remembered now as the personification of hypocrisy, the English Tartuffe: but Dickens describes in some detail his office, with trainee architects working there (the young Martin Chuzzlewit is one) whose designs Pecksniff adapts, without full acknowledgement, to meet his own commissions. Phiz's illustration *Martin much gratified by an imposing ceremony* (illus. 46) shows Pecksniff in his professional activity, attending the laying of the foundation stone of a school he claims to have designed, with a look of butter-hardening virtue. Pecksniff is a satiric figure, but the satire is a refraction of practice: and what Mr Pecksniff illustrates is both the dignity, or pomp, new-professional man had acquired, together with the tactical incorporation – serving to reinforce his standing – of the older black robing of the man set apart by humility, piety, learning and virtue. In J. P. Knight's portrait of Sir Charles Barry (illus. 47) in London's National Portrait Gallery we may see a black-suited architect represented *not* satirically, but with the proper respect, the respect due to genius, though Pecksniff also, in order not to miss inspiration striking at night, slept with pencil and paper beside him (as did, for example, William Blake). One may easily find in the National Portrait Gallery many nineteenth-century black-suited new-professionals (alongside, of

46 Hablôt K. Browne ('Phiz'), *Martin much gratified by an imposing ceremony*, 1843–4, etching for *Martin Chuzzlewit*.

course, black-suited *old*-professionals – physicians to the distinguished, judges, divines).

In *Fitz-Boodle's Professions*, his sequel to *Fitz-Boodle's Confessions*, Thackeray offers, through the mouth of his character George Fitz-Boodle, advice on the new professions now available 'to the unemployed younger sons of the nobility' ('Does not the world want new professions? Are there not thousands of well-educated men

panting, struggling, pushing, starving in the old ones?'). His first profession, or mock-profession, is that of Auctioneer; his second, his own invention, is that of Dinner-master or Gastronomist, and he prescribes the appropriate dress and mien:

You will make your appearance, dressed in a dark dress, with one handsome enormous gold chain, and one large diamond ring. . . . You will be yourself a portly grave man, with your head a little bald and grey. In fact, in this, as in all other professions, you had best try to look as like Canning as you can.

The dress scholar Elizabeth Wilson has referred to 'the discreet and secretive style of the business or professional man'.[34]

Though the novelists were amused by professional *gravitas*, the professions and new professions were a force. A man who has subdued himself to an arduous training, and who shows by his dark suit that he denies himself still, is clearly the servant of his hard-earned skill: which is then his power and gives him power, however humble his manners may be. And a professional had power in the nineteenth century, as a priest had power in the late Middle Ages: it is not surprising they are synchromatic. You may not understand all the professional says, for every profession has its necessary jargon, serving, as had Latin in the past, to make command manifest, through command of a language the layman cannot speak. But, however powerful, he can also be relied on; his black also tells you that, for it says he is unseduced by cheap pleasures and temptations. A man in black is a man you can trust. He is a man, to come to the bottom line, whom you can trust with your money. It was important, by extension, for stockbrokers to wear black, and for black to be a prominent colour not only in the city (for black is especially urban) but in the City. At the same time black is good cover for a rising élite, aspiring but not yet sure of arrival, and the new-professionals were on course to be the new élite.

The move of menswear into black in the nineteenth century is not surprising when one sees how, while the aristocracy qualifies its sumptuary display (for there were recurring revolutions to be seen on the Continent), the black armies of the Nonconformist merchants and ironmasters, and the learned professions and the new professions, and of course the dandies, and Evangelical preachers, converge with new confidence on the same tailors. The change spread steadily to more walks of life, and to those in service as well as in employment, to the gentlemen's gentlemen as well as the gentlemen. In 'The Dorsetshire Labourer', written in the 1880s, Hardy records that agricultural labourers no longer wore their smocks and gaiters, but now wore dark or black clothes and 'might be tailors or undertakers' men, for what they exhibit externally'.[35]

Seeing these cooperating workers in black, one might think not only of Weber but of Durkheim, and recur to Durkheim's concept of a social church. One might speak of a society, or at least of a gender within the society, that states in its colour a sense of common cause shared by people in diverse roles. Black cannot here be called, without serious qualification, what Baudelaire called it – that is, 'democratic'. Yet its general use does surely testify to an underlying coherence within Victorian society, and a desire to present at least an appearance of equal claims, however stratified and divided that society may also have been. One sees this in those London scenes, photographed or painted, where the many men in black, rich and less rich, go about their different businesses with a common erect self-respect, a shared sober self-importance.

Society was much preoccupied with its differences of rank. But still black was apt, if one accepts – as suggested earlier – that black has been associated with bonds of authority: with the acceptance of authority and its obligations both by those who order and by those who obey, a relationship that might be represented by those *Punch* cartoons where a gentleman, tall and lean and black-suited, is at ease in his command, exercised lightly, of his valet or manservant, who is also tall and lean and black-suited, and at ease in his service, which he tends with self-respect and with his own secure pride. It could even be hard, according

48 George du
Maurier,
'Inconvenience of
Modern Male
Attire', wood
engraving, from
Punch, date
unknown.

INCONVENIENCE OF MODERN MALE ATTIRE

First Stranger. " Here—hi ! I want a knife and fork, please ! "
Second Stranger. " Con-found you—so do I ? "

to at least one *Punch* cartoon, to tell who was a servant and who was a guest (illus. 48): both the men in Du Maurier's cartoon are 'Strangers', and men in black are simultaneously strangers and brothers (as earlier the *fratres*, or friars, were). The black-clad servant has his own dignity, and if the master does not keep his end up, the result is unhappy, or the material for comedy, as in P. G. Wodehouse, where Bertie is minded by the power-figure Jeeves. The power-black of the butler – a figure who becomes a black priest of class values – was not invented by Wodehouse, or by J. M. Barrie, the creator of the 'perfect butler', the 'Admirable Crichton'. It is already there complete in *Little Dorrit*: the 'vulgar' tycoon in that novel, Mr Merdle, is reduced to a timorous slinking when he meets his butler, 'the stateliest man in company. He did nothing, but he looked on as few other men could have done.'[36]

It is clear that however rich and smart black might be, it also was, even when not ascetic, serious – serious, often solemn, and not infrequently gloomy. The dominant feature for Dickens of the world he inhabited was oppressiveness, and the oppressiveness is localized in people's clothing, as with Mr Tite Barnacle, a head of the Civil Service:

His wristbands and collar were oppressive, his voice and manner were oppressive. He had a large watch-chain and bunch of seals, a coat buttoned up to inconvenience, a waistcoat buttoned up to inconvenience, an unwrinkled pair of trousers, a stiff pair of boots. He was altogether splendid, massive, overpowering, and impracticable. He seemed to have been sitting for his portrait to Sir Thomas Lawrence all the days of his life.[37]

There are happily dressed men in Dickens, of course, dashing blades and sparks, comfortable fathers of families; but often the relation between men and their clothes is negative, and either dark or constraining or both. He has two antithetical conceits to express this; in one, what is dark in the clothes merges into the man, as with Mr Murdstone. Mr Jaggers in *Great Expectations*, who as a lawyer would necessarily wear black, is recognizable to Pip by 'his dark complexion, his deep-set eyes, his bushy black eyebrows, . . . his strong black dots of beard and whisker'. Alternatively, Dickens registers a maladjustment between men and their apparel, as with Mr Tite Barnacle, massively incommoded; or Mr Merdle in the same novel, with 'a somewhat uneasy expression about his coat-cuffs, as if they were in his confidence, and had reasons for being anxious to hide his hands'; or Mr Turveydrop the dandy, 'pinched in, and swelled out, and got up, and strapped down'; or Mr Gradgrind in *Hard Times*, with 'his very neckcloth, trained to take him by the throat with an unaccommodating grasp, like a stubborn fact, as it was'; or Bradley Headstone, the schoolmaster in *Our Mutual Friend*, in 'his decent black coat and waistcoat, and decent white shirt, and decent formal black tie. . . . He was never seen in any other dress, and yet there was a certain stiffness in his manner of wearing this, as if there were a want of adaptation between him and it.' They are secure for the time being in their different social grades, and any oppression in their clothes is chosen by them: it 'suits' them. So, for instance, the tension between Bradley Headstone and his clothes is a tension between his passions and the mechanical constraints he has wanted to put upon his nature, in pushing to make his career as a new model teacher.[38]

In other words, whether men merge with their clothes or are at war with their clothes, the oppression in the clothes is an oppression in them also, which they maintain however secure or successful they are. Dickens does not rest in his early vision of the ethical drama of Scrooge versus Pickwick. The world of his later novels from *David Copperfield* on has a shadow on it at every level: which makes it appropriate, I hope, for me to try at this point to broaden my argument, and to consider the whole ambitious picture Dickens attempted to paint of his much-troubled triumphal society.

49 Gustave Doré, *Ludgate Hill – A Block in the Street*, wood engraving from *London:
A Pilgrimage*, London, 1872.

5 England's Dark House

Oppression, in Dickens's late novels, is ubiquitous. It is outside and inside, in the atmosphere of his cities and in the bloodstream of his people. It is in the rhythm of transactions with inferiors and superiors, and even of the transactions men have with themselves. The point is made repeatedly in the presentation of Mr Jaggers, who is a savagely overbearing bully, and not only to others but also, it appears, to himself and his own feelings. There is the famous, perhaps schematic, case of Jaggers's clerk Wemmick, who only lets himself be human when he is at home. When he and Pip return to the office, 'by degrees, Wemmick got dryer and harder as we went along, and his mouth tightened into a post office again'. The point is made more subtly – indeed, beautifully – in the scene in the office where both Jaggers and Wemmick, recording the history of Estella from childhood, let their feelings become involved, and afterwards are irritable with each other. They are saved by the arrival of the client Mike, whose daughter has been taken up for shoplifting, and who starts to cry. Both Jaggers and Wemmick join in bullying him ferociously ('I'll have no feelings here', says Jaggers, 'Get out'), and Dickens records:

So the unfortunate Mike very humbly withdrew, and Mr Jaggers and Wemmick appeared to have re-established their good understanding, and went to work again with an air of refreshment upon them as if they had just had lunch.

The 'good understanding' is professional-ascetic; they relish the functional frost of the office.[1]

There is a constant tension in Dickens's England. Though he depicts many pompous people, he does not, in his large-scale political canvases, depict a complacent society. On the contrary, those in command are often in a state of irritable nervousness with regard to those who are supposed to be under them: this applies not only to his schoolmasters and tyrannical parents, but also to his aristocrats, and his magnates in the City. And British politics at large, and more especially since the late eighteenth century, had manifestly been a politics of alarm, with successive governments watching anxiously the upheavals on the Continent, and passing a string of measures, such as the Seditious Meetings Bill, to ensure the same thing did not happen here. That Dickens himself shared these alarms is clear from his comments on the Chartists and on the early trades unions; but he also had what his friend Forster called his 'old radical leanings', and at times shared the revolutionary impulse:

I declare I never go into what is called 'society' that I am not aweary of it, despise it, hate it, and reject it. The more I see of its extraordinary conceit, and its stupendous ignorance of what is passing out of doors, the more certain I am that it is approaching the period when, being incapable of reforming itself, it will have to submit to be reformed by others off the face of the earth.[2]

Dickens did not have great contact with working men, but some of their feelings reached him directly, for instance in his correspondence with the cabinet-maker John Overs, a relatively mild man who, none the less, told Dickens:

The working-man . . . toils from dawn to sundown merely for the liberty to exist. He feels that the curse of Cain is upon him – every man's hand is against him – and he concludes that he ought to have Cain's revenge – his hand against every man.[3]

He also wrote to Dickens that 'the working-man has no method in his thoughts, *but the scythes are a-sharpening*'. Dickens could share such feelings to an extent, as when he wrote the part of Will Fern in 'The Chimes': 'There'll be a Fire to-night. . . . When you see the distant sky red, think of me no more; or if you do, remember what a Hell was lighted up inside of me.' But still Dickens keeps the rick-burning 'distant', and there is something painfully double-edged in the rhetoric he puts into Will Fern's mouth. For the 'Hell' that is lit inside Will Fern must tend to put him among the damned, even as others are blamed for lighting it. And in fact, for all his radical leanings, powerful as they really were, Dickens is still busy, within the correspondence, in keeping John Overs in his place. When Overs criticized Dickens's friend Macready, Dickens wrote 'You have shown a deficiency of that moral sense which I have believed you to possess . . . you have lost sight of your true position in regard to that gentleman, and all other gentlemen with whom you have come in contact.' Dickens himself is as willing as any of his own pompous characters to employ, when he needs it, that greatest, most universal, and possibly most powerful resort of oppression in Victorian England, the 'moral sense'. The 'moral sense' of the Victorians was a good deal concerned with keeping people in their social place, as in the 'moral' education offered at the Academy of Charlotte Brontë's Mr Brocklehurst.[4]

The moral sense, in this sense, was a powerful agent, both policing society and making each person his own policeman. In Dickens's fiction there is a growing suggestion from novel to novel of unruly forces tightly pent, both in Society and in individuals too: as the emotions that threaten a late creation like Mr Jaggers – or, much more, Bradley Headstone – are powerful indeed and are kept down with power. Indeed, a large part of the Dickens 'gallery' of characters consists of variations on the theme not so much of tension as of torsion. Many of his people are eccentric or odd, and not a few of them are more or less crazy, as a result of strains, internal and external, which are close to being too much for them. He shows a society that is not static in a frozen way, but is unhappy with baulked and frustrated energy, and which uses its energy to keep itself so. It is a society, in his own term, 'dedlocked', which he also thought was like a social bomb, and bound sooner or later to explode. The oppressiveness of his world is not a cloud but a smoke, the pall of a fire damped but not out (an image he liked to use). If then the black clothes show a certain coherence in the society – a society militantly respectable and militantly pious – and show also the acceptance of the bonds of authority, a degree of self-effacement in the impersonality of 'station', still this coherence and acceptance are far from serene. They are the product of a will and effort to maintain them, and from this point of view black must seem, as it had at an earlier period, the insignia also of misgiving and anxiety, the uniform of an effort and assertion of discipline.

It is a society marked not only by oppressiveness, but by a more painful anguish of frustration – as in the long war fought by the inventor Daniel Doyce (who wears 'decent black') to make and market his new invention, against the labours of the Circumlocution Office (Whitehall) to frustrate and prevent him; or as in the efforts of Dickens's litigants to obtain justice from a court busy mainly in devouring those who resort to it. This is the pattern of social movement in Dickens's world, and it is the pattern of movement in his fiction also. His novels advance from confrontation to confrontation, while the main action consists of the efforts of people to combat powers that in the end will defeat them. His heroes may win a respite and a personal solace – a marriage, a home, a modest prosperity – but in their bigger campaigns they are disappointed. Indeed, it is not easy to imagine them being otherwise, for they are born from the start into closed situations, into prison or immemorial webs of litigation, into roads that are blocked, deep-rooted double binds. And they are complicit in the fates that defeat them, like Pip who wants to be a gentleman, though gentility also does him great damage.

The oppressiveness of this world can be presented by Dickens as overwhelming and defeating, as something before which one can feel only helpless, as does the crossing-sweeper Jo:

And there he sits, munching and gnawing, and looking up at the great Cross on the summit of St Paul's Cathedral, glittering above a red and violet-tinted cloud of smoke. From the boy's face one might suppose that sacred emblem to be, in his eyes, the crowning confusion of the great, confused city; so golden, so high up, so far out of his reach.[5]

Both the milling, choked confusion, and the high cross in the sky, are caught in Gustave Doré's wood-engraving *Ludgate Hill – A Block in the Street* (illus. 49); a Victorian hearse, with mutes, may be seen in the centre. The whole series Doré made, to illustrate *London*, the book he produced with Blanchard Jerrold, are intensely significant – and relevant to this chapter, though I reproduce only two of them – just because Doré was a foreigner, and therefore registered with an unfamiliar, naked vision both what was extraordinary, and what was socially and politically appalling, in the over-thronged city with its social extremes.

Of this confusion, Dickens had his analysis: he contrasts England with the Continent, where social upsets occurred, and relates the oppressiveness he describes to the old-fashionedness of so many English institutions. He traces that old-fashionedness back to the Conquest, and the point merits development. Several times, even in the last two centuries, it has been Britain's role in Europe to lead a conservative crusade. We still possess – as we have uninterruptedly, even throughout the Interregnum – the nobility established by the Conqueror. People come and go but structures persist, and we might, reviewing our history, remark the peculiar situation of England, as a country subdued by a foreign invasion which never afterwards went away: so there is (to use the ironic phrase Dickens enjoyed) a merry-old-English tradition of oppression running back not just for decades but for nearly a millennium.

It is true that Victorian England hardly seems to us a scene of deadlock, especially when we think of the age's innovations. England was first in the field in the Industrial Revolution, and was a hugely inventive commercial dynamo. Dickens reported the innovations, especially in the pages of the magazines he edited, and he clearly shared the popular exhilaration in his age's 'mighty course of civilisation and improvement'.[6] But still, in the new works, he found blackness and oppression: in the new railways, which he compared to death; in the factory-machines, which he compared to mad elephants; in the burgeoning Utilitarian philosophy of Fact. Dickens saw his world as a wonderland of new mechanical marvels, and yet also as a big rich prison of materialism. It is clear too that he saw the new national order as continuing the pattern of old subjugations. The *nouveau riche* mill-owner Mr Bounderby, in *Hard Times*, who believes his workers want to be fed on turtle soup and venison with a gold spoon, is identical in his reactionary politics to the landed aristocrat Sir Leicester Dedlock, obsessed with his fears of a new Wat Tyler.

It would have to be said too that, even as regards big business, the century did not have an untroubled course. There were periods of depression, for instance at the end of the Napoleonic Wars and again in the later 1830s. There were crises in 1841–2 and 1847–8, and a new crisis and price-collapse in 1855. As the century aged, England faced increasing competition from the industrial revolutions of other countries. What Dickens describes in *Little Dorrit*, which was written in the mid-1850s, is an England that is falling behind its competitors; that neglects its best talents, like those of Daniel Doyce; and that is failing to make as good use of its resources as even imperial Russia was doing. Dickens's vision in that novel was perhaps darkened too much by the exigencies of 1855, for the business world recovered quickly and British exports boomed in the later 1850s in a way one certainly would not have guessed from reading *Little Dorrit*. It still was the case that Great Britain faced increasing international competition, and by the Paris Exhibition in 1867 it was clear that pre-eminence had passed to other countries, and to new growing companies, such as Krupp. Though Dickens saw darkly, he was not wrong to see Britain facing decline, and it would be hard now to say he was wrong in connecting Britain's frustration of its own best possibilities with the survival, in so many departments of the country, of a reactionary apparatus. It was there not only in the law courts and the country estates, but in the Civil Service also (the Circumlocution Office), which Dickens still saw as 'a politico diplomatico hocus pocus piece of machinery, for the assistance of the nobs in keeping off the snobs'. Dickens's vision is of an England dominated finally by ancient privileges, which pen and oppress its newer energies, so the whole thronged and hugely opulent vessel, increasingly turning its gaze to its past, gloomily sinks.[7]

One might, in this light, see British black, although a variation of Protestant black, as having also its similarity to Spanish black, the black that wrapped Philip II's domain, the black that is not only of a nation, but rather of an empire, both feeling its grandeur and yet observing with displeasure the likely erosion of its power. For there is certainly a connection between black and empire. It is not a connection that works both ways, for what an empire wears must depend on the character and history of the empire, and manifestly not all empires have wanted to wear black. But it is notable, from the other side of the argument, that whenever a European nation as a whole has taken black as its fashion, this has occurred at that nation's greatest moment of international power. This is true of Burgundy in the fifteenth century, of Venice in the fifteenth and sixteenth centuries, of Spain in the sixteenth century, of the Dutch republic in the seventeenth century and of England in the nineteenth century. It is not hard to see how the values of black discussed earlier in this study – self-effacement and uniformity, impersonality and authority, discipline and self-discipline, a willingness to be strict and a willingness to die – might assist in maintaining an imperial order. Beyond these considerations, one might again naturally connect the use of black by the Spanish, the Dutch and the English, during their centuries of power, with the fact that each of these nations placed a large reliance, both for the internal discipline of their functionaries, and also for their general licence to see themselves as a power for good, on an ascetic and fear-filled cast of Christianity. Imperial black would, then, be the final, most potent, and most fully secularized translation of the black of the Church. One might, adapting Durkheim's notion, speak of a society held darkly together by grave faith in itself, not so much as a 'social church', but rather as an imperial church.

An attendant fact – due to black's many solemn associations – is that black, if smart, is also *important*: black is a good colour to wear if you are sure you should be taken a great deal more seriously than any mere prosperous peacock. The sense of importance is visible and strong in many portraits and photographs of the dark-clad great of the dominant nations. Whether at the same time, as I have suggested earlier, imperial black contains an element of the *Angst* of empire is hard of course to prove. Burgundy was in the event cut in two, and Venice, at the turn of the sixteenth century, was briefly at risk of being destroyed. It is true, too, that Spanish black reaches its deepest at a period when Spain had achieved its largest expansion, and was especially concerned to keep secure hold of its increasingly restive possessions. The United Provinces, both through their rise and in their greatest prosperity, lived with the constant threat of invasion, either by their immediate neighbours or by Spain, or of course by the sea. In the case of England, however, it is harder to argue for a continuing anxiety. For during a large part of the period in which black was fashionable – in the years from the mid-1840s to the mid-1870s – there was an enormous English accumulation of wealth, facilitated by new commercial treaties with the nations of the world, from France to Japan. Against this, one can only note that a period which in retrospect looks so serenely profitable still had, at the time, its causes for concern, not only with the crisis of 1855, but with, for instance, the American Civil War (1861–5), which seriously interrupted trade. There were also the more patent upsets of empire, such as the Indian Mutiny of 1857–9. But in any case the boom period came to a close, and the late years of the century, from the mid-1870s on, saw Great Britain wane as a commercial power, though the empire, now become an Empire (Victoria was titled Empress in 1876), continued to grow geographically until the end of the Great War. One can certainly say that High Victorian black was important black, and, however rich, was accompanied by cares.

The importance shows in Dickens's novel of the mid-1860s, *Our Mutual Friend*, which features very early on the extreme new-money opulence of the Veneerings. It was in the mid- to late century that Victorian black, as worn by high life, was at its most sumptuous. The novel echoes with well-fed voices, that are more complacent than the power-voices heard in the novels of the 1850s. The fortunes are shown, however, to have shaky foundations, and there is a clear element of self-protection in the closed-mindedness Dickens shows in a figure like Podsnap: a closed-mindedness that is more marked, the more Podsnap has to speak of other nations, even though his own income depends on foreign trade:

Mr Podsnap's world was not a very large world, morally; no, nor even geographically: seeing that although his business was sustained upon commerce with other countries, he considered other countries, with that important reservation, a mistake, and of their manners and customs would conclusively observe, 'Not English!'

Podsnap is 'in the Marine Insurance way' – a dealer in what, at the time, were called 'incorporeal earnings' – and must, I think, be one of the first portraits in fiction of the figure of the insurance broker. He is also necessarily a man in black, since he is allowed by Dickens to exist only in the City and at dinner parties; and his main feature is that being 'thus happily acquainted with his own merit and importance, [he] settled that whatever he put behind him he put out of existence': 'I don't want to know about it; I don't choose to discuss it; I don't admit it!' He is ponderous, cumbersome, oppressive in the extreme, and seems, in this late novel, Dickens's conclusive depiction of a swollen national ego keeping up its spirits with the echoing hollowness of its superior patronizings, a depiction that has moments of frank sublimity:

'We Englishmen are Very Proud of our Constitution, Sir. It Was Bestowed Upon Us By Providence. No Other Country is so Favoured as This Country' . . .

'It was a little particular of Providence,' said the foreign gentlemen, laughing, 'for the frontier is not large.'

'Undoubtedly,' assented Mr. Podsnap; 'But So it is. It was the Charter of the Land. This Island was Blest, Sir, to the Direct Exclusion of such Other Countries as – as there may happen to be. And if we were all Englishmen present, I would say,' added Mr. Podsnap, looking round upon his compatriots and sounding solemnly with his theme, 'that there is in the Englishman a combination of qualities, a modesty, an independence, a responsibility, a repose, combined with an absence of everything calculated to call a blush into the cheek of a young person, which one would seek in vain among the Nations of the Earth.'

It is a passage in many ways suggestive, since it shows how English moralism – the ascetic strain in English life – equates with respectability and is twined with English religiosity in composing an imperial English conceit. So Dickens remarks later in the novel, 'See the conquering Podsnap comes, Sound the trumpets, beat the drums!' At the same time, the supreme privilege Podsnap gives to the *absence* of everything that could lead to blushes makes black, the colour with no colour – the colour that makes a point of absence – seem the natural colour for the conqueror to wear.[8]

The whole picture Dickens paints is of an England that has risen to massive wealth and international power, which is none the less a sombre place, run by men, and sometimes by women, who wear black often, and who, even apart from their black wear, are frequently reserved, nervous and oppressed, however rich and powerful they may personally be. There is the image that grows to increasing prominence in his fiction of the dark house, the black or blackening or blackened house, the house in mourning. One may think at first of the black and darkened houses of his most frightening women, the sardonically misnamed Satis House of Miss Havisham, or the house of Mrs Clennam in *Little Dorrit*. The latter may be seen, in the grimy blackness that Dickens emphasizes, in James Mahoney's illustration (illus. 50); Arthur Clennam, in black, is lowering his black nineteenth-century umbrella in preparation to enter. There is also the mourning house of Mr Dombey: 'Through the whole building white had turned yellow, yellow nearly black . . . it had slowly become a dark gap in the long monotonous street'. The inhabitants of these houses have property and power (Mr Dombey presides over a vast import and export business), but they are also often solitary and unhappy, and may be physically immobilized, as are Mrs Clennam and Miss Havisham in their

50 James Mahoney, illustration to *Little Dorrit* in the Household Edition, 1871–9, wood engraving.

wheelchairs, and also Sir Leicester Dedlock after his stroke in his gloomy town-house in its street of 'dismal grandeur', and Mr Tite Barnacle, a head of the Civil Service, immobilized by gout in his dark and dingy mews residence. Through Dickens's novels there develops a cumulative image of a large dark house, which is the home of power but is also a prison.[9]

One of his great novels is even called *Bleak House*. It is true that the Bleak House in the novel is notably not bleak: the solitary man who lives there has invited youth, beauty and imagination into the house, and the house itself is of the old-English, richly rambling kind that Dickens always loved. But still it would seem that in giving the novel that title, Dickens did mean to represent, in a larger sense, a bleak house. The world of this novel is otherwise bleak, as are the other buildings there, whether they are country houses, like Chesney Wold, or warehouses like Krook's, or law-courts, or slum-buildings like those in Tom-all-Alone's. As the novel showed its emphasis, coming out month by month, the illustrator, Hablôt Browne, was moved to develop for it a style wholly different from his usual vivacious jostle of characters. Instead he used a ruling machine to produce plates with dense darks and blacks precisely to render the novel's unhome-like

51 Hablôt K.
Browne ('Phiz'),
Tom-all-Alone's,
1852–3, etching for
Bleak House.

homes (illus. 51). The only figure in the grim slum-study *Tom-all-Alone's* is the doll hung for a shop-sign, which looks like a person hanged, while the wooden beams at the top of the plate, holding the tottering tenements apart, repeat on each side the shape of a gallows. In general, in illustrating the nineteenth century, I have chosen black-and-white engravings and book-illustrations, for this was the great age of black-and-white, of an art that drew and shaded its visions in black printer's ink – as, a little earlier, it had been also the great age of the silhouette, of an art that portrayed people in flat shapes of black-on-white. In an elaborate silhouette of 1835 (illus. 52), a young dandy in tight pantaloons is poised in dangerous calculation, while his gouty elder takes snuff watchfully: the two being engaged in that household game, itself checked black-and-white, which most intricately codifies the plays of power, aristocratic, ecclesiastical and regal, in a hierarchic warrior society.

CHECK MATE.

52 Augustin Edouart, *Check Mate*, lithograph, 1835. Victoria & Albert Museum, London.

Not every home in Dickens is bleak: he will show homes warm in family happiness. But these tend to be humble homes, small and crowded (the poor may be together in Dickens, while the rich are lonely), and they are more like cheerful cellars in the big house of his fiction, which one may I think, without too great licence, see also as being the House of England. It is a house where, as we ascend the social storeys, we find ourselves increasingly in the house of lonely pride, of discipline and resentment and the habit of using people like tools, of the human ego cut off from life, and jealous and ill-willed but also disabled for all the wealth at its command, as if just to be very rich and powerful were also to be – with all the force of the poetry Dickens gives these black houses – in the dark.

It would not be hard to connect this cumulative image with the elements of radicalism in Dickens's politics, and also with his gospel-Christian agreement with the proposition of Christ that the rich are further from Heaven than anyone else (for Dickens himself was not a Calvinist). But it is not a matter only of Dickens's beliefs. When he writes of these dark houses his prose both lifts with the exaltation of the writer truly moved, and thickens with a vividness of new convincing details, such as the fungus-trees in Mr Dombey's cellars, or the cobwebbed centrepiece of Miss Havisham's wedding-breakfast table, rising black from the yellow expanse with speckled-legged spiders 'running home to it'. Looking around the world he lived in with imaginative vision, Dickens saw again and again the dark house, which is not the house only of power and wealth but the bleak house also of the righteous spirit, harsh, jealous and puritanic – the house become the church of a sightless cold materialism and a merciless upright ethic.[10]

It is not a matter of houses only. The words 'dark' and 'black' recur in his descriptions of docks, railways, workshops, offices, churches, prisons – and, needless to say, of slums like Tom-all-Alone's, 'a black, dilapidated street', 'deep in black mud and corrupt water'. His many dark buildings, poor and rich, accumulate into the greater image of the nighted city, the black city, the city itself in mourning. Most famously this city is London, whose smoke-filled sootiness never failed as a black inspiration. London, in *Bleak House*, is the great metropolis of riches and influence, but still has 'the dirtiest and darkest streets that ever were seen in the world', with 'smoke lowering down from chimney-pots, making a soft black drizzle, with flakes of soot in it as big as full-grown snow-flakes – gone into mourning, one might imagine, for the death of the sun'. London buildings, in *Great Expectations*, wear a 'frowsy mourning of soot and smoke'. The soot itself was due to the nineteenth century's massive increase in the use of coal-fires, but it is clear from Dickens's recurrence to this imagery that the sootiness and smokiness were more than facts, they were images too of the city's sad spirit, which was equally manifest in its 'melancholy little squares', its 'dismal trees', its truly mournful burying grounds, and which was most manifest of all on its Sundays:

It was a Sunday evening in London, gloomy, close, and stale. Maddening church bells of all degrees of dissonance, sharp and flat, cracked and clear, fast and slow, made the brick-and-mortar echoes hideous. Melancholy streets in a penitential garb of soot, steeped the souls of the people condemned to look at them out of windows, in dire despondency.

London, which in *Our Mutual Friend* is 'such a black shrill city . . . such a gritty city; such a hopeless city, with no rent in the leaden canopy of its sky', is clearly for Dickens, for all its grandeur and its eminence in the world, a heart-chilling city of dreadful night.[11]

But if London is the old dark city, the new city of Coketown is equally dark:

It was a town of red brick, or of brick that would have been red if the smoke and ashes had allowed it; but as matters stood it was a town of unnatural red and black like the painted face of a savage. It was a town of machinery and tall chimneys, out of which interminable serpents of smoke trailed themselves for ever and ever, and never got uncoiled. It had a black canal in it, and a river that ran purple with ill-smelling dye. . . .

Coketown is, from a distance, more just a darkness on the landscape than a city, as in these wonderful sentences (a kind of industrial Turner):

You only knew the town was there, because you knew there could have been no such sulky blotch upon the prospect without a town. A blur of soot and smoke, now confusedly tending this way, now that way, now aspiring to the vault of Heaven, now murkily creeping along the earth, as the wind rose and fell, or changed its quarter: a dense formless jumble, with sheets of cross light in it, that showed nothing but masses of darkness; – Coketown in the distance was suggestive of itself, though not a brick of it could be seen.

The dark and black, it should be said, are not only symbolic and scenic. The nineteenth century's places of industry were often heavily smoke-filled. The coke used in blast-furnaces, to take one instance, was made by the open-air burning of coal spread out over acres of ground. But at the same time the smoky shadowiness signals also the mood of the town, a mood identified, on a nearer view, with the innumerable steam-engines shaking their pistons like elephants 'in a state of melancholy madness'. Melancholy madness is the product of the work ethic – 'You saw nothing in Coketown but what was severely workful'. And again, the oppression is reinforced by religion, and by the ugly churches of the 'eighteen religous persuasions'.[12]

Beyond the cities is the English landscape, which Dickens in the later novels increasingly visualizes in terms of fens, marshes, mud-flats, as in the doomed voyage down the Thames late in *Great Expectations* (a passage that Samuel Beckett picked out for special praise):

. . . a little squat shoal-lighthouse on open piles, stood crippled in the mud on stilts and crutches; and slimy stakes stuck out of the mud, and slimy stones stuck out of the mud, and red landmarks and tidemarks stuck out of the mud, and an old landing-stage and an old roofless building slipped into the mud, and all about us was stagnation and mud.

Dickens's fenscapes tend more and more, like this one, to be seen as evening closes in. Both *Great Expectations* and *Our Mutual Friend* begin by the slime and ooze of the Thames as evening darkens, setting the mood of the novels. The image of the dark house and dark city expand to the image of a muddy, cold, darkening land.[13]

It seems, then, that the image of oppressiveness, of oppression, in Dickens's England is most markedly an image of darkness. And if one asks what *is* this shadow that hangs on house and city and land, it is clear that more is involved than general gloom and malaise and oppressiveness, and the frustration of baulked, blocked forces at odds. For there is sharper suffering and misery there, among the poor and

53 Luke Fildes, *Houseless and Hungry*, wood engraving from *The Graphic*, 4 December 1869.

disinherited most obviously, as they shiver in alleys or hovels or slums, and die in epidemics or watch their children die. They may be seen, as Dickens also saw them, in the illustration *Houseless and Hungry* (illus. 53), engraved for *The Graphic* by the artist Luke Fildes, who was also the illustrator of Dickens's last novel, *Edwin Drood*.

It is not, however, only the poor who suffer: children suffer, neglected by harsh parents and guardians; wives suffer from heartless husbands, husbands suffer from tyrannic wives; even his cruellest people suffer – Miss Havisham is cruel precisely from suffering. Of cruelty in Dickens's world there is a great deal. In the early fiction it may be exaggerated and part comic, as in Mr Bumble the beadle, and Squeers: but even their cruelty is not all fantasy, and the cruelty of Mr Murdstone is far from fantasy. There is cruelty in the workhouses, in the family, in the schools; there is cruelty to daughters, to employees, to governesses, to wards. It is a country, or a world, with cruelty in its heart; almost, one might say, where cruelty is salient. This is not a matter of Dickens having a cruel eye, or liking cruelty, or practising an early theatre of cruelty; for if anything, the world he lived in was even more cruel than it is in his depiction of it. There were, for instance, the conditions of child labour, which Dickens meant to depict, though in the event he did not. Had he done so, he could hardly have created a more frightening father than the following overseer in a cotton mill, whose testimony to a parliamentary inquiry had become infamous. He was questioned on his treatment, not only of child-workers in general, but of his own six and seven-year-olds when put to work in the mill. It is true that he differs from some characters in novels, in that he does not sound sadistic: in his case, it is rather the practicality that chills:

While they have been almost asleep, they have attempted to work? – Yes, and they have missed the carding and spoiled the thread, when we have had to beat them for it.

Could they have done their work towards the termination of such a long day's labour, if they had not been chastised for it? – No. You do not think they could have kept awake or up to their work till the seventeenth hour, without being chastised? – No.[14]

Though Dickens exaggerates, he also edits, and does not in sum show a world with more suffering in it than in reality there was. It is not surprising, then, that in his presentation of cruelties he is corroborated alike by social historians and by other novelists.

What is distinctive to the cruelty the novelists show is that it is conscious cruelty, cruelty made a virtue of, cruelty for self-congratulation, and, frequently, Christian cruelty. It is un-Christian, of course: all the novelists stress that, but still they study the way in which their society may use the Christian faith to subsidize a consciousness aware of being harsh. If one turns to the popular apologetics of the time, even to apologetics addressed to children, one finds something like a cult and care of cruelty. In the issue of *The Children's Friend* for May 1847 (edited by the Revd W. Carus-Wilson, Rector of Whittington), the first article, militantly Protestant, is 'Burning Heretics':

'They had to die cruel deaths'. Yes, very cruel deaths, for sometimes they pulled out their eyes, pulled limb by limb off their bodies, threw them on spikes; put them into casks of boiling oil, and tormented them in the most horrid and cruel ways.

This past cruelty is revived as present fear: 'there is no saying how long England will remain free from such fetters. Popery is spreading fast. O! how we ought to value our Bibles while we may have them.' A later article in the same issue (following an 'Address to the School Children of Sedgeford, at the Funeral of Elizabeth Gill – 'It is not easy, I know, for young minds fully to understand what a serious thing it is to die') is titled 'The Cruel Boy Punished', and describes an episode of a boy tormenting a dog (in Sweden) that sound sufficiently sadistic. The article describes the punishment awarded in Sweden (25 stripes), illustrates it with a woodcut, and then concludes:

Cruel boys, make haste to get your hard hearts softened. In England, you may not get punished for your crimes; but a severer punishment, and a more angry judge, awaits you. The torments and anguish of hell exceed that of any pain and punishment on earth.

The protest at cruel practices accompanies a cultivated consciousness of cruelty not only in this life but in the next. There is much virtuous cruelty in the England Charlotte Brontë shows, as in the Reed family where Jane Eyre lodges, and in Mr Brocklehurst and the system of his academy. Not all the cruelty in fiction is Calvinistic, of course. Dickens's Mrs Clennam may voice a cruel faith, but others in Dickens are cruel who are neither Calvinistic nor religious, as again is Miss Havisham. There is much cruelty also, and little reference to Calvinism, in the England of Thackeray.

As to where the pain and cruelty come from, that make the hard centre of darkness in this world, one has to say I think that they amount – at least as they are registered by novelists – to more than may simply be ascribed to cruelty inherent in the workings of capitalism; or to cruelty inherent in reactionary politics; or to cruelty enshrined in old harsh laws; or to cruelty inherent in a mechanistic philosophy of fact; or to cruelty inherent in ascetic Calvinistic religion. One cannot for instance prove that political (or economic) factors were the *cause* of the steady intensification, through the mid-years of the century, of a harshly puritanical sexual morality. Nor could one prove, *pace* Max Weber, that ascetic strains in both established and Nonconformist religion had a decisive causal role in the sudden great development of industrial capitalism: if they had, they would have loomed larger at the start of the Industrial Revolution, and they would have loomed larger during the Regency than they do. Apropos of Weber's argument, one would have to say that, if anything, the ascetic and puritanical motive, becoming more thorough-going and harsh through the century, seems to follow the business and industrial expansion, and to be at least as much a result as a cause. The Calvinistic motive was there before, however, running back through English business history to puritan projectors in the late sixteenth century; and the causal link in either direction is hard to prove conclusively. Yet all of the separate elements I have mentioned clearly cooperated with, and assisted, the others, indeed they seem to reinforce and feed each other. The whole situation, as to the course English history took in the nineteenth century, seems less a matter of a main cause with attendant effects, than of several harsh forces working together with mutual increase to make what, in a longer perspective, might look like a slow-wheeling, intensifying cyclone, a cold storm in history fed by currents of cruel attitude. But however the processes of cause and effect work, it cannot be by chance that all these developments coincide with the rise of Great Britain to its highest-ever position of worldly wealth and international power.

If the reference to a storm seems Romantic, one may note that it is an image the century used of itself. It is not a question only of Dickens, whose storms develop from his early, exhilarated reworkings of King Lear's storm, to the dark storms of his late novels, chilly as reality – like 'the hard implacable weather' of *Our Mutual Friend*: 'It was not that the wind swept all the brawlers into places of shelter, as it had swept the hail still lingering in heaps wherever there was refuge for it, but that it seemed as if the streets were absorbed by the sky, and the night were all in the air' (chapter Twelve). There is (in the same chapter) a harshness in the wind described that is more than meteorological:

The grating wind sawed rather than blew; and as it sawed, the sawdust whirled about the sawpit. Every street was a sawpit, and there were no top-sawyers; every passenger was an undersawyer, with the sawdust blinding him and choking him.

But apart from Dickens, and other storms in fiction (for instance in the Brontës and Hardy), there is the case of Ruskin, and the extraordinary belief he became obsessed with, to the effect that the weather really was changing, and was actually growing darker as 'the plague wind' – which was for him both a moral wind and a real wind – blew more cruelly. Describing this wind, in *The Storm-Cloud of the Nineteenth Century*, he notes:

1. It is a wind of darkness, – all the former conditions of tormenting winds, whether from the north or east, were more or less capable of co-existing with sunlight; but whenever, and wherever the plague wind blows, be it but for ten minutes, the sky is darkened instantly.
2. It is a malignant *quality* of wind, unconnected with any one quarter of the compass. . . .
5. It degrades, while it intensifies, ordinary storm . . .[15]

In describing the new storm-clouds, he implies that they have a connection with industry: 'Thunderstorm; pitch dark, with no *blackness*, – but deep, high, *filthiness* of lurid, smoke-cloud; dense manufacturing mist . . .'. He says too, at one point, 'It [the wind] looks partly as if it were made of poisonous smoke; very possibly it may be: there are at least two hundred furnace chimneys in a square of two miles on every side of me.' There is a connection too with the more general vast increase in the century of coal-fires: he refers to 'the sulphurous chimney-pot vomit of blackguardly cloud'. But the issue is more than ecological ('Thunder returned, all the air collapsed into one black fog ... the darkness seeming each time as it settles more loathsome'). When he comes to his peroration, he makes no bones about attributing the climatic gloom to moral wrong:

Remember, for the last twenty years, England, and all foreign nations, either tempting her, or following her, have blasphemed . . . and have done iniquity by proclamation, every man doing as much injustice to his brother as it is in his power to do. Of states in such moral gloom every seer of old predicted the physical gloom, 'The light shall be darkened in the heavens thereof, and the stars shall withdraw their shining'.

And so he concludes, 'that the Empire of England, on which formerly the sun never set, has become one on which he never rises'.

In the portrait by John Everett Millais (illus. 54), Ruskin stands by a chilly waterfall, at Brig o' Turk in the Trossachs, in a close black coat and black cravat. Though he stands in a shady gully, it is a portrait of a man on a moral height: 'he looks so sweet and benign', Millais wrote, 'standing calmly looking into the turbulent sluice beneath'.[16] Ruskin is keen but cold like the water, and indeed was himself so damaged by strains of the most intimate British asceticism that he was unable to be a husband to his wife. It was during this walking and painting trip in Scotland that Effie Ruskin turned from her unconsummated marriage to the younger artist's warmer care. There are elements of personal pathology in Ruskin's obsession with the plague-cloud, as possibly there are in Dickens's darkness: but their pathologies were of their culture, involving as it were ethical injury, and sensitized them to a greater pathology.

It is, of course, a delicate question as to what actual, historical conditions one might seek to identify with the embracing darkness which both Dickens and Ruskin see as descending on their world. Ruskin identifies the darkness not only with 'blasphemy' but with 'iniquity', and in particular with 'every man doing as much injustice to his brother as it is in his power to do' – in other words with an habituated and general injustice. It is relevant, then, to note that nineteenth-century observers saw the cruel divide between rich and poor, which became more extreme as Britain 'prospered', both as dark in itself, and as placing the great numbers of the poor and the totally unprovided, in their cramped housing, slums, tenements, squats and doorways, specifically in 'darkness'.

Darkness was the image later chosen by William Booth, founder of

54 John Everett Millais, *John Ruskin*, 1853–4, oil on canvas. Private collection.

the Salvation Army, who titled his book *In Darkest England and the Way Out*: 'As there is a darkest Africa is there not also a darkest England? . . . May we not find a parallel at our own doors, and discover within a stone's throw of our cathedrals and palaces similar horrors to those which Stanley has found existing in the great Equatorial forest?' And the image is extended and detailed, with references to predators and exploitation, to slavery and the slavery of women, to physical deprivation, stunting, disease ('Darkest England, like Darkest Africa, reeks with malaria'), even as it is also augmented: 'Talk about Dante's Hell, and all the horrors and cruelties of the torture-chamber of the lost!' There is perhaps the assumption, in the texture of Booth's imagery, that the 'natives' of the slums are men black at once with the misery of destitution and with spiritual deprivation.[17] When he turns from the sodden squalor and despair of the slums to proposing solutions, Booth changes his image from that of a jungle to that of an ocean. It is an ocean of misery, but a sea may bear lifeboats, and thus he introduces the Salvation Ship, which is a floating temple and a floating island, a small blessed travelling England, and which also is an actual vessel, taking emigrants to the colonies. But the ocean, too, is an image of darkness, raging in the chart that accompanies the book around the great lighthouse of Salvation, which has large letters over it proclaiming The City Colony. This is to say, the building is at once a metaphorical lighthouse, and one of the brightly lit warm city refuges which Booth organized, as the first place of escape from the darkness of the slums. I have concentrated on Booth's imagery precisely because he is not writing as a literary man, but as an intensely practical person moved to imagery by his detailed, quantified and analysed knowledge of homelessness, starvation and the economics of the sweating system, of crime and alcoholism and prostitution-to-survive, of mortality, despair and desperate lunacy, in the actual black jungle, swamp and Hell of the late nineteenth-century London slums.

The social light and darkness of 1870s London is most graphically shown in Gustave Doré's illustrations to *London*, in which, as Alan Woods has pointed out, the extreme differences of lighting are emphatically economic, 'consistently gloomy for the scenes of poverty, invariably light and airy for the scenes of wealth'.[18] And it is true that the poor, in *London*, are generally depicted in dusk, fog or darkness. The illustration *Bluegate Fields* (illus. 55), described in Jerrold's text as showing 'the densely packed haunts of poverty and crime – in the hideous tenements stacked far and wide', shows young and old loitering in the street as by day, though it is dense night (the lamp is 'the flaring public-house lamp – hateful as the fabled jewel in the loathsome toad's head'). As Woods notes, Doré applies to the London rich and poor the imagery of Heaven and Hell he had developed in his illustrations to *The Divine Comedy* and *Paradise Lost*: 'it could well be that Doré, a Frenchman and a stranger to London, imagined himself as an artist being guided round an earthly hell'. And the radical-minded Jerrold, who knows his London well and is less tempted by infernal imagery, still picks out insistently (what were doubtless really there) houses that 'are black and grim', 'dark byeways', 'black pools of water', 'a low black door', card-players with 'black hands', 'dark corners'.[19]

It is pertinent, therefore, that similar imagery had been used by Dickens, describing the slum-area Tom-all-Alone's in *Bleak House*, and the life of the poor who live there. The 'dark plate' illustration of Tom-all-Alone's was reproduced earlier (illus. 51). The slum is first described, in chapter XVI, as 'a black, dilapidated street', and Dickens concentrates on its character at night ('these tumbling tenements contain, by night, a swarm of misery. . . .'), while Jo the crossing-sweeper who dosses there is mentally 'in utter darkness'. Daylight is slow to arrive ('Jo comes out of Tom-all-Alone's, meeting the tardy morning which is always late in getting down there'), and his working weather is bad – his day (spent sweeping horse-dung off the road)

55 Gustave Doré, *Bluegate Fields*, wood engraving from *London: A Pilgrimage*, London, 1872.

'becomes dark and drizzly'. When Mr Snagsby and Mr Bucket penetrate Tom-all-Alone's in chapter xxii, it is at night: their only lighting is a policeman's bull's-eye lamp. They pass down 'a villainous street, undrained, unventilated, deep in black mud and corrupt water – though the roads are dry elsewhere – and reeking with such smells and sights that he, who has lived in London all his life, can scarce believe his senses'. As the undrained streets and courts multiply, Mr Snagsby 'feels as if he were going, every moment deeper down, into the infernal gulf'. They meet a poor funeral:

'Draw off a bit here, Mr Snagsby,' says Bucket, as a kind of shabby palanquin is borne towards them, surrounded by a noisy crowd. 'Here's the fever coming up the street!'

Ruskin's black wind is a plague wind, and Dickens's allusions to 'corrupt water' and 'polluted air' are allusions to nineteenth-century popular understanding of how infection spread (carried by bad or evil air). Dickens records elsewhere in *Bleak House* the real epidemics of smallpox and typhoid that spread through nineteenth-century London from the slums; it is pertinent to the sense of a 'plague wind' at large that Prince Albert himself died of typhoid (in 1861). In Tom-all-Alone's, houses and ceilings and the rags people wear are black or blackened. They do find, in a dark tenement, a mother nursing 'a very young child':

'Why, what age do you call that little creature?' says Bucket. 'It looks as if it was born yesterday.' He is not at all rough about it; and as he turns his light gently on the infant, Mr Snagsby is strangely reminded of another infant, encircled with light, that he has seen in pictures.

Presently they prepare to leave 'black and foul Tom-all-Alone's', and 'by the noisome ways through which they descended into that pit, they gradually emerge from it; the crowd flitting, and whistling, and skulking about them . . . like a concourse of imprisoned demons.'[20]

Making the slum the pit of Hell, and the majority of the wretched inhabitants 'demons', allows Dickens to preserve a dramatically imaginative distance from the poor (the gulf is also between him and the 'demons'), even as his generous sympathy means to plumb the depths. He does, at all events, acknowledge the hostility with which the poor saw their intermittent higher-class visitors, however charitable, and the police who guarded the visitors and moved on the poor.[21] What is clear is that 'darkness', in nineteenth-century idiom, is not only where the heathen live, it is also where the poor and the destitute live: and this darkness in turn is part of the moral 'darkness' – 'moral gloom' Ruskin called it – of the society that corporately consents to such misery. The 'black wind' shows a further connection with poverty – but abstracted and seen less generously – when Ruskin at one point refers to the 'plague cloud' as 'that thin, scraggy, filthy, mangy, miserable cloud'. In the literature of the time, these several darks are focused in the figures of child labour to be met with in the London streets, such as Jo from Tom-all-Alone's, or, especially, the chimney-sweep's boy, black with the soot of prosperous chimneys – black, that is, with the substance that literally blackened nineteenth-century London – but black also with poverty, deprivation and paganism: a blackness that kindness would wash with fresh water, as sin is washed from those born in sin – as happens to Tom in *The Water-Babies* of Charles Kingsley. I quote, though, from Charles Lamb, whose pity is more lightly witty, and in one sentence plays innocence against several blacknesses, including black and clerical dress:

I have a kindly yearning towards those dim specks – poor blots – innocent blacknesses – I reverence these young Africans of our own growth – these almost clergy imps, who sport their cloth without assumption; and from their little pulpits (the tops of chimneys), in the nipping air of a December morning, preach a lesson of patience to mankind.[22]

It would be hard, none the less, to see a close connection between the 'black' slums and the black clothes the respectable wear; and it is noticeable that in pursuing his paradisal imagery, and presenting the rich as living in light, Doré tends to lighten dress-colours, to draw the outlines of the rich but not to tone them in; and then they do seem like spirits of opulence. As to the black dress of the comfortable and the wealthy, it is perhaps not irrelevant that both Dickens's 'darkness' and Ruskin's 'plague-wind' are associated with death. For the plague-wind is a death-wind: the cloud borne on it is 'a dry black veil'; mornings are 'grey-shrouded'; the wind, so recurringly described as 'black', also looks 'as if it were made of dead men's souls'. Ruskin compares its effect to a performance he has seen of *Faust*, where he was impressed 'in the phantom scenes, by the half-palsied, half-furious, faltering or fluttering past of phantoms stumbling as into graves; as if of not only soulless, but senseless, Dead, moving with the very action, the rage, the decrepitude, and the trembling of the plague-wind'. The plague wind is a death-wind, and again Ruskin seems to have its deathliness in mind when he describes 'the most important sign of the plague-wind and the plague-cloud: that in bringing on their peculiar darkness, they *blanch* the sun instead of reddening it'.[23]

Since Dickens himself repeatedly describes the darkness he sees in homes, streets, slums and cities in terms of funerals and mourning, and also repeatedly associates men's black dress with mourning – as also do Baudelaire, Gautier, Musset, Wilde – it does seem legitimate to connect both the large imagined 'darkness', and the black clothes men wear, with the fact that the century did elaborate its own form of a cult of death. There were of course many deaths in Victorian urban life – the more visible because corpses were laid out at home. And the increased awareness of a drastically increased mortality perhaps did contribute to the Victorians' elaboration of, as it were, the formal theatre of death. Certainly there was an increase in the use of black at funerals, black hearse-plumes, horse-plumes, black-wrapped wands and staves, and trays of black feathers to be carried by mutes, rested on the head. There were also funeral furnishings at home, black trimmings for furniture, bird-cages, women's underwear. If the social darkness was to be found especially among the poor, the black funeral and the newly prolonged period of mourning – and then half-mourning – was to be found only the more, the higher one ascended the social hierarchy. It is true that men did not need to make many adjustments to their dress, but then, as Henry Mayhew noted, 'a gentleman of the present nineteenth century, attired for the gayest evening party, would apart from his jewellery, be equally presentable at the most sorrowful funeral'. Indeed, the sole specific requirement of even the most formal mourning was that the black frock-coat should have no buttons on its sleeves or pockets. And it was men, in the first half of the century, who actually attended funerals: women mourned at home. But whether at home, or in later years at funerals, women too were elaborately blackened. A widow was required to spend twelve months in entire crape, then six months in widow's silk, then three further months in more varied black, with fringes. There then followed the further six months of half-mourning, when such colours as grey, lavender, mauve and violet could be worn together with black.[24]

A further use of black-for-death was to be seen at executions. At 'A Dinner in the City', in *Sketches and Travels in London*, Thackeray is amused by the stentorian usher, 'a fellow with a gold chain, and in a black suit, such as the lamented Mr Cooper wore preparatory to execution in the last act of *George Barnwell*'. It is not surprising that the popular stage had a tradition of the condemned man dressed dramatically in black: but the same tradition applied on the real scaffold, and applied both to the condemned man and his executioner. Executions in the nineteenth century were *seen*, they were public deaths, a form of death-theatre cut into consciousness. In 'Going to see a man hanged', Thackeray records:

Just then, from under the black prison-door, a pale, quiet head peered out. It was shockingly bright and distinct; it rose up directly, and a man in black appeared on the scaffold, and was silently followed by about four more dark figures. . . . Courvoisier bore his punishment like a man, and walked very firmly. He was dressed in a new black suit, as it seemed: his shirt was open. . . . He went and placed himself at once under the beam, with his face towards St. Sepulchre's. The tall, grave man in black twisted him round swiftly in the other direction. . . .

Women, too, might wear black on the scaffold, as famously did Marie Manning, who, with her husband, murdered her lover, in the case known as 'The Bermondsey Horror'. Both at her trial and at her execution she wore a handsome black satin gown, described by

Dickens's friend John Forster, who, together with Dickens, saw her execution, with a somewhat morbid mix of admiration and delectation:

You should have seen this woman ascend the drop, blindfold, and with a black lace veil over her face – with a step as firm as if she had been walking to a feast. She was *beautifully dressed*, every part of her noble figure finely and fully expressed by close fitting black satin. . . .

At her request she had been blindfolded with her own black silk handkerchief, and she had a black lace veil thrown over her head and tied under her chin, before she came out. Her black satin dress passed into myth as the cause of a depression in the satin trade. It was claimed, for instance by Charles Kingston, that 'for many years afterwards no woman would think of wearing black satin . . . and numerous small traders went bankrupt'. It does however now appear, as Albert Borowitz has argued, that these 'reports of the death of black satin have been greatly exaggerated'. The dress itself was faithfully replicated for Madame Tussaud's waxwork of her – 'Maria Manning, as done in wax, is really a *chef d'œuvre* . . . the black satin gown is unexceptionable' – and she was to live again, her black satin dress gone into black eyes, in Mlle Hortense, the murderess, in Dickens's novel *Bleak House*. It should be reported that, at the execution, her husband, Fred Manning, also wore a black suit, though he was thought, by contrast, to make a shabby figure.[25]

The enhanced performance of mourning in the high nineteenth century is reflected, most 'materially', in the number of new mourning cloths in use, so that in addition to serge (used from at least the twelfth century), bombazine and sarcenet (from at least the thirteenth), taffeta (from at least the fourteenth), armozine, broadcloth, crape, cypress, Norwich crape (from at least the sixteenth), grosgrain and lutestring (from the seventeenth), there were available in the nineteenth century: Albert crape, alpaca, barathea, barege, barpour, byzantine, Courtauld crape, crepe anglais, crepelle, crepe imperial, crepe-de-chine, crepe myosotis, crepon, de laine, Henrietta cloth, radzimir and voile.[26] Perhaps most significant was Courtauld crape – indeed the whole prosperity of the firm of Courtauld was based on manufacturing materials for mourning. And, as in Burgundy, with its black fashion and its Dances of Death, Philip the Good had mourned long; and in Spain, with its black fashion and its elaborate mourning rituals, Philip II had mourned long: so in the nineteenth century, with its black menswear and its stately funerals, Queen Victoria wore full mourning for 40 years. At her own funeral, in 1901, every spectator of the procession wore black.

56 Gustave Courbet, *Burial at Ornans*, 1849, oil on canvas. Musée du Louvre, Paris.

It is a question why, in these cultures, an elaborated ceremonial of death has marked their periods of greatest power. One may, of course, note that the rituals of mourning are rituals of attending, of following, of a community totally deferring – and deferring to the importance of at least some of its members, and, in a sense, to the principle of importance. A great funeral says both that the dead mattered massively, and also that their commemoration, and indeed that the commemorators themselves, matter massively, and matter publicly. In Courbet's great painting *Burial at Ornans* (illus. 56), the coffin is borne in from the left, draped in a white pall; ahead of it a crucifix is raised against the sky. But still, both cross and coffin are off to the side, and no one actually is looking at them: they are not the centre of interest, which rather is the whole visible community of the mourners. There is, in fact, reason to believe that in painting the *Burial at Ornans* Courbet was thinking of, and was in part inspired by, Baudelaire's 'Salon of 1846', the article cited earlier, in which Baudelaire describes no actual funeral, but the way in which, in general, men in his century looked like mourners at a funeral.[27] The suggestion, in other words, is that Courbet's painting was not conceived as a portrait of an interment, so much as a portrait of nineteenth-century bourgeois society – a delegation of it, that is – assembled in the ritual that most characterized its moral economy, and that best manifested its serious purposive strength.

It is, of course, formal wear that most resembles mourning. As many commentators of the time remarked (and not only literary people, taking a Romantic view, but the alert and the curious generally), the difference between formal and funereal dress could, even in the highest circles, be a matter virtually of a button more or less. It is men in their smart wear, men on their dignity, men of importance, men of standing, whose dress most approaches the style of mourning: as if smartness, dignity, importance, standing, had themselves an affinity with grief. Yet formality, for its part, should not need to be black, and in other periods formality had worn other colours, as for instance scarlet, or white, or white and gold. It is distinctive to nineteenth-century formality to be black, as it is also distinctive to it, to judge from the novelists, to be often stiff, unwieldy, rigid, to be gravely graceless in its pomp compared with the pomp of earlier periods – to be, in short, funereal even when feasting. It is the idiosyncrasy of mid-nineteenth-century Victorian culture to achieve more completely even than Spain had, at the height of its black-clad 'Golden' age, the formality/mortality equation, of which the vehicle is dress.

The culture of appearances is a register of consciousness: it is the character of consciousness that is manifest in clothes, and it is not so much Victorian morals that are black, as the Victorian moral consciousness of its own strong prosperity. It is a question of inflection and accent of awareness, and it would be hard not to infer a deep unease that could lay such a mark on the consciousness of a society that in showing its dignity must simulate privation and in enacting its rich state must dress and act as if bereaved. This is not to suggest that men's black may be read directly as conscience or social conscience, though it does seem to me to emerge from the whole case presented in this chapter that a part of the work of men's black in this period is the deflection, or placation, of conscience, by reconstituting comfort and power as formality-unto-death.

That funerals themselves confirm standing in society is a truth vigorously illustrated in nineteenth-century novels, with reference to virtually every level of society. The classic instance is the funeral of Pip's sister in *Great Expectations*:

At last I came within sight of the house, and saw that Trabb & Co. had put in a funeral execution and taken possession. Two dismally absurd persons, each ostentatiously exhibiting a crutch done up in a black bandage – as if that instrument could possibly communicate any comfort to anybody – were posted at the front door . . .

Inside, the undertaker, Mr Trabb, arranging everyone's mourning, looks as if he is holding 'a kind of black Bazaar'. The bereaved husband, Joe, is 'entangled in a little black cloak tied in a large bow under his chin'. Dickens indeed alludes to the Dance of Death, making clear at the same time that it includes a social dance:

'Which I meantersay, Pip,' Joe whispered me, as we were being what Mr Trabb called 'formed' in the parlour, two and two – and it was dreadfully like a preparation for some grim kind of dance; 'which I meantersay, sir, as I would in preference have carried her to the church myself, along with three or four friendly ones wot come to it willing harts and arms, but it were considered wot the neighbours would look down on such and would be of opinion as it were wanting in respect.'

'Pocket-handkerchiefs out, all!' cried Mr Trabb at this point, in a depressed business-like voice. 'Pocket-handkerchiefs out! We are ready!'

The narrator notes, 'we were much admired as we went through the village'. Similarly, in *Middlemarch*, old Featherstone 'had been bent on having a handsome funeral, and on having persons "bid" to it who would rather have stayed at home'; on the day:

there were pall-bearers on horseback, with the richest of scarves and hatbands, and even the under-bearers had trappings of woe which were of good well-priced quality. The black procession, when dismounted, looked the larger for the smallness of the churchyard; the heavy human faces and the black draperies shivering in the wind seemed to tell of a world strangely incongruous with the lightly-drooping blossoms and the gleams of sunshine on the daisies.

Nor did all at a funeral grieve: the incongruity between funeral and funeral feeling is nicely evoked by Thackeray when he speaks of the undertakers' men, in the aftermath of a stately funeral, 'speckling with black the public-house entrances'. The funerals of the distinguished were of commensurate social pomp: where indeed grief, condolence, and tribute might be enacted by a solemn succession of the empty coaches of the great – a sight of the times which moved Dickens and Thackeray to almost identical comment: 'the amount of inconsolable carriages is immense' (Dickens); 'the neighbouring gentry's carriage . . . empty, and in profound affliction' (Thackeray). For the supremely great there was the funeral car: that which bore Wellington's coffin was a six-wheel juggernaut weighing more than ten tons, heraldically embellished with spears, helmets, breast-plates, lions, cannons, and cannon-balls – but with no ecclesiastical symbol – and towed by 'twelve of the largest and finest black horses that could be procured'. The city itself was clothed in black for the occasion; the whole of Temple Bar was draped in black cloth and black velvet for the procession to pass through it, an event that lasted two hours.[28]

But if the funeral was an external demonstration of stature and importance – and, on the grander scale, of the stature and importance of that society – the observances of death were not only external. There was a culture of grief, as well as of public mourning: men as well as women were respected for weeping rather than, as later, for hardly showing they were moved. Within the family, 'the bereaved and their comforters all write enormous letters, symptoms are dwelt on, dying speeches and death-moments repeated and extended, the Will of God is bowed to again and again, sorrow is so persistently exhibited as joy that both become meaningless'.[29] How deeply death and grief were taken to heart is evident from Tennyson's masterpiece, *In Memoriam*, which was the record less of a death than of a much extended and profound process of mourning, and which had on publication an instant great popularity. What other society has had, for its popular epic, an elegy?

> I sometimes hold it half a sin
> To put in words the grief I feel;
> For words, like Nature, half reveal
> And half conceal the Soul within.
>
> But, for the unquiet heart and brain,
> A use in measured language lies;
> The sad mechanic exercise,
> Like dull narcotics, numbing pain.
>
> In words, like weeds, I'll wrap me o'er,
> Like coarsest clothes against the cold:
> But that large grief which these enfold
> Is given in outline and no more.   (*In Memoriam*, V)

As Tennyson's title reminds us, the preoccupation with death and the dead involved also a resistance to death, a piety in commemoration, in remembrancing, which worked to let the dead not die. ('My own dim life should teach me this, / That life shall live for evermore', *In Memoriam*, XXXIV.) In so far as there was a cult of death, there was a cult of memory also, of preserving, of not only not letting people die wholly, but of not letting past experiences die, or past phases of life (such as childhood, remembered and recreated in the nineteenth century as never before in human history, though still recreated as something also past and over). The cult of remembering structures many novels, and structured many lives lived in the shadow of dead parents, or lives blighted by ancient misfortunes: so that Miss Havisham in *Great Expectations* is an odd negative correlative of Queen Victoria. Miss Havisham lives on secluded in Satis House in her white bridal dress, in a permanent white mourning for her being jilted long ago (and white was for the Victorians a further mourning colour, worn especially but not solely for children). The commitment to remember, never to forget – consummated for French culture in *À la recherche du temps perdu* – is necessarily retrospective: it preserves but looks back, it is another means of affirming existing importances, almost, the idea or fact of importance (the *important* is what is not forgotten), and in this sense is continuous with the death-preoccupation. As Tennyson says, 'O Death in Life, the days that are no more.'[30]

It would not be sufficient to suggest only that important funerals, and important grievings, were the reflections of an existing national importance: there does seem a further process involved, in the role played in some triumphal societies by their enhanced preoccupation with death. Humanity draws power from its awareness of death. In the case of Tennyson, death frequently is his inspiration, or lies half-concealed at the heart of his subject; often it seems it is just this inspiration of death that furnishes his poetic language with its energy and life. Nor did his preoccupation, in his best poetry, with the intimate metamorphoses of grief in any way inhibit his nineteenth-century commitment to the social dignity of the public funeral. So he was able to offer, as the last two lines of *Enoch Arden*, 'And when they buried him the little port / Had seldom seen a costlier funeral' – lines that probably seem bathetic to us, but which Tennyson defended as 'quite necessary to the perfection of the Poem'.[31] His sensuous aesthete's love of a kind of swooning dying (as in the Choric Song to 'The Lotus Eaters'), which seems on the literary side Hamlet's death-reverie ('To die, to sleep . . . perchance to dream') received via Keats ('half in love with easeful Death'), is complemented by his exhilaration at imagining joining up, by his willingness to put heart into those who enlist:

> For the peace, that I deemed no peace, is over and done,
> And now by the side of the Black and the Baltic deep,
> And deathful-grinning mouths of the fortress, flames
> The blood-red blossom of war with a heart of fire.
>
> > (*Maud*, part III. VI. iv. 50–53)

Indeed, even in the aftermath of an appalling 'blunder', he will readily rise, with banking exaltation, to the heroic determined headlong embracing of death:

> Their's not to reason why,
> Their's but to do and die:
> Into the valley of Death
> Rode the six hundred.[32]

Ruskin had chosen to relate the 'storm-cloud' to Empire. And it may be that what one is facing – taking together the various 'dark' factors so far cited – is the operational necessity of cooperating forms of solemnity, harshness and death-readiness in a nation that is on course to own a quarter of the globe. It goes without saying that foreigners are contemned, and not only through the lofty dismissal of the Podsnaps. There is the more general phenomenon of the maintenance of ego through severity to 'natives', guyed – to return to Dickens – in the pointless savagery with which Major Bagstock treats his Indian servant always: 'You villain! Where's my breakfast?' ('The native', Dickens explains, 'had no particular name, but answered to any vituperative epithet.') Even the philanthropists are, in Dickens's picture, not disinterested: Mrs Jellyby, in *Bleak House*, is committed to 'the cultivation of coffee, and natives'. And harshness is not directed only at foreigners, it is turned inwards also, and at the centre of much nineteenth-century art, and certainly of Dickens's art, is a vision of the way England is harsh with itself. I have concentrated so far on the testimony of authors. If I wanted to cite an illustrative historical figure it would not be Dickens, Hopkins, Tennyson; or Isambard Kingdom Brunel, posed dark-suited among the links of gigantic chains; or John Henry Newman in his priestly black; or ministers of the crown in black morning-coats; or Queen Victoria herself in black; or her consort, Prince Albert, magnificently posed for his portrait by Winterhalter in the black regimentals of the Rifle Brigade.[33] None of these famous figures made a change so much felt by so many as did the administrative reformer Edwin Chadwick. Chadwick is now best, and worst, remembered as the inventor of the New Poor Law. Under the New Poor Law, pauper families were broken up, and the men, women and children were confined to separate wings of the new workhouses. They were deliberately given tedious and unpleasant work, and fed on gruel, since these measures together must be the best way to make them want to leave the workhouse quickly, and return to the world of real hard work. Chadwick, who sounds, so described, like a prophet of Britain's 1980s, believed that salvation was to be secured through harshness, and one father was duly prosecuted for visiting, during the night, one of the children, whom he had heard crying elsewhere in the workhouse.

It is not hard, then, to present Edwin Chadwick, in all the rigour of his practically applied Benthamism (he had been chosen by Bentham to be his secretary), as the harsh spirit of the age in person: a figure who makes Dickens's Mr Gradgrind resemble a kindly uncle. He does not, however, look like Mr Gradgrind in the photographs that survive (illus. 57), where he makes the most of thinning hair and is somewhat unkept at mouth and chops; and he was a disinterested spirit in whose debt we all are. His greatest passion was for sanitation: he truly was a pioneer in the cause of public health, and it is especially to his insistent, his obsessive practical diligence that we owe the eventual installation in our cities of comprehensive sewage and drainage systems – supplied by

57 *Sir Edwin Chadwick*, photograph.

the corollary, which again Chadwick fought for, the universal public supply of piped water. The same man who inflicted new misery on the destitute helped vanquish typhoid and contributed to the saving of innumerable lives. And he acted in both causes in the identical spirit, for the more one studies his benignly obsessive commitment to hygiene, the more that commitment seems, in its fervour, yet one new twist of the governing ascetic and puritanic impulse – the translation into a zeal for efficiency of that Victorian morality which was on all levels so vigilant against staining, adulteration and soiling. Chadwick himself became a byword for the harsh scouring of everything. As *The Times* complained in 1854, life, when Edwin Chadwick was influential,

was a perpetual Saturday night, and Master John Bull was scrubbed, and rubbed, and small-tooth-combed, till the tears came into his eyes, and his teeth chattered, and his fists clenched themselves with worry and pain.[34]

In Chadwick we see the ascetic impulse acting as a social will. He seems the very personification of the spirit that Dickens found generally dominant, the spirit of all that was 'severely workful'. And if at times Dickens applies his imagery of darkness and blackness to just those things that Chadwick hated – the hovering infections of the slums and the standing black water nursing epidemics – still his more general vision is of darkness and black as the shadows that were cast by a harsh philosophy, and by the morality that sustained his society. It was a morality that was black not only because it was cruel – many societies are in practice cruel – but because it made a conscious Christian virtue of the harshness it applied. It was cruel not only in its hurt to the spirit, to pleasure, to light-heartedness, to sexual pleasure, but cruel also in the licence, even relish, it nurtured for all manner of actual punishments and confinements, from caning and shutting up in cupboards at home to the new interest, in the prison service, in solitary confinement.

One might ask what it could mean for a morality to be black. The answer, surely, would be that black is the only colour one could choose for a morality that rests on fear. It does not seem that Jesus himself based his moral teachings on fear, but fear, whether of Purgatory or of destined damnation, has loomed large in later Christianity, and perhaps especially in those Churches that have become built into the disciplinary structure of an ambitious but beleaguered nation. Whatever relation one may posit between England's internal repressive politics and the savagery of her resurgent Calvinism, the result was clear: prosperous nineteenth-century England was pale-faced with guilty fear. Both the Evangelical Movement in the Anglican Church, and the broader evangelicalism of the dissenting sects (notably the Calvinistic Methodists) insisted on the natural depravity of man, and the extreme danger – the likelihood – of eternal damnation. How English Calvinism could feel from the inside had been expressed, in the late eighteenth century, by the poet Cowper:

> Hatred and vengeance, my eternal portion,
> Scarce can endure delay of execution: –
> Wait, with impatient readiness, to seize my
> > Soul in a moment.

The strict morality of a terrifying faith was taught in the schools as well as the churches, and could be taught in both places with an appalling moral terrorism which one can see recorded alike in the work of novelists like Dickens and Charlotte Brontë, and in the actual hymnody prepared for children by such a figure as the Rev Carus-Wilson, editor of *The Children's Friend*:

> It's dangerous to provoke a God
> Whose power and vengeance none can tell;
> One stroke of His almighty rod
> Can send young sinners quick to hell.

That, in the language of writers, 'black' is associated with the most strict forms of Christian morality is apparent not only in Protestant authors such as Dickens and Charlotte Brontë: it is apparent even in the poetry of Gerard Manley Hopkins – himself a Jesuit priest in black, a palely patient long-suffering figure. His great sonnet 'Spelt from Sibyl's Leaves' offers itself, precisely, as a sybilline prophecy directed at his age: he speaks of 'Óur évening . . . óur night', 'Our tale, O óur oracle!', marking his stress each time on the *our*. The event that is 'óur tale', 'óur oracle', is nightfall – in which all the rich variety and sensuous beauty of the day, all its 'dapple', is ended, so that a tree of foliage becomes a nightmare silhouette, a black shape of dragon-limbs with beaks growing from them. What makes this night black is just the process of an unremitting moralization of everything, carried to such lengths that it becomes sterile, tormenting and self-tormenting. Hopkins could not evoke the anguish more powerfully than he does in the sestet of this extraordinary sonnet, the most momentous in the language:

> Only the beakleaved boughs dragonish ˈ damask the tool-
>   smooth bleak light; black,
> Ever so black on it. Óur tale, O óur oracle! ˈ Lét life, wáned,
>   ah lét life wind
> Off hér once skéined stained véined varíety ˈ upon, áll on twó
>   spools; párt, pen, páck
> Now her áll in twó flocks, twó folds – black, white; ˈ right,
>   wrong; reckon but, reck but, mind
> But thése two; wáre of a wórld where bút these ˈ twó tell, each
>   off the óther; of a rack
> Where, selfwrung, selfstrung, sheathe- and shelterless, ˈ thóughts
>   agáinst thoughts ín groans grínd.[35]

Invasive moralizing has, for Hopkins, turned Nature to a Night-Dragon. In a lighter, more surreal vein, there is Edward Lear's Old Person:

> There was an Old Person in Black,
> A Grasshopper jumped on his back;
>   When it chirped in his ear,
>   He was smitten with fear,
> That helpless Old Person in Black.

The grasshopper, in Lear's drawing, is as big as the Old Person, who therefore perhaps is right to be frightened. Or it is his fear that has made the insect man-sized. Either way, the grasshopper is a green quick creature, and a part of that Nature from which the man in black is separated in fearfulness.[36]

For some contemporary commentators, the greater part of the

English middle class was damaged by a moral self-incarceration. Matthew Arnold felt he must paint

the picture of a class which, driven by its sense for the power of conduct, in the beginning of the seventeenth century entered, – as I have more than once said, and as I may more than once have occasion in future to say, – *entered the prison of Puritanism, and had the key turned upon its spirit there for two hundred years.* They did not know, good and earnest people as they were, that to the building up of human life there belong all those other powers also, – the power of intellect and knowledge, the power of beauty, the power of social life and manners . . . they created a type of life and manners, of which they themselves indeed are slow to recognise the faults, but which is fatally condemned by its hideousness, its immense ennui, and against which the instinct of self-preservation in humanity rebels.[37]

The italics are Arnold's, and in the essay from which the passage comes, 'Equality', the faith of the puritanical middle class is equated with England's 'religion of inequality', its anti-Continental piety towards the principle of hierarchy, of social division of rank above rank in a structure severally unequal. Both for Arnold and for his contemporaries, the things dimmed or extinguished in this harsh, rich century were social feeling, fellow feeling, Charity, kindness, warmth, passion, foregiveness – above all, love. It is clear, too, in Dickens that if what is positively present in his dark houses is ethic, what is absent from them – whose absence makes them dark – is again love. This is patently so in the shuttered house of Miss Havisham, who was jilted on her wedding-day and cut to the soul, and who is unable to love afterwards, though able to be hurt. But the same is true of his other dark houses, where love, if and when it comes, is by contrast associated with light: often with a young woman, who enters both with and like a light, whether it is Florence Dombey coming to her father – 'there shone into the room a gleam of light; a ray of sun' – or, much more subtly, Little Dorrit, bringing light either into the black Clennam House, or into the Marshalsea prison, to her lost father and later to her despairing lover: 'As they sat side by side, in the shadow of the wall, the shadow fell like light upon him'. And Dickens is not of course alone in associating light, love and young women: the association is so general as to be a cliché, but it was a cliché of great suggestiveness for the Victorians, who saw the womanly and the feminine as the antithesis of blackness. They liked to see men dark, and women, like Christ, as the light of their world. Even so, many women in Dickens are eccentric, hurt and even vengeful: but still his men are the darker case. Most of his men in black are both severe with ethic and also loveless – that is, both unloving and unloved – and jealously resentful of love if they meet it. His whole depiction is of a strong great country with not much love in it: with not much love in the places where one might seek it – in families, in marriages – and with not much capacity for love in most people (though he also, often with more piety than convincingness, respects the convention that the close of a novel should include a happy betrothal). The ability to love seems almost bred out, a casualty of the combining severities; though Dickens does then depict his very many children of loveless childhoods as feeling some need, some permanent unappeasable want. What he seems most to feel, as he reviews the combined changes occurring in English life, is the cost to the heart, an unplumbable sadness. His cities mourn, his landscapes are desolate, there is a bereavement in his prose: 'a wintry shudder goes among the little pools on the cracked uneven flag-stones, and through the giant elm-trees as they shed a gust of tears'.[38]

The large question this raises is to what extent Dickens, as novelist, was able to feel *with* the men in black, whose growing numbers dismayed and depressed him. In *Bleak House*, for instance, it is not only the deadly lawyers who wear black: a number of the sympathetic figures are also in black, but Dickens's feeling for them is muted. There is not a great deal of Mr Rouncewell, the industrialist. Mr Bucket the detective is enigmatic: you cannot tell what Dickens's attitude to him is. And the official hero of the novel, Alan Woodcourt – a professional man, a doctor, a dark man – is curiously shadowy. Not, of course, that Dickens himself should simply be taken as the proponent of colour and the enemy of black. Black has several values for him. It is, for instance, the colour of false piety and of obnoxious hypocritical fawning obsequiousness: Uriah Heep in *David Copperfield* is 'dressed in decent black'. In Frederick Barnard's illustration to the Household Edition (illus. 58) he squirms in his unction of obsequious fawning, even while his pallid narrowed eye appraises the dogged David shrewdly. Uriah Heep merits more than a passing comment, for he is another personification of Protestant asceticism, evangelically pious (his father is 'a partaker of glory'), endlessly self-castigating and self-chastizing ('we are so very umble'), intensely industrious (he will make himself a lawyer 'with the blessing of Providence'). Actually he uses his emphatic self-effacement ('There are people enough to tread upon me in my lowly state, without my doing outrage to their feelings by possessing learning') as a placatory verbal camouflage while he pushes to take over the firm. But with all that said, black still is also for Dickens the colour of a worthiness really to be respected: Daniel Doyce, the inventor in *Little Dorrit*, is also described as being 'in decent black', and here decent *is* decent, no irony is attached.[39]

58 Frederick Barnard, illustration to *David Copperfield* in the Household Edition, 1871–9, wood engraving.

And Dickens himself, for all his campaigning, cannot be placed easily on one side or the other. He was no ascetic, but he was hardly *l'homme moyen sensuel*. He fought against puritanism, but still had his own sentimental puritanism, which inhibited his treatment of masculine passion. It is a sad fact that his most virile creation should be Quilp, a deformed dwarf. He denied body and sexuality almost entirely to the women in his fiction that he liked. He campaigned against all that was 'severely workful' – against those who lived for work and worked for money – but he was himself an indefatigable worker who never stopped, just as he never stopped making money. He was himself a dandy – sometimes he was thought a vulgar one, with his liking for crimson or green velvet waistcoats – but he could also be dashing in his tight-fitting black pantaloons with buttons at the ankles, his new black hat, his brilliant white cravat, and his 'very handsome blue cloak with black velvet facings'.[40]

Dickens is so various and so good on these things because he stands in an uneasy relation to them: and that uneasiness is best resolved when he seeks for his heroes not among the bright, but among the darkened men. There is a slow change in his heroes. In his early novels they are bright, priggish and unconvincing, whether they are juvenile leads like Oliver Twist or young gentlemen like Nicholas Nickleby. His heroes only begin to convince, and to be interesting in themselves, when they are sadder people, like David Copperfield, who always feels 'the vague unhappy loss or want of something'. *Bleak House* is a curious transitional novel: after the abundance of its opening it loses impetus because none of the principals can take a strong hold on us. It is only with Arthur Clennam, in *Little Dorrit*, that Dickens is able to sympathize truly with a man whose life is deeply darkened. He can do this because the man is suffering the darkness, and wanting to escape it, though achieving this is terribly difficult.

Clennam, it should be said, is another of Dickens's illegitimate children. Illegitimacy is a subject that looms large in his fiction; larger than is perhaps compatible with his popular reputation as a safe sexless read for the Victorian family. Invariably he associates illegitimacy with darkness and shadow, and if in a broad survey one were to seek Dickens's most intimate application of his 'dark' imagery, one would, I believe, locate it in his representation of the consciousness of bastardy – in the consciousness of others, that is, as they perceive the illegitimate person; in the persona the illegitimate person may project; and in the illegitimate person's consciousness of the way in which they are 'different'. The subject is one on which Dickens becomes subtle, as his early sentimental interest in 'orphans' gives way to a keen and feeling curiosity as to how these children deal with what they are told they are. It would seem indeed that the reason he returns to this subject is that he finds in it the most moving demonstration of the way his age's morality was wrong at the centre, eschewing charity and opting for harshness, and operating concepts of 'taint' and 'stain' that made most guilty those who were most innocent, and laid on them as infants a burden of sinfulness for which all their lives they should labour to atone – for birth out of wedlock was something else never to be forgotten, always to be re-remembered. The stain of illegitimacy was blackest when laid on women. Dickens investigates the different ways the 'stained' person may react. Esther Summerson is brought up under the 'darkened face' of her godmother – 'Submission, self-denial, diligent work, are the preparations for a life begun with such a shadow on it' – and even when walking in the sun she watches 'my long shadow at my side'. Esther's reaction to her birth is to be apologetic for life, and be always good and self-effacing (there is an odd, ferocious irony in the way her life-situation is then re-enacted, when she alone among the principals is infected with smallpox, and is disfigured by it – though she meets the catastrophe with strength, Dickens being interested in the sources of strength). Of Miss Wade, in *Little Dorrit*, we are told 'the shadow in which she sat, falling like a gloomy veil across her forehead, accorded very well with the character of her beauty'. The course she takes is the opposite of Esther's: treated by everyone as a child who is 'different', she develops a paranoia, and on her wasted life and her waste of other lives Dickens is acute.[41]

Clennam's case is more particular: he is the son of his father's mistress, but is brought up by his father's wife, who is financially placed so as to be able to blackmail both her husband and his beloved. Since she both separates the lovers, and also separates herself and her 'son' from her husband, it seems her main motive is jealous vengefulness. She, of course, presents her course as labour to redeem her son: her faith is the severest capitalist-calvinism, and an extreme of 'Victorian moralism':

I devoted myself to reclaim the otherwise predestined and lost boy; to give him the reputation of an honest origin; to bring him up in fear and trembling, and in a life of practical contrition for the sins that were heavy on his head before his entrance into this condemned world.[42]

Needless to say, his 'life of practical contrition' is a life of hard work in the family business: he is as nice a case as Max Weber could have wished for of fearful religious sanctions conducing to the work ethic, and a solemn dedication to business. But though Clennam has grown up in the black house – literally the black house – of his mother's loveless severity, his own reaction to his 'sins' has been neither permanent apology nor paranoia, but rather a deep withdrawal and reserve. He is described, on his first appearance in the novel, as 'a grave dark man of forty', with, again, a 'dark face'. From within his reserve, he watches the world, with a hurt, alert and sympathetic gaze. Maybe one could speak of emotional damage: in his relationship with Little Dorrit he responds, on the one hand, to the ways in which she is small and like a child, and on the other to the ways in which – quiet as she is – she is like a strong mother. But they both are, when they need to be, markedly strong people. It would seem, both in their case and in that of Esther, that Dickens is interested not only in damage, but also in the strength and the sympathetic imaginativeness that may develop in a person as they learn to live with a continuing deprivation. They make for themselves what they have needed and not been given, giving value to loss, and meeting lovelessness with love.

They represent, in other words, special strengths and values, which the ascetic and puritanic tradition may actually nurture in spite of itself. For it should not be argued that black and darkness are a curse only, and that only colour is good. It is surely at the intersection of the dark and coloured worlds, where ascetic spirituality and passion and zest pull on each other, that life is deepest? The spirit divided against the body may be also the creative spirit.

The plight of the profoundly subdued English man – a problem not gone – becomes, finally, one of Dickens's great themes. Both Clennam, and Pip in *Great Expectations*, are very un-Dickens-like men with whom, notwithstanding, Dickens feels a profound bond. Pip is not, I think, to be imagined as wearing black every day: he is financed in the acquisition of a gentleman's wardrobe, which would have included light garments as well as black smart wear. *Great Expectations* is, none the less, a fair sequel to *Little Dorrit*, in a still grimmer, and a barer, vein. Moving starkly between social extremes, between black rich London and a village blacksmith's house, and between high society and the life of a convict transported to Australia, it seems Dickens's most drastic translation into story of what was most cruel in the frame of mind of the time. It is a nightmare parable of those who have been denied and made wretched making use of other people to deny and despise and make wretched yet others in their turn – and to do so both by their use of social class and by the incitement and denial of love. Both Pip and Estella are vehicles of revenge, as well as being repositories for such starved affection as their tormented patrons have. And, as with Clennam, we see the process from the inside, we see Pip both moved and hurt by his close contacts with the world of privilege. He is trained to despise and patronize, and trained so that the only woman who can thrill him is the woman who has treated him with contempt. His love and shadowy sexuality is bound to Estella's frigidity, as she binds herself to the sadistic thug Drummle. The whole savage story is rendered from the start and throughout with a brief poignant poetry:

I saw her pass among the extinguished fires, and ascend some light iron stairs, and go out by a gallery high overhead, as if she were going out into the sky.

The novel depicts a society as class-ridden as the eighteenth century had been; but how twisted and darkened in heart and libido! Here it is denial above all that is power: as in the black-clad lawyer, Mr Jaggers, for this is another Victorian novel governed by the law. At the root of its complicated plot, behind both the transportation of Magwitch, and also the desertion of Miss Havisham, is the shadowy, oddly absent figure of Compeyson – of whom all there is to say is that he has been a gentleman, with a gentleman's spoiled selfishness, and carelessness and ruthlessness. He is the blackest sort of gentleman, as Pip in time becomes the better sort. It is gentleman's black that he wears in court, as Magwitch recalls from the day of their trial:

59 James Mahoney, illustration to *Our Mutual Friend* in the Household Edition, 1871–9, wood engraving.

When we was put in the dock, I noticed first of all what a gentleman Compeyson looked, wi' his curly hair and his black clothes and his white pocket-handkercher.[43]

Dickens's inquiry, in such a world, could not rest with figures like Clennam and Pip, with the good heart in the shadowed life. An inhibited life has had violence done to it, and a continuing inhibition entails a continuing friction. The men in black in his last novels are figures of enclosed passion gone black and murderous. Mention has already been made of Bradley Headstone in *Our Mutual Friend*, 'in his decent black coat and waistcoat . . . and formal black tie. . . . He was never seen in any other dress, and yet there was a certain stiffness in his manner of wearing this, as if there were a want of adaptation between him and it.' Within, increasingly, there is 'raging jealousy and fiery wrath', especially as he and Eugene Wrayburn, rivals for the affections of Lizzie Hexam, become obsessed with one other, and night after night each haunts the other through the London streets, the schoolteacher increasingly consumed with hatred, the gentleman with contempt, in the most negative relationship Dickens ever presented, at once passionately personal and a thing of class, an extraordinary *danse macabre* of two dark figures, the gentleman and the respectable man, in

60 Luke Fildes, 'Jasper's Sacrifices', *The Mystery of Edwin Drood*, 1870, wood engraving.

a deadlock of hatred tending to murder. Mahoney's illustration (illus. 59) catches them at a moment when Wrayburn has turned, so as to pass back under the eyes of his follower, whom – and whose bitter frustration – he pretends not to see, even as he talks about Headstone for Headstone to overhear, and describes loudly the 'grinding torments' Headstone undergoes. He relishes the cruelty his status makes easy. At another point in the chase, Bradley Headstone's black clothes make possible Dickens's macabre dream image of him: 'he went by them in the dark, like a haggard head suspended in the air'.[44]

The figure everyone remembers in Dickens's last novel, *The Mystery of Edwin Drood*, is John Jasper, the dark, black-scarved choirmaster. He is black-suited also – he is compared to a rook – and is another of Dickens's ominous men 'with thick, lustrous, well-arranged black hair and whiskers. He looks older than he is, as dark men often do. . . . His room is a little sombre, and may have had its influence in forming his manner. It is mostly in shadow.' He has elements both of Eugene Wrayburn and of Bradley Headstone, being securely a gentleman but also a man secretly devoured by passion, and possibly a murderer. He is clearly intended by Dickens to be seen as a man explosively divided. Luke Fildes's illustration (illus. 60) shows him approaching the heroine Rosa, who recoils as he sets 'his black mark upon the very face of day'. He concludes his menacing declaration to her with the odd, modernesque phrase 'Rosa, I am self-repressed again'.[45] Though Jasper is no Nonconformist, it fits the larger argument that this last figure of baulked emotion, cased in black, is himself enclosed in an ecclesiastical close. It is notable both in his case and in Headstone's that their murderous passion and violence stem especially from sexual jealousy, without their seeming men who have much positively loving love for the women they desire. Both Lizzie and Rosa, the women they love, are frightened of them and shrink from them, and the dark murderousness of their anger seems the blacker side of a sexual desire that is itself a dark quantity, desire in its dark aspect. The man in black may have at his centre a dark secret indeed – one of the primal drives of life shifted into its deadly form.

There is a good deal of murderousness in the late Dickens. It lies both in the heart of his black intense men, and also in the heart of his oppressed societies, as he shows in his late novel *A Tale of Two Cities*, in which he describes the maddened bloodletting of the French Revolution with an urgency reflecting his current fears for England. The violence was not only something seen, or foreseen – there is murderousness also in the late Dickens himself, which emerged in the exhausting hot passion with which he carried through, again and again, his star public reading of the murder by Bill Sikes of Nancy. In those readings, his contemporaries observed, Dickens was on both sides: he was the killer, but also Nancy being killed. Perhaps the passions of the readings are connected with Dickens's circumstances at that stage in his life, having deserted his wife but being not easy in his relationship with Ellen Ternan. But also violence done to women has the same value in Dickens that it has in Shakespeare, it represents hurt done both to women themselves, and also at large to what is tender and loving and benign in human beings: to the side of human life that often is characterized *as* the feminine. Which is only to say again that Dickens belonged to the world he described – a world he more and more depicted as inflicting on itself intimate injuries. Moving in that world as an important public figure, he was not only the recorder but also a representative of a period when if black had the values of smartness, decency and respectability, it had also the values of oppressiveness and grief – of the mourning for something missing from the heart of man, of men – and beyond that again had also the darkness of impulses, from sociability to sexual love, constricted, distorted, and ready to rise in murder. Which again is to say that black in the nineteenth century has its affinity with ancient black, and not only with mourning black, but that it also has some tincture of a black fatality, of the black that is of the Furies.

61 Peter Paul Rubens, *Self-portrait with Isabella Brant, c.* 1609–10, oil on canvas.
Bayerische Staatsgemäldesammlungen, Munich.

6 Men in Black with Women in White

Colour dies in menswear in the nineteenth century, leaving colour and brightness to women. This raises the question – Why is it that women do keep their brightness, when the men have passed into shadow? It is a large question, that lies, really, beyond the scope of the present study; as does the whole enormously abundant subject of the significance of colours – of all the colours – in dress, especially women's dress. I shall venture some considerations.

In so far as dark menswear signifies work, the world of work and professional dignity, the brightness of women's clothes is not hard to understand: the professions, and most jobs, were closed to women. But in so far as the darkening of menswear reflects either a certain sombre gravity of power, or, more at large, an ascetic temper, women's colour and brightness is problematic, for one might expect the wife's dress to be as strict and monochromatic as that of her husband. This was certainly the tendency with black fashions in the past: the courtly black, so favoured by Spain, was worn with grave dignity both by lords and by ladies; and again the Calvinist black of the United Provinces was worn both by burghers and by burghers' wives. This is very clear in portraits of couples: where, if the wife or fiancée does not wear black itself (quite often she does not, the man being the appointed 'head' of the household), she wears dark blue or dark brown in a tone very close to her husband's. Again, she may wear more jewellery, a more elaborate ruff, maybe a skirt of rich dark stuff; but often she wears with these things a black mantle, a black jacket or a black overskirt, while the husband may be as much decorated as she is, with cut velvet, brocaded silk, woollen damask. Often there is an elaborate complementarity, as in Rubens's beautiful portrait of himself with his young wife Isabella Brant (illus. 61). He wears black breeches but she wears a black over-gown, the sheen on his deep-coloured doublet matches that on her deep-coloured skirt, while his warm-pink hose are light-toned like her satin stomacher, itself richly worked, as is his doublet. Her cuffs and ruff are richly edged with lace, so is his shoulder-wide shirt-collar.

Similarly, he sits higher but she is in the foreground; he leans towards her, it is she who has laid her hand on his. In many ways at once, their looks, their look and their clothes say both they are themselves, and they are each other's.

The eighteenth century preserved a reciprocity. In that period, as Fred Davis has observed, 'both men and women . . . were equally partial to ample displays of lace, rich velvets, fine silks, and embroideries, to highly ornamented footwear, to coiffures, wigs, and hats of rococo embellishment, and to lavish use of scented powders, rouges, and other cosmetics'. Men's embroidered satin suits might be as colourful as women's gowns. Men's coats had lifted skirts that quietly complemented the pannier-propped skirts of women. Women adopted 'le redingote' from the riding-coat of men. Both genders, it seems, were at peace with the fact that there is a thread of the masculine within the feminine, and of the feminine within the masculine. As to black, it is true that men wore more black than women, but then women would use black for provocative cosmetic details, like the black ribbon at the neck, or the beauty-spot (which men also wore). In Russia, women might have their teeth 'dyed black and shining as if japanned'.[1]

In contrast with such affected and affectionate intrication, the nineteenth century's way of using colour to differentiate gender, according to the stark formula of black men and bright women, seems another of that century's sharpened severities. It is a delicate question, whether one should align this contrast with those readings of gender that relate masculinity to a negation of the feminine. This negation is made especially necessary, in Nancy Chodorow's analysis of gendering, because the boy-child grows up knowing mainly his mother, while his father is absent at work. And as to the connection between dress and gender, one may note that this most stark black/light, man/woman contrast did develop in a period of commercial and industrial expansion. Work-patterns had changed. In the past, the father was often near, ploughing in a field within sight of home, or at work in the downstairs front room of the house, at a shop-counter, a loom, or a bench. Then, as the factories and offices multiplied, the father was more likely to be away many hours. It is true that in the – indeed – working class, women and children might themselves be slaving in the mills, or the mines: but the black/light, man/woman division is not so marked in working-class dress. That division was nurtured by the middle class especially, and it was middle-class mothers who stayed at home, absorbed in raising their children, whom also they had breast-fed, as the use of the wet-nurse by the well-to-do passed increasingly from fashion.[2]

It is not hard to point to qualifying circumstances, or to find quite different colour-combinations, used in other societies where the father might be often away (seeking merchandise, at war, at sea). Nor can one read all male dress as negation: the erect bracing of the figure, the sharp cut of a strong-coloured coat, the well-calved leg in close-fitting light trousers – all these had their positive male assertion. But black, on the other hand, is negation: very frequently it has had a negating value – of life, of the world, of the frivolous self – however smart it has also been. Indeed, if any colour has seemed to be made of meaning, it is black, in the sense that to negate something is an act of pure meaning. *Something* is negated when a person wears black. But even putting black aside, the distinctly plain style which men's dress developed in the nineteenth century does seem, however well-cut and smart, to embody a downgrading of the pleasure of dress, while dress as such, a high pleasure in dress, and indeed a readiness to talk of dress and nothing else, comes to be seen, in nineteenth-century superstition, almost as constituting the feminine. It is a superstition perpetuated, severely yet with a nod and a wink to both men and women, especially by women novelists: most notably Mrs Gaskell. So the father, in one of her novels, says to his daughter, with obvious complacent-indulgent belittlement, 'It seems people consider you as a young woman now, and so I suppose you must run up milliners' bills like the rest of your kind'. Mrs Gaskell will record that 'the ladies started back, as if half ashamed of their feminine interest in dress', that 'the ladies, for the most part, were silent, employing themselves in taking notes of the dinner and criticizing each other's dresses', that two women's 'chief talk was of fashions, and dress'.[3] And though I have stressed the value of remarks on dress in novels, it is true too that there is some redundancy in the ordinary run of clothing-comment in novels. What is most often said is that an interest in dress is frivolous, and that this interest is especially a feminine frivolity.

The corollary, certainly, is that it is in the novels by women, writing on women's dress, that the best light is shed on the real and serious importance of dress: as when, in *North and South*, the true nobility of Margaret Hale, both of her figure and of her spirit, is made visible by a particular dress, or as when Dorothea Brooke in *Middlemarch*, preparing for a difficult interview with the woman she believes to have seduced the man she loves, draws strength from the attention she gives to her toilet: 'the tradition that fresh garments belonged to all initiation, haunting her mind, made her grasp after even that slight outward help towards calm resolve'. The world of dress, and of talk about dress, is, in the nineteenth century especially, a woman's world. And the suggestion that male dress is influenced, on various levels, by a concern to cancel the feminine, might be reinforced by the arguments of Jo Paoletti that a major motor of change in men's dress (which, otherwise, seems not impatient to change) is fear of ridicule – ridicule, that is, for dressing in a way that strikes observers as feminine. The subject of Jo Paoletti's study is the change of male dress in the 1880s in America, in particular to escape the label of the 'dude', who was lampooned at the time as a womanish figure. But her argument might equally be applied to European dress earlier in the century, when some divisions of the dandies were satirized in caricatures, by Cruikshank and others, with distortions that especially feminized their look. And it would seem that the plain style of Beau Brummell himself, which was notably spare and manly, accompanied a negation not only of the feminine but of sexuality too.[4]

Clearly at all times there is a negotiation between men's dress and the feminine, as between women's dress and the masculine: and it does seem reasonable to suppose that, in the nineteenth century even more than previously, there was a negotiation at a deep level between men's black and the feminine. It is important, however, not to overstate the rigour of the divide of men from women. In the 1840s, for instance, men's coats were padded so as to make their shoulders appear rounded, and their waists nipped in, in a shape of body that was cultivated also by women. And women's dress itself was not, in that century, always and uniformly luminous. Deep tones were available, and had periods of fashion in, again, the 1840s, and in the 1850s. There also were women in black, women who regularly wore black by choice; and the black they chose to wear had some of the assertive values it had when worn by men. George Eliot tells us of her Mrs Transome that 'her tight-fitting black dress was much worn': Mrs Transome is gentry and no widow, and even if her black dress is over-used (she is not as well-to-do as she would like), it is still part of her smartness and state and style ('rare jewels flashed on her hands, which lay on her folded black-clad arms like finely cut onyx cameos').[5] Her decision to wear smart black permanently goes with her sense of her presence and importance, and also with certain sombre notes in her life, certain secrecies and reasons for unease: her black is felt in the novel as belonging with her uncommon force of will. Outside the world of fiction, the smart black clothes of such a figure as the pioneering Africanist Mary Kingsley serve as the emphasis of her force.

Mrs Transome, one might say, wears the proud black dress; there was also, as in menswear, a more humble black wear – the black dress, plainer in cut, that was at once respectable and self-respectful, but

62 Richard Redgrave, *The Governess*, 1844, oil on canvas. Victoria & Albert Museum, London.

which also partook of the un-lustrous black which was the colour of dutiful service. This is the form of black dress that might be worn (for instance) by governesses. In fiction, the career-governess Jane Eyre has an almost all-black wardrobe. For outdoor wear she has a black stuff travelling dress, a black merino cloak and a black beaver bonnet. Indoors, she normally wears a 'black stuff dress', but on smarter occasions changes it for 'one of black silk'. Her black clothes fit not only her situation, but also, growing out of it, her strong serious self-awareness. They fit her emotional temper, which is strengthened by losses and griefs, as well as by grief as such. They fit her intensity, her gathering clarity of will and decision. In her black Jane complements Mr Rochester, who is dark-haired, swarthy, and especially smart in black, as well as being a figure of sombre and damaged power. 'My master' she calls him, though she is by the end a governess who has risen to govern, a woman – as he is a man – whose black has command as well as duty.[6]

Since not all Jane's clothes are black, it does not seem her black is to be construed directly as mourning for the parents she has lost some years before. Of course, the death of a parent, or parents, could lead to a young woman becoming a governess, and Richard Redgrave's governess is clearly in mourning, as the letter in her hand confirms, for it is on black-edged paper (illus. 62). The caption in the catalogue, when this painting was first exhibited in 1845, read 'She sees no kind domestic visage here', and she is isolated at once by her position and by her grief, seated in the sombre foreground of the picture, though clearly in the shadowy background of the family, whose children skip laughing near the sunny garden (or wait wistfully, with nothing better to hand than a book, for their turn to skip). She does, none the less, look smart and distinguished in her black mourning wear: this is not everyday governess's black, but something more formal. A commentary on the picture added in 1870 begins 'An orphan, whose mourning dress shows her loss is recent . . .', and this painting may serve to show, as men's dress also shows, the close relation there could be between the smart use of black and the mourning use of black. It is a characteristic of Victorian society that its formality and its grief wear nearly identical clothes. There is by the same token an affinity – or an ambiguity – between the humbler everyday black of employees and the commemorative but everyday black of those, like widows and orphans, whose condition is importantly defined by death, though the loss is no longer recent. As with formality and grief, so also there is an affinity between service and long loss.[7]

One might mention here the black of Lord Fauntleroy, although it is not only he who wears black. His mother wears black constantly, not because her loss and grief are recent, but because she is a widow. And Lord Fauntleroy wears black not because he is a little lord, and so naturally garbed in a black velvet Van Dyck suit, but because his father is dead. He wears black in America, not always but often, before he is a lord. At an early age he wore, as the cook says, 'his bit of a black velvet skirt made out of the misthress's ould gownd'; at seven he is 'a handsome, cheerful, brave little fellow in a black cloth suit and red neck-ribbon'. He has with him, on his trip to England, a black velvet cap that is not necessarily aristocratic, and when going to see the Earl he is dressed by his mother in the smart clothes he already has, 'a black velvet suit, with a lace collar'. Thereafter he regularly is, as he also is in the well-known illustrations, 'a little boy in a black velvet suit'. Black velvet had in the past been the wear of the very rich, indeed of the dukes of Burgundy, and it is in order that, inheriting his lordship, Lord Fauntleroy should once again wear, for his grand introduction to the neighbourhood gentry, a black velvet suit – augmented this time with 'a large Vandyke collar of rich lace'. The lace is evidently new, though he wore lace before. We are not told whether the velvet is new, and tailored at patrician expense. The uncertainty perhaps suits Frances Hodgson Burnett's ingenious tenderness for, at one and the same time, the American open-hearted democratic spirit, and a British nobility redeemed by love. The uncertainty also enables Lord Fauntleroy and his mother (he is dressed by his mother) to illustrate, as also does Redgrave's dignified governess, the resemblance there could be not only between grief and formality, but between grief and rank.[8]

As to the truly smart, it is apparent that if women were required to mourn at length, still mourning dresses were so fully adjusted to fashionable society that one could almost think fashion was set by bereavement. The 1860s brochure of the London General Mourning Warehouse (247, 249 & 251 Regent Street, proprietors Jay & Co.) is called 'Jay's Manual of Fashion', not Jay's Manual of Mourning Fashion. It makes haste to point out that the mourning colours are anyway the height of fashion – 'it is also well worthy of remark, that in Paris, at the present time, Black and White enjoy a decided favouritism', and adds that all its dresses may actually (like men's clothes) be worn equally by the bereaved and the smart:

It is necessary to explain that the subjects of the Illustrations are made up in various materials, suitable either for Ladies who adopt Mourning, or for those who wear Black in accordance with the taste of the day.

Constrained as she was by convention and grief, the widow could, none the less, in due season, choose from among the Madeline (mantle of black velvet, with a crochet insertion of jet, the bonnet of black *velours epinglé*), the Euphrasie (mantle of black ribbed cloth or crape, trimmed with slashed velvet bordered with braid, bonnet of violet terry and black velvet), the Agatha (mantle of black velvet, trimmed with Maltese lace, and headed with Vandyck crochet trimming, tassels of silk with jet headings), the Corinne (dress of black tulle, trimmed with goffered tulle and edged with black satin ribbon, with a coiffure of white frosted leaves and black velvet coral, and with jet necklace and bracelets), and the Druid (mantle of superfine black cloth or velvet, dress of black *gros de tour* or black *moiré antique*, bonnet of black velvet with crown of satin and black ostrich feathers on either side). For the Druid (illus. 63), which looks, from the back, like a Victorian Gothic church made in cloth, Jay's proudly declare they have taken out a patent:

The configuration of the 'Druid' Mantle having been registered by the Messrs. Jay, no other persons can make it without their permission. This exclusiveness will ensure its being worn by families of distinction. . . . It is equally suited by its form for evening wear, carriage, promenade, or travelling, and is made up for these specialities. When trimmed with crape, either on cloth or silk, it is one of the most appropriate mantles for mourning ever invented. And when made in velvet, it folds with unusual ease from the shoulders.

63 'Druid' Mantle (Back), from *Jay's Manual of Fashion Illustrated*, published by The London General Mourning Warehouse, lithograph, *c.* 1860.

The prices vary between two and twenty-five guineas, crape additions coming in normally at a half guinea extra. It is clear that evening wear, carriage, promenade and travelling were occasions where smart wear and mourning could be virtually identical, and that in dressing to honour the dear departed, one could (as in earlier periods) dress in present luxury. The observances of death set the high style for life.

The black dress in the wardrobe, reserved for mourning, might be put on for other serious events, even if these were wholly private. Perhaps the most moving instance, in fiction, of black put on to share in loss, arises in *Middlemarch* when the severe, suave dissenting banker Bulstrode has at last revealed to his wife his secret crisis – now on the verge of becoming public – of sharp practice and, effectively, murder. Mrs Bulstrode, we are told,

locked herself in her room. . . . She took off all her ornaments and put on a plain black gown, and instead of wearing her much-adorned cap and large bows of hair, she brushed her hair down and put on a plain bonnet-cap, which made her look suddenly like an early Methodist. . . .

He raised his eyes with a little start and looked at her half amazed for a moment: her pale face, her changed, mourning dress, the trembling about her mouth, all said 'I know'; and her hands and eyes rested gently on him. He burst out crying and they cried together, she sitting at his side.

She had decided she would only go down to see him when she could 'espouse his sorrow, and say of his guilt, I will mourn and not reproach'. What they must face together is not actual death, but social death: disgrace, the situation of outcasts in the tight town world.[9]

On a lighter note, but only slightly, Gwendolen Harleth, in George Eliot's *Daniel Deronda*, says when she is preparing as she thinks to refuse Grandcourt's proposal of marriage, 'I shall put on my black silk. Black is the only wear when one is going to refuse an offer.' And there were other, non-mourning, forms of black dress, for instance, a woman's smart riding-habit might be all black, going with the man's black hat she would wear when on horseback. In the riding world, the normal colour-coding was reversed, as in Mary Ellen Edwards's engraving for *The Graphic*, *The Special Train for the Meet* (illus. 64), where two handsome young women stand with assurance in the centre of the carriage, both in long trailing black riding-habits and with neat, too-small black top-hats fastened tilted over their brows (one holds up her riding-crop as a fence between her and an amiable gentleman). The men attending them wear lighter-coloured clothes, and the man on the left is clearly in his hunting gear, including the pink coat. The smart black of the riding-habit, together with its pretty mock-masculinity, doubtless enhanced the excitement of escaping from the crinoline by getting on a horse. Of Gwendolen Harleth we are told, 'She always felt the more daring for being in her riding-dress'.[10]

It remains the case, however, that black was the exception in women's clothing, as it was the norm in men's. Preponderantly, women's clothing was light. It could also use bright colours – cyclamen, deep blue, saffron – either for whole dresses, or for such accessories as bonnets, shawls, sashes, ribbons. The developing use of aniline dyes from the 1850s on made available a brighter register of colours again, and English women might use the new colours in a way that could strike a foreign visitor as garish. Hippolyte-Adolphe Taine, for instance, complained of 'bonnets resembling piled-up bunches of rhododendrons . . . with packets of red flowers or of enormous ribbons, gowns of shiny violet silk . . . the glare is terrible'.[11]

Taine, however, was a habitual exaggerator. Women wore purples, reds and blues, but they also wore a good deal of white, as is clear from paintings of promenades, *fêtes-champêtres*, horse-races, railway stations. Frequently women wear white dresses, white pelisses, white shawls, white caps. Often these garments are decorated, but the decoration again may be either white lace, or a light stitching of pale blue or pink. Ribbons and bows seems actually more often white than coloured, and materials that are not white are very often decidedly pale

64 Mary Ellen Edwards, *The Special Train for the Meet*, wood engraving in *The Graphic*, 23 March 1872.

in tone. The dress of young women especially is etiolated or virginal, as in Whistler's *The White Girl* (illus. 65), which he subtitled 'Symphony in White, No. 1'. One may say the painting plays with the conventions, since Whistler knew intimately his red-haired model. But in the painting itself, the white girl is a whiteness, as white within as out, standing erect loosely holding a white lily (the Virgin's flower), a white curtain behind her. Her eyes are alive but expression-less. The bearskin rug she stands on suggests that any animality in her is dead, unless one gives credit to the not-quite-dead look of the bear's head, tipped out towards us by the painting's steep perspective. It may be, too, knowing that the White Girl was Whistler's mistress, that one should speculate about an alternative under-association, and see the white dresses, beneath their profession of purity, as being open to a less cold affinity, with white linen and bed-sheets, the boudoir and the bed. And bed-sheets were embroidered, as were dresses. But yet the White Girl holds her lily; and it seems that white, in the world of Whistler's paintings, is, chiefly, purity. There is a wanness to his white vision, and a certain air of melancholy. This painting pays its odd oblique tribute to the age's wish for women to be angels; while men, who move in the soiling world, might turn its stain to a black sober smartness.

For whiteness too, it should be said, had over the centuries changed in its associations. When Peter the Venerable was discussing with Bernard of Clairvaux the pros and cons of black monks and white monks, he spoke of white as the colour that in the Scriptures represents 'gaudium et sollempnitas', that is, joy, and 'solemnity' in the sense of festive formality: it is the colour of the radiant transfigured Christ; similarly, it is the dress of weddings, where it represents 'nuptiali gaudio', nuptial joy.[12] White was not, then, worn only by the bride, or mainly to symbolize – as it did in the nineteenth century – a virginity she had and which the bridegroom, in black, probably lacked. And when older women wear white, it may represent virtue, fidelity, fineness, but hardly seems, often, the dress of joy.

White was, of course, also a mourning colour: worn especially for children, and also by young women. Mrs Gaskell gives a graceful, but wary, picture of mourning white, when she describes Edith Lennox in *North and South* (in mourning for an uncle), 'dancing in her white crape mourning, and long floating golden hair, all softness and glitter'. White, like black, could be a colour of death, and was also the colour of ghosts and the ghostly. Wilkie Collins plays on many of white's associations when his hero, Hartright, is crossing Hampstead Heath by bright moonlight:

every drop of blood in my body was brought to a stop by the touch of a hand laid lightly and suddenly on my shoulder from behind me. . . .

There, in the middle of the broad, bright high-road – there, as if it had that moment sprung out of the earth or dropped from the heaven – stood the figure of a solitary Woman, dressed from head to foot in white garments, her face bent in grave inquiry on mine, her hand pointing to the dark cloud over London, as I faced her.

For an instant the Woman is ghost, angel, moon-goddess, corpse, bride, mourner, virgin in one. She is pale, like her clothes. Later we observe her white is humble: 'her dress – bonnet, shawl and gown all of white – was, so far as I could guess, certainly not composed of very delicate or very expensive materials'. Her whiteness may have a more disturbing strangeness, when we hear, at the chapter's end, 'She has escaped from my Asylum. Don't forget; a woman in white'.[13]

In the event, her whiteness, we learn, had been chosen for her years before by a benefactress, Mrs Fairlie, 'explaining to her that little girls of her complexion looked neater and better in white than in anything else'. The Woman in White – she is now named as Anne Catherick – continues in white from 'the old grateful fancy': that is to say, her white is a piety to charity. If this explanation dispels some of the aura Collins has conjured for her, he has at the same time added a new strangeness by introducing a second 'woman in white', Laura Fairlie. She also wears white because it suits her: and it suits her because, in one of the novel's mysteries, she is in her physique the double of Anne Catherick. She also, in white muslin, is to be met at night, on 'the terrace, walking slowly from end to end of it in the full radiance of the moon'. And white as worn by Laura Fairlie has some of the values of black as worn by men. In her we see that this other colour of mourning may be at once formal, and self-effacing, and to a degree classless and money-denying:

Miss Fairlie was unpretendingly and almost poorly dressed in plain white muslin. It was spotlessly pure: it was beautifully put on; but still it was the sort of dress which the wife or daughter of a poor man might have worn, and it made her, so far as externals went, look less affluent in circumstances than her own governess.

The narrator later learns she dresses thus because of her aversion 'to the slightest personal display of her own wealth'. She is beautiful, and pure, and, like her half-sister Anne Catherick, is white in her innocence and her goodness: she is technically the novel's heroine, and the technical hero, Walter Hartright (who, so named, could scarcely not be the hero), marries her at last. And yet, even as she focuses the snow-values of Wilkie Collins's world, she is a figure to some extent faint and weak, and could be said, to some degree, to personate

65 James McNeill Whistler, *The White Girl (Symphony in White, No. 1)*, 1862, oil on canvas. National Gallery of Art, Washington, DC.

femininity as absence. She is contrasted throughout the novel with another kind of woman, whom Collins warms to more, though he has to call her 'ugly': the woman of character, of strong colour, who wears colour, Marian Halcombe. She is vigorously intelligent and acts with vigour, she has elements of 'manliness', even to 'her large, firm, masculine mouth' and to 'the dark down on her upper lip'. She is outlawed by the colour-code, but truly is a heroine. Indeed, she not only has 'thick, coal-black hair', but has blackness in her, she is 'swarthy'. Within the person of Marian Halcombe, a masculinity which may be read as a blackness both negates her femininity and gives her strength. Thus she, not the white woman, is a fit antagonist for the Napoleonic villain, fat Count Fosco. She is the woman, not in white, that one best remembers from a reading of *The Woman in White.*[14]

One should not, however, overstress the cold side of white: the century was not in a constant frost. It was in the ballroom, for instance, that the colour contrast of the genders was greatest, but can hardly have been at its coldest, as partners approached, alert to each other, attracted, touching. If the colour-patterning made men and women opposites, the dances themselves – waltzes, not quadrilles – let couples keep hold. And in fact one finds, in ballroom scenes, a quietly stated complementarity: as in Tissot's *Too Early* (illus. 66), where the couple that lean apart in the doorway do at the same time lean symmetrically, their feet toe to toe and their bodies flexing forward again (but her fan, held in white gloves, guards her breast and lips). He is in black, with white cuffs, collar and neck-tie; she is in white, with black ribbons at wrists and neck. They are formally dressed but they are also relaxed. They are clearly acquainted, and wait with a degree of lassitude for other arrivals to allow them to move. The central group is partnerless, mainly, and not all the women's dark ribbons are black, but when their partners come their tones will reciprocate. The principal figure is in pink: her dress, as it were, blushes for her, since she has made the *faux pas* of arriving 'too early'. A disturbing element, possibly, is the way the women's collars end in stray ribbons trailing down their backs, as though they are ready-tethered for as yet unseen controlling hands.

If white was not always cold, often there was a chill. In Manet's *The Balcony* (illus. 67), women and man are dressed so as to press sexual difference to the maximum of difference: the women wholly in white; the man in black coat, dark-grey trousers, dark-blue necktie. The colour contrast gives them a complementarity, but that complementarity here seems purely formal and somewhat enigmatic. One cannot actually tell what the relationship between these people is: and though the models for the painting were friends of Manet's – the painters

66 James Tissot, *Too Early*, 1873, oil on canvas. Guildhall Art Gallery, London.

67 Edouard Manet, *The Balcony*, 1868–9, oil on canvas. Musée d'Orsay, Paris.

Guillemet and Berthe Morisot, and the violinist Fanny Claus on the right – they seem a group only by juxtaposition, looking different ways, thinking their own thoughts in quite different moods. The most powerful face is that of Berthe Morisot (seated): her look is concerned and penetrating, and perhaps marks her as a separate soul. The man seems also apart, on his own, though he does stand with an air of proprietorial assurance.

While the women's white may be virtuous white, still virtue seems not the main point of their dress: rather, one would say, all three have dressed smartly. These are not casual clothes: they are special, and becoming – they are clothes for show, and what they show is the possession of a certain status. If one stands back from the painting, and tries to read in a generalized way its postures, it may suggest the thought that while women's brightness does still have the brightness of display, often what is at issue is vicarious display by men – women serving as leisure-bright accessories to a prosperous head of household standing black-garbed behind but over them. For it is apparent, especially if we return to England, that even the most severely workful bourgeois felt that a measure of show was called for, to make clear his success in his labour in his calling: and the lighter and more luminous part of the display is delegated to his woman or women. The result is the somewhat icy form of display, marked in nineteenth-century women's wear, which is bright and may have some colour – and occasionally may have rich colour – and which may imitate sexual display and the display of warm feeling, because these things are the pattern of display, but still seems not to be these things.[15]

Perhaps the best description of this joylessly dutiful conspicuous non-consumption is that given apropos of Mr Merdle, the *nouveau riche* financier in *Little Dorrit*:

This great and fortunate man had provided that extensive bosom, which required so much room to be unfeeling enough in, with a nest of crimson and gold some fifteen years before. It was not a bosom to repose upon, but it was a capital bosom to hang jewels upon. Mr Merdle wanted something to hang jewels upon, and he bought it for the purpose. Storr and Mortimer might have married on the same speculation.

Like all his other speculations, it was sound and successful. The jewels showed to the richest advantage. The bosom moving in Society with the jewels displayed upon it, attracted general admiration. Society approving, Mr Merdle was satisfied. He was the most disinterested of men, – did everything for Society, and got as little for himself, out of all his gain, as a man might.[16]

This notably cold bosom is Mr Merdle's, he has bought it; and in general it is apparent, in nineteenth-century paintings, that the women in white belong to men in black. Maybe they belong to them as the soul does to the body – this does seem one suggestion of the contrast, where women shed a pure light, while men enjoy the taint of property and power. Black often is a power colour, but white seldom is (with the strong exception of the tropics, of course, where Governors wore white, as they still do in Hong Kong and Bermuda). The white power of women is rather that of mothers over children (and white is the colour of mother's milk, as well as of the chaste snows). But both black and white are colours of denial; and what they deny is colour.

The dangerous power that colour could have is indicated – if we cross the Atlantic to another great Puritan country – in Hawthorne's mid-century fable 'Rappaccini's Daughter'. In the secluded Paduan garden of Dr Rappacini, the plants that he has bred are luridly rich in colour: they are sensuously and almost sexually gorgeous, but also poisonous. He has a daughter whom he keeps at home to look after the garden. She is of a deep and vivid beauty like the plants, and calls the most richly purple and splendid of them her 'sister'. This is also the most poisonous plant in the garden, and she has become poisonous from her contact with it. The story is a prose analogue to Blake's 'Sick Rose', a parable of secretive nurturings. The principal poison, however, is neither in the flowers nor in the girl. 'Farewell, Giovanni!' says Beatrice, the daughter, to the young hero at the end, 'Oh, was there not, from the first, more poison in thy nature than in mine?'[17] It is in the hero's righteous mind that the poison is. The story, in other words, seems a nightmare-poem, where the poison-garden and the poison-girl are a Puritan's eye-view, with both thrill and anguish in it, of sensuousness, sensuality, fragrant luscious carnality. If such is the Puritan's suspicion in the garden, his husbandry will be severe and cruel: he may choose to array his wives and daughters in white, he will do right to wear black himself.

In the Protestant countries especially, it appears, strains of asceticism were liable to blanch women as they darkened men. It is very clear in English nineteenth-century fiction, which has no Emma Bovary or Anna Karenina but does have a Puritan St Theresa, Dorothea Brooke; and Gwendolen Harleth; and Sue Bridehead; and Estella in *Great Expectations*. There are two powerful symbolic figures in Dickens, who surely are complementary: Mrs Clennam in her black, Miss Havisham in her discoloured white. Both are paralysed, and have stayed in their rooms, indoors, for decades: the one woman frozen in intolerant moralism, the other waiting eternally for a bridegroom who does not come, bringing up her ward in frigidity and malice. They are both in darkness, the one in black, the other in white, but a terrible white – the colour of love and death at once. They make a joint image of damage done to women, at least as grievous as that done to men, in the rich but mourning mansion of Victoria's England – Satis House it is called at last – which in Dickens's presentation is at once the home of power, and a desolation, a prison, and a tomb.

It is customary now to argue that sexuality, in the Victorian period, was not as greatly scarred by puritanism as used once to be thought. As Valerie Steele has observed, historians today argue that 'we have greatly exaggerated the prudishness of Victorian women (and men) and have neglected their celebration of sexuality', and she notes, from her own research, that 'despite their long skirts, high collars, and corsets, Victorian women were neither prudish nor masochistic'. That there still was a blanching, that went deeper than dress, is I believe clear if one turns from the stylized art of Dickens to the fuller, inward picture of feminine life given in the novels of George Eliot. In particular there is Dorothea Brooke, the heroine of *Middlemarch*. Certainly Dorothea represents a serious attempt – an attempt scarcely made by Dickens – to present what is admirable in the ascetic and puritan strains of English character as they might appear in an energetic, beautiful, and vigorously intelligent woman. Dorothea is specifically identified with 'the hereditary strain of Puritan energy': we are told 'it glowed alike through [her] faults and virtues'. She is handsome, healthy, emotion-ally ardent, and it is no surprise that she is fascinated by deep and rich colour: though she is quick to spiritualize any sensuous beauty. Examining her mother's jewels with her sister, she exclaims:

How very beautiful these gems are! . . . It is strange how deeply colours seem to penetrate one, like scent. I suppose that is the reason why gems are used as spiritual emblems in the Revelation of St John. They look like fragments of heaven. I think that emerald is more beautiful than any of them.[18]

She admires colour but has not herself much colour – we are told most often of her whiteness – and does not wear colour. She has a black dress, in which, her sister thinks, she would look well with jewellery. But especially she is represented in the novel as wearing grey.

In pursuing black, then white, I have not so far mentioned their compromise, grey: but it was a further un-coloured colour the Victorians valued. It was a virtuous colour, associated in Christian use with the faithful conjugality of doves. In menswear it figured especially in trousers – the trousers one might wear with a black frock-coat. And in women's wear the grey dress was clearly a precious item. It is the one dress Jane Eyre has that is not black: she records that her black silk dress was her best, 'except one of light grey, which, in my Lowood notions of the toilette, I thought too fine to be worn, except on first-rate occasions'. Dorothea is dressed exceptionally finely, as well as simply, when she is observed in Rome by two young art-lovers, in an extraordinary scene that, for all its set-piece explicitness, does eloquently juxtapose the two great epochs of womanhood as the Victorians conceived of these:

The two figures passed lightly along . . . towards the hall where the reclining Ariadne, then called the Cleopatra, lies in the marble voluptuousness of her beauty, the drapery folding around her with a petal-like ease and tenderness. They were just in time to see another figure standing against a pedestal near the reclining marble: a breathing blooming girl, whose form, not shamed by the Ariadne, was clad in Quakerish grey drapery; her long cloak, fastened at the neck, was thrown backward from her arms, and one beautiful ungloved hand pillowed her cheek, pushing somewhat backward the white beaver bonnet which made a sort of halo to her face around the simply braided dark-brown hair.

'What do you think of that for a fine bit of antithesis?' one of the young men exclaims, 'There lies antique beauty, not corpse-like even in death, but arrested in the complete contentment of its sensuous perfection: and here stands beauty in its breathing life, with the consciousness of Christian centuries in its bosom.'[19]

George Eliot very much *sees* her heroines. Presenting Dorothea she makes a large use of colour, or rather of bleached colour, and of different shades and values of whiteness. The most remarkable instance must be that passage, long recognized as symbolizing Dorothea and her world, when she has just arrived at her marital home and looks out on a snow-world, a privileged prisoner:

A light snow was falling as they descended at the door, and in the morning, when Dorothea passed from her dressing-room into the blue-green boudoir that we know of, she saw the long avenue of limes lifting their trunks from a white earth, and spreading white branches against the dun and motionless sky. The distant flat shrank in uniform whiteness and low-hanging uniformity of cloud. The very furniture in the room seemed to have shrunk since she saw it before: the stag in the tapestry looked more like a ghost in his ghostly blue-green world; the volumes of polite literature in the bookcase looked more like immovable imitations of books. The bright fire of dry oak-boughs burning on the dogs seemed an incongruous renewal of life and glow – like the figure of Dorothea herself as she entered carrying the red-leather cases containing the cameos for Celia.

She was glowing from her morning toilette as only healthful youth can glow; there was warm red life in her lips; her throat had a breathing whiteness above the differing white of the fur which itself seemed to wind about her neck and cling down her blue-grey pelisse with a tenderness gathered from her own, a sentient commingled innocence which kept its loveliness against the crystalline purity of the out-door snow. As she laid the cameo-cases on the table in the bow-window, she unconsciously kept her hands on them, immediately absorbed in looking out on the still, white enclosure which made her visible world.[20]

The enclosure is social as well as emotional: George Eliot equates 'the snow and the low arch of dun vapour' with 'the stifling oppression of that gentlewoman's world'. Imprisoned in cold whites and greys, Dorothea is, in her own whiteness, associated with fire, warmth and redness; yet still she seems, in many senses of Blake's phrase, and even though newly married, 'a pale virgin shrouded in snow'. The narrative makes it clear that Dorothea is damaged by her asceticism, even though George Eliot hesitates to criticise her heroine explicitly. It is apparent, for instance, that Dorothea lives very much in fantasy – extraordinarily much, when one considers how blind she is to the repulsiveness (George Eliot insists on it) of her first husband. Even when she finds a man more suited to her, in the second half of the novel, she would rather live away from him and fantasize about him, than actually be with him. The only level on which she can meet him intimately is the level of childhood – he himself being already in some ways a child-man, whom she does not wish so much to mother, but rather to join as a sibling ('and so they stood, with their hands clasped, like two children').[21]

The main picture one takes of Dorothea is, however, probably of her sadness in her first marriage – a radiant figure of grey and different whites, married both spiritually and literally to English Puritanism, personated for her and for George Eliot by one of fictions's memorable men in black, the theologian Edward Casaubon ('the black figure with hands behind and head bent forward continued to pace the walk where the dark yew-trees gave him a mute companionship in melancholy'). Casaubon, it should be said, is a figure of upper-class, anglican, academic puritanism, as the other dark husband of the novel, the banker Nicholas Bulstrode, represents England's middle-class, dis-senting, business-world puritanism. In her fiction at large, George Eliot has her own cast of memorable men in black, which includes Matthew Jermyn in *Felix Holt* and Savonarola in *Romola*.[22]

At the centre of her work, however, are the pilgrimages of her virginal puritan heroines. The type is first presented in Dinah Morris, the beautiful Methodist preacher in *Adam Bede* (a woman in black), but its fullest embodiment is Dorothea herself, a white woman in grey and a modern St Theresa. The puritan heroine is likely to be contrasted with a shallow, pretty worldly woman, as Dinah is with Hetty Sorrel, and Dorothea is with Rosamond Vincy, until, most interestingly, the two types are combined in Gwendolen Harleth in *Daniel Deronda*. Gwendolen is in principle no puritan, and is notably weak on the philanthropic side. She is pretty, vivacious, worldly and daring; but still she is virginal, her prettiness has a 'stinging' quality. Like Dorothea, she can't stand a warm man and is glad to marry a cold one, especially when marrying coldness means marrying class. Even more than Dorothea she seems a snow-queen, markedly white and chill to the touch: she is convinced she cannot love, and does not want to love. Her colour, when first presented, is sea-green: she strikes onlookers as a nereid, silvery and serpentine, a creature from cold waters. Dorothea too was seen in surroundings of an underwater character, in the passage quoted earlier where she hovers in a blue-green, blue-grey world. Gwendolen is more provocative and sprightly than Dorothea, but moves in colder colours. Her figure is set off, at the dancing following the archery meeting, by 'the simplicity of her white cashmere with its border of pale green'. As noted, she thinks to wear her 'black silk' to reject Grandcourt's impending proposal; she is often in a riding-habit, which would be dark or black; she meets Deronda after her husband's death, in which she feels implicated, draped in a long white shawl. In her last meeting with Deronda, we are told, 'slowly the colour died out of face and neck, and she was as pale as before – with that almost withered paleness which is seen after a painful flush'. She is left alone and suffering, the pale heroine in cold-coloured robes, whose story is shaped by the chilled heart she has inherited and could only ever be – it seems written into the novel throughout – a tragedy.[23]

Such a heroine is harder to find in French fiction. In Catholic Christendom, the gender opposition of black *vis-à-vis* white seems often to have a less puritan value. So while one may find many French paintings, for instance many Impressionist paintings, where all the women in gardens, or at picnics, or at dances, wear virginal white, lightly relieved sometimes with rose or azure, there is also, in France especially, another combination, which I shall represent by that sub-genre of French art, the picture of a danseuse in a white toutou haunted by a man in black evening dress. Degas, especially and famously, endlessly reworked this theme, but it is familiar in the work of other artists too.

In Forain's *Behind the Scenes* (illus. 68), the picture is split nearly down the centre, so that we see also some of the scenery. We see the edge of a flat, and the white danseuse in her whiter dress patiently awaiting her cue. She is slightly plump but long-necked, and shows in her face a slightly foolish complacent awareness of the figure behind her, the denizen or master of the behind-the-scenes world – for the behind-the-scenes space is solid black, and he wears solid black, you cannot see where he ends and dark space begins. His face and collar

68 Jean Louis Forain, *Behind the Scenes, c.* 1880, oil on canvas. National Gallery of Art, Washington, DC.

are picked out brightly: so brightly there is an ambiguity as to recession, for the head and shirt seem to hover as far forward as her face, though necessarily he is behind her and might be expected to be more in shadow. He is middle-aged, comfortable, standing with raised head, hands in his pockets, the connoisseur-possessor of his body's desire, her body. His assured still figure leans slightly back, while she tips slightly forward, ready to move, to dance – to his appreciation especially, but perhaps to that of all the gents. For if his smart black is the uniform of his power in the social élite – the money élite – her white also has its distinction. Clearly, for the black-clad men of the world,

69 Paul Cézanne, *A Modern Olympia*, 1872–3, oil on canvas. Musée d'Orsay, Paris.

there also was an erotic élite, composed precisely of star danseuses, ballerinas, actresses: a different élite, often brilliant in limelit white, from that to which the men in black ultimately returned, the moral élite of virtuous women, kept waiting at home in wifely white.

The subject of the man of the world with his mistress is not always handled in the serious mode. Cézanne's *A Modern Olympia* (illus. 69) depicts him and his hat with satiric largesse, leaning back in prosperous well-fed awe before the vision of his desired, who seems to float high on a luminous cumulus cloud of bed-clothes, while her black servant with a wonderful flourish sweeps clear a white sheet to show her plump lovely pinknesses, drowsily nestled but just raising her head to acknowledge her desirer. The picture is, however, uncharacteristic of Cézanne, and uncharacteristic of paintings of men of the world, which tend to show their geniality in a less than genial light: especially when the location is not so much the opera-house, or the kept apartment, but the nineteenth century's form of night-club, where the woman desired may be a prostitute in white.

In Toulouse-Lautrec's painting on card, *The Englishman at the Moulin Rouge (William Tom Warrener)* (illus. 70), the woman Mr Warrener likes is in her skin colour white as her dress (though she also

70 Henri de Toulouse-Lautrec, *The Englishman at the Moulin Rouge (William Tom Warrener)*, 1892, oil and gouache on cardboard. Metropolitan Museum of Art, New York.

wears a black neck-band, black armbands, and close-fitting, elbow-length black gloves). Their eyes don't quite meet, it's her flesh he wants and seems to gloat over, while she, leaning back but drawing tall in the face of his lurch towards her, seems – in the black dot of her eye – perhaps alarmed, perhaps appraising. There is something canine about William Warrener's snout, and something sinister in the face of the woman looking on, with a gleaming slanted eye. And if the prostitutes of Toulouse-Lautrec may at times seem sinister – dangerous, though desirable – so too can be the evening-dressed men, both in his and in other artists' paintings: where they can seem, in their standardized black wear, less like individuals than like automata of male desire. There is a sinisterness in a man wanting to make love who presents himself not in personal plumage, rather in an impersonal, formalized antiplumage, which has acquired its formality from earlier associations with the virtues of seriousness and self-denial. The men in these pictures may still have a gravity, and stand like black totems, ominously immobile among mobile women, seeming full of desire but less than fully alive – very different figures from the young lover in black in earlier art, whose black was grieving love, where these men's black is class and money.

Both Toulouse-Lautrec, and other French artists handling this milieu, convey, with the eroticism, a sense of the sordid, the soiled, a sense of the mercenary side of the coin, of a transaction in the body market. In Degas's ink-drawing *The Customer* (illus. 71) the customer, dressed in black, keeps his black hat on as he decides his preference, and the women are white – as white as paper, they are coloured chiefly by the absence of ink – not because they are wearing white clothes, but because they are naked. In others of his drawings, Degas represents dancers by deepening the tones all round their shapes, while

71 Edgar Degas, *The Customer*, 1876–85, ink on paper. Pablo Picasso Museum, Paris.

they stay blank areas, suggesting again that what is recapitulated in the whiteness of the dancer's toutou (or of her petticoat, or of her white dress) is, especially, the whiteness of her skin. Nor should one discount the possibility that whiteness had sometimes this sensuous value in the respectable white worn by ladies, or young ladies: the different pearly whitenesses of some Renoirs suggest this. One might even draw a confirmation of the point from Sacher-Masoch's novel *Venus in Furs*: for the Wanda the hero loves is his Venus, white either in her 'white muslin dress' or out of it, and he derives the same erotic charge from seeing sable fur wound either round her bare body, or round her white-dressed body. In *Venus in Furs* one sees the final inner work of dark clothing in the psyche, as black-on-white ascetic harshness is naturalized (fur not cloth), wedded to death (the furred animal is dead), and eroticized in a desire for punishment, to be inflicted by a whitened woman both bare and clad in black.[24]

The opposition of men's black and women's white seems in nineteenth-century night-life (and in the brothels of London, doubtless, as well as those of Paris) another instance of separation: an alienation confirmed by the *purchasing* of intimacy. In other words, though one may find various expressions of the complementarity of men and women, still the century's black/white gender-coding does seem to reflect an exacerbated sense of sexual difference, a magnified sense of sexual distance. This is not of course to deny that one can find pictures of lovers, he in black and she in white. Even, though very occasionally, one may see a closely loving couple, as in Renoir's wonderful *Dance in the Country* and *Dance in Town* (illus. 72, 73), where the country lover wears dark blue and clasps his girl more or less kissing her, but even so does not hold her as closely, affectionately and lovingly as the town-dancer in black (and white gloves) holds his partner to him.

Another benign image is of the man in black as family man, leading his daughter to her first communion, a subject handled by Toulouse-Lautrec with charm, poignancy and humour in his *First Communion* (illus. 74), where the paterfamilias, a man in his best black, pushes a pram with a little daughter in white, with his elder daughter behind in such brilliant-white clothes that she is an area of pure paper. (The mother and another child are somewhat grey behind her.) Father and daughter at a first communion was one of the first subjects the young Picasso painted.

How great, on the other hand, the black/white, man/woman distance could be, we may see if we return to where we began, to the nineteenth-century dandy – to the French dandy in black of the literary sort. For while the man in black in the brothel may be a very different

72 Auguste Renoir, *Dance in the Country*, 1883, oil on canvas. Musée d'Orsay, Paris.

73 Auguste Renoir, *Dance in Town*, 1883, oil on canvas. Musée d'Orsay, Paris.

figure from the earlier, devastated lover in black, the more sensitive dandies combined both personae. That, at all events, is the case with both Charles Baudelaire and Gérard de Nerval. Baudelaire, who wrote both of men in black and of dandies, commissioned for himself an especially long and straight coat of black broadcloth with narrow pointed tails, which he wore with slim black trousers buttoning under patent leather shoes and a lustrous silk top-hat. Though when young he experimented with a red cravat and rose gloves, he later confined himself to black with black: with the coat, trousers and hat went a black cravat and a black kerseymere waistcoat, and at leisure in his black-and-red striped apartment he wore a black velvet tunic pinched at the waist by a golden belt. He saw the black fashion as a stylish form of

74 Henri de Toulouse-Lautrec, *First Communion*, 1888, halftone gravure from the *Paris Illustré* of 7 July 1888.

mourning, and the black he wore was perhaps also Hamlet's black. His mother's remarriage had encouraged him in his sympathy with the prince, and he had a set of Delacroix's illustrations to the play hung around the walls of his apartment, together with Delacroix's painting of Grief. Like Nerval, he preferred to love women from a distance, and hymned his white 'ange', Mme Sabatier, as Nerval wove the luminous fantasies of his Aurelia, an actress, around the figure of Jenny Colon; it seems Nerval did not want closer contact, while Baudelaire demonized the woman he slept with.

Both were dandies in black who were lovers in black who also wore the black of the melancholy man, of the mourner, the man in the shadow of death. The black they wear is continuous with the use of black in their verse – the recurring 'noirs', Baudelaire's chiming of 'ténèbres' and 'funèbres' – and continuous too, in Baudelaire's case, with the construction he liked to place on the fact that his mistress, Jeanne Duval, was of mixed parentage and was herself dark-skinned: 'Sorcière au flanc d'ébène, enfant des noirs minuits. . . . O démon sans pitié! verse-moi moins de flamme. . . . Dans l'enfer de ton lit' (Sorceress with thighs of ebony, child of black midnights. . . . O demon without pity! pour less of your flames on me . . . in the hell of your bed). The sky of 'Spleen' poured on Baudelaire a 'jour noir' sadder than night. Nerval saw a black sun rise above Paris, and thought 'the eternal night begins': his Christ, seeking the eye of God, finds only a black socket radiating thickening night on the world.[25]

Though dramatized, their black is profoundly depressed. It is the black of death in the heart, even as at the same time it may involve black eroticism – from out of which they gaze towards a white high radiant angelic feminine figure, whom they want to keep at that far distance. In their different ways, each commits his genius to an eroticized fatality of absence: Baudelaire undoubtedly the greater genius, but Nerval standing in deeper shadows:

> I am the shadowed man – bereaved – unconsoled,
> Aquitaine's prince by his ruined tower,
> My only star's dead and my spangled lute
> Bears the black sun of melancholy.
>
> In the night of the tomb, you who consoled me,
> Give me Posilipo and the Italian sea,
> The flower which pleased so my desolate heart
> And the trellis where the vine and the rose are allied.
>
> Am I Love or Phoebus? Lusignan or Biron?
> My forehead's red still from the kiss of the queen;
> I've dreamed in the cave where the syren swims . . .
>
> And twice a victor I have crossed Acheron:
> Weaving in turn on Orpheus' lyre
> The sighs of the saint and the fairy's cries.

He was in love with being in love with his fantasy-Aurelia, and yet more poignantly in love after Jenny Colon died. Loving so her loss was a way of loving absence, negation and death. Still, he is the only man in black to have taken a lobster for a walk in the Palais Royale gardens; and he committed suicide in evening dress.[26]

75 John Singer Sargent, *Madame X* (Mme Gartreau), 1884, oil on canvas.
Metropolitan Museum of Art, New York.

7 Black in our Time

If women had worn mainly light, pale or blanched materials for much of the 1800s, the situation was to change towards the close of the century, when the striking and assertive new use of black in dress is in women's clothes, not men's. The new force can be seen in Sargent's famous paintings of handsome society ladies *decolletées* in black. The woman in his *Madame X* (illus. 75) is wearing not mournful or grieving, or moral or puritanical, or modest or humble, black – her bearing is quite other – but rather an assured, serious, powerful black. There is an awareness of personal and social force, with the added vibration of confident daringness, playing off the potency of sexuality against the power of the serious. It is the black of women stepping from behind, as it were, white shadows.

The changed balance shows in Sargent's portrait *Mr and Mrs Isaac Newton Phelps Stokes* (illus. 76), so unlike a Victorian couple (though, strictly speaking, they were one). He is the more daunted and somewhat recedes. The vigorous confidence is especially hers, it shows in her bearing and her expression, and shows too in her black jacket, which works in the portrait like a strong emphasis – like an emphasis of strength. The use of black in women's dress, sometimes modest, reserved, respectable, but often much more positively both strong and elegant, has continued throughout the present century both in handsome black wear, especially appropriate for the professions or executive position, and also in recurring waves of *haute couture*, where, however light the material, black still is arresting and important. Of course, black was often worn by women in the past: but mostly by nuns and by widows, that is, by women both without men and largely without power. Whereas in the new use there is no implication of lack, but rather, it would seem, an allusion to the power-confidence in black which used to be associated especially with menswear. And of course if black is no longer, predominantly, a colour used in men's dress, that goes with the fact that men are no longer conceded the predominance that, in earlier times, they took for granted as their birthright.

It is true that at the close of the nineteenth century, black was distinctly smart and sumptuous for men as for women: a point that makes against Anne Hollander's argument that black begins in smartness and then tends to the drab.[1] The period might be seen, by contrast, as working out the last stage of Max Weber's logic: for Weber had been impressed by John Wesley's apprehension that, as Christian diligence must lead in time to wealth, so wealth, long continued, will undermine the piety that assisted its growth. Weber posited that as the work ethic led to riches, so the spirituality attached to the ethic would wither, and indeed in time the ethic itself. And it would seem in the latter years of the century that the 'Victorian' elements of puritan sobriety, gravity, moral gloom, *had* withered, ushering in precisely the fat-necked sensualist in rich evening dress that one is familiar with from late nineteenth-century paintings. This is not, of course, to deny that the ascetic habit kept a powerful hold, especially in many strata of the 'respectable' middle class. But the wearing of black by men in these years does seem more a matter of inertial survival, than of its spreading use like a growing black tree, as had earlier been the case.

At the close of the century, as earlier, the dandy might still emphasize himself with a striking use of black. It is true the long prevalence of serious black had provided the dandy – and especially the aesthete dandy – with an incentive for startling colour. Oscar Wilde wrote to *The Daily Telegraph*, in 1891, to protest against 'the uniform black that is worn now', which he found 'dull and tedious and depressing' and unable to be 'in any way beautiful'; Lord Henry Wotton says, in *The Picture of Dorian Gray* (1890), that 'the costume of the nineteenth century is detestable. It is so sombre, so depressing. Sin is the only real colour-element left in modern life.' When young, Wilde liked scarlet and lilac shirts and later plum breeches; he commissioned a red suit; he appeared with his wife, who was independently interested in dress reform, in matching suits of Lincoln green. But also, both early and late, he was a passionate devotee of men's black evening wear, and, famously, he commissioned in New York, for an American lecture tour, a suit of black velvet, which consisted of 'a plain black velvet doublet fitting tight to the body, without any visible buttons, after the style of Francis I', with sleeves 'of embossed velvet with embroidered field-flower designs . . . the upper part of the arm is to be in large puffs . . . the breeches are to come to the knee and to be tight-fitting . . . the stockings are to be of black silk and the shoes cut low and secured with a silver buckle'. So described, the suit scarcely sounds funereal, though it may be that for Wilde himself his black-dandy clothing had something of the daring and the emphasis of death-wear. For if there is

76 John Singer Sargent, *Mr and Mrs Isaac Newton Phelps Stokes*, 1897, oil on canvas. Metropolitan Museum of Art, New York.

anything in his writing that resembles this suit (his writing generally eschews black), it is the mourning-bed in *The Picture of Dorian Gray* which Catherine de Médicis had 'made for her of black velvet powdered with crescents and suns. Its curtains were of damask, with leafy wreaths and garlands . . .'.[2]

Wilde's dress is a late, baroque variant on the black style of dandyism, which initially had been as simple as it was dark. Broadly, the use of black was diminishing as the economy of assurances and anxieties, which had sustained the high nineteenth century, altered in many processes of change, challenge, usurpation, relaxation. The changes are reflected in the wider tonal range of the new lounge suit, and the new prominence given to leisure fashions – Homburg and 'blazer' in the city, knickerbockers and deerstalkers on the moors – as the nineteenth century is succeeded by the Age of Edward. It becomes a matter of choice whether one wonders more at the speed with which black broadcloth is eclipsed by light flannels, thistly tweeds, crisscross-coloured knitwear; or at the actual continuing tenacity of black (embodying continuing pieties of power), as it keeps its hold in evening dress (the white tuxedo was to be short-lived), in formal dress, in wedding wear; in wear for work, in the professions, in the office; and indeed in the wear of politics. For the black suit became, in the early years of the century, the distinctive wear of the Labour Party – as distinct from the continuing use by the Tories of the black frock-coat. The frock-coat could be worn with trousers other than black: most frequently, trousers had a fine black stripe, from which uniform evolved, or rather survived, the livery of the City of London, of a black jacket no longer frock, worn with black-and-white pinstripes. It was a uniform shared by business and bureaucracy – in short by the governors – which had earlier given the uniform of the other governors, the Labour government in waiting, the serious all-black look of an insurgent movement within a polity.

Black, in other words, survived as formality, thus giving piquancy to the supple modern dinner-jacket, now a form of fun black, apt for the cocktail bar, with loose trousers to charleston in. Even Franz Kafka had mused:

I'd love to go on an excursion with a pack of nobodies. Into the mountains, of course, where else? How these nobodies jostle each other, all these lifted arms linked together, these numberless feet treading so close! Of course they are all in dress suits.

This lightly surreal fancy ripples in a quicker dance when one realizes the linked dancing 'nobodies' resemble letters in a line of Kafka's Gothic script, or indeed of Gothic print.[3] It was at the same time Kafka who had demonstrated that if grave evening wear had become, through long use, slightly comic (and thus ready to be worn by Charlie Chaplin or Oliver Hardy), still at the same time the broad shadow of its 'black' values now rested with a gravity deep in human consciousness: witness his novel *The Trial*, decidedly and in many senses Europe's novel in black.

The men who arrest Joseph K wear an incongruous form of black dress. The first warder 'wore a closely fitting black suit, which was furnished with all sorts of pleats, pockets, buckles, and buttons, as well as a belt, like a tourist's outfit, and in consequence looked eminently practical, though one could not quite tell what actual purpose it served'.[4] It is not only K's comic-ominous visitors who wear black, he himself, dressing to meet the Inspector, is told what he must wear, 'It must be a black coat'. K, who evidently has thoughts of judicial and execution black, retorts 'But this isn't a capital charge yet'. In the event, he opens his wardrobe, 'where he searched for a long time among his many suits, chose his best black one, a lounge suit which had caused almost a sensation among his acquaintances because of its elegance, then selected another shirt and began to dress with great care'. K will play the dandy in black: he is, as Kafka was, an elegant, and will don a self-contained black stylishness to confront the black fatality that has so mysteriously invaded his life. Kafka's own drawings associated with this novel show mobile, angular matchstick-men in black.

K's way of dressing is one among the many ways in which he does not so much flee, as advance to meet, or even seek out, the shadowy judicial process, enigmatic and contradictory, which is drawn inescapably to the fact of his guilt. When he attends his 'First Interrogation', in a public room which, with dream-incongruity, is entered from a fifth-floor tenement flat, we are told of the audience, 'Most of them were dressed in black, in old, long, and loosely hanging Sunday coats. These clothes were the only thing that baffled K, otherwise he would have taken the meeting for a local political gathering.' Presently the audience are all bearded old men, and could be elders in church or synagogue. K discovers that each of them wears under his beard an official badge. So also does the Examining Magistrate, up on the platform, whose developing eyebrows – they become 'great black bushes' – re-enact in little, invertedly, the frightening black-clad staring which the whole gathering brings to bear on K. Thus K concludes they are all officials of the Court, as if all men might prove to be this. At the same time, ranks and roles in the novel may reverse. The officials who pursue K may themselves be pursued and punished, and even at K's behest: there is a lumber-room in K's bank where, whenever he opens the door, even after a delay of days, he finds the two warders who first arrested him stripped and being whipped by a man 'sheathed in a sort of dark leather garment which left his throat and a good deal of his chest and the whole of his arms bare'. ' "Sir," they cry, "We're to be flogged because you complained about us." '[5]

It does seem, from mysterious references to its ineffable higher levels, that the Court has a metaphysical and spiritual dimension: a later chapter is set 'In the Cathedral', itself disappearing in deepening darkness, in which K's interlocutor is a priest – one who proves to be a priest of the Law. The men in the interrogation chamber had been wearing Sunday clothes, and even K's landlady had said of his arrest, 'It gives me the feeling of something very learned, forgive me if what I say is stupid, it gives me the feeling of something abstract'. In its study of guilt, *The Trial* clearly is a metaphysical work, a kind of surreal religious satire, but one that expresses an intuition shared with Greek tragedy, to the effect that we live in a darkness in which the divine itself appears divided and contradictory.

It is, however, at the same time a novel about men and women, and, especially, about bachelors who work in offices and women employees. All the guilty and the accused are men, and the charge against them is precisely that of guilt. '"Yes," said the Law-Court Attendant . . . "all of them are accused of guilt."' The lawyers and court officials (of course) are men, while the not-guilty women, almost all, are the inflamed, promiscuous sexual property of the men, made-love-to in sordid circumstances, competitively wooing the perversities of men:

'That's no advantage,' said Leni. 'If that's all the advantage she has over me I shan't lose courage. Has she any physical defect?' 'Any physical defect?' asked K. 'Yes,' said Leni. 'For I have a slight one. Look.'

If the novel engages a metaphysical hierarchy, still its dream logic allows it to depict at the same time the mystificatory hierarchies of man-made power. The movement of the writing is to manufacture hierarchy, envisaging a machinery of authority on authority, pedantic, high-priestly, claiming sexual property, which men principally have made in the world – indeed, in the universe, under God the Father and Jehovah. It is a structure of limited power and of unlimited guilt, in which each man is only comically individual, for all wear the black uniform, expressing authority and anonymity, of those who build guiltily inexorable Law, on whom notwithstanding judgment is passed.

At 'The End', the black of the Court is death. Two men call for K: they are pallid and plump, dressed in black frock-coats and top-hats. They find K 'sitting also dressed in black in an armchair near the door, slowly pulling on a pair of new gloves that fitted tightly over the fingers', an action as appropriate to an executioner as to a man (a solemn dandy, now) who knows his own execution is come. With the arms of all three locked together – so they are like a tighter version of the dancing letters in evening dress, the 'nobodies' in the mountains – they proceed through the streets. The surreal comedy continues – the comedy of K's complicity in his own 'Trial' – and when they confront a bushy-moustached policeman, who might, if asked, release him, K quickly pulls the others away, fleeing like a guilty man to the place where, like a guilty man, he lets them thrust the knife in his heart, killing him 'like a dog'.

In Kafka's fiction, black clothing belongs especially to the pursued, accused, judged world of *The Trial*. The world, and clothes, are not dark in his quest-novel *The Castle*, where the colour-emphasis is rather white. The early chapters of this novel have a brightness of light not usual in Kafka ('But one morning – the empty, quiet market-place had been flooded with sunshine, when had K ever seen it like that either before or since?'). There is a radiance on his brief glimpse of mother-and-child: 'a pale snowy light came in . . . and gave a gleam as of silk to the dress of a woman who . . . was suckling an infant at her breast'. Silken too, and distinctively, almost angelically white, are the clothes of Barnabas, the messenger from the Castle: 'He was clothed nearly all in white, not in silk, of course; he was in winter clothes like all the others, but the material he was wearing had the softness and dignity of silk'. The chief figure in *The Castle* to wear black is Klamm, that fugitive potentate of the castle's bureaucracy whom we see but do not meet, and whom we come to know as resembling a remote lover, a remote father, a remote god. He has no fixed appearance, and is more an absence than a presence (the word 'Klamm' means a deep gorge), and yet also he is the novel's most potent presence, and 'he always wears the same clothes, a black morning-coat with tails'. We are told, in a prolonged discussion of menswear in the Castle, that 'the officials . . . have no official dress . . . the officials go about in their ordinary clothes, very fine clothes, certainly. Well, you've seen Klamm.' Their 'ordinary' clothes, it would appear, are at the same time the most formal form of dress available to men: the dress, at the time, of civil ceremonial, of high public dignity and state, which might at the same time be more a matter of persona than person. And the officials, we are also told, exist in peculiarly cramped conditions (like the spectators in the gallery at the interrogation in *The Trial*, stooped down under the ceiling), tight-pressed behind a formal bench, where they do no more than read 'great books', and sometimes whisper as they read, for the clerks beyond the bench to hear.

In the art of the 1920s and 1930s, the 'man in black' is ominous, mysterious, and seems also the trope of the impersonal man, the man abstracted in social order, as in the paintings of René Magritte. In one famous painting, *Not to be Reproduced* (1937), a dark or black-haired man, in a neat black coat, stares over a mantelpiece into a mirror, in which he sees not his face, but the black back of himself that we see. It is as though there were no face, as though he were more coat and hair than a man; and again as though there were many of him, so this exact 'reproduction', whose face no mirror may reproduce, might itself be repeated again for ever. In another, much later, painting (*Golconda*, 1953), the men in dark suits, dark coats, black bowlers – men in the clothes Magritte wore for photographs – fill the sky and grow faint in distance. Those nearest to us hang their shadows on the house-fronts, in which the windows are curtained and closed. Nearer to Kafka in both date and spirit is the painting *The Threatened Assassin* of 1926–7, in which two men in black bowlers, in black suits, ties and coats, wait – one holding a club, one holding a net – on either side of a large doorway, through which we see, standing, a handsome light-haired man, elegant in such a black lounge-suit as K wore, with a black coat and grey trilby on the chair beside him. He gazes into the yellow flower-form of a phonograph speaker. On the divan behind him lies a naked woman, decapitated it appears (a white towel hides the cut), with blood running from her mouth. Beyond her is an open doorway and balcony, over which three further men in black look in, as impassive and waxwork-faced as all the men here. Beyond are a dark and a snowy mountain. Perhaps the body, and the other, menacing men, are dreams in the head of the man gazing at the phonograph: perhaps they are his music, a frozen music, for all feeling is frozen here, in a scene of dream-death with no dream fear in it, a scene of menace and murder 'without affect', dressed in formality and in social good form.

Black evening dress, and business wear (bowler-hatted), and the black lounge suit, could all be perceived as suits of death. In the meantime a more literal black dress of death was, through the 1920s and 1930s, preparing. The first appearance of what was to be Fascist black was in a more simply patriotic context: in the black shirts permitted to the young volunteer *arditi* in the Italian army in the Great War, an élite group of shock-troops that most famously included D'Annunzio. Disaffected after the War, and retaining their organization, they quickly attached to the Italian Fascist Movement on its foundation, and became the Italian Fascist Black Shirts. Their black had been in origin patriotic, it signified their willingness to die for the nation. It was in effect a kamikaze black, a young warrior's honest facing of death, even his daredevil embracing of it. It had the authority of heroism, it claimed the entitlements of the brave, and this gave it special appeal to the Fascists – as its use turned in peacetime to pose and rhetoric. Then its daring turned to ruthlessness, its carelessness of the wearer's own life to a carelessness of other lives while the wearer, himself, took power – his dress changing in the process from a black shirt to black full uniform.[6]

The Fascist administration operated different colours of uniform, it should be said: non-black uniforms being worn with the black shirt, and the black uniform itself being worn by various officials and divisions of the movement: for instance the 'Musketeers', the élite corps assigned to protect Mussolini himself. At a march-past (illus. 77), they practised the 'Roman Step', which augmented the impersonality of the uniform by making their movements different from the

77 Mussolini's bodyguard of Fascist Musketeers.

normal human lope, more severe, more regimented, more like a dangerous mechanism.

Fascist dress was not necessarily black. In Spain, the Falangists wore blue shirts (theirs was the 'Era Azul', the Azure Age), Hitler's SA in Germany wore brown (the party having inherited a large consignment of ex-army shirts). Greek Fascists wore either blue, derived from Spain, or black: Greek Fascist black being influenced by Italian black, but having, independently, its own patriotic authority. The original μελανοχιτονες (black tunics) had, I believe, been the Macedonian freedom-fighters, at the beginning of the century, fighting the Turks and Bulgarians. But in Germany, too, there was a background of patriotic black: and as the Nazi movement, increasing in power, began to mark off from within itself its own élite troop, of men of the most absolute loyalty and ardour, it made its own growing resort to black.[7]

In their first embodiment as an SS, as the Schosstrupp Adolf Hitler (Adolf Hitler Shock Troops) of 1923, this Praetorian élite was distinguished by the famous death's-head cap-badge, a compact version of the pirate flag, with a grimacing skull overlaid on crossed bones. Hitler then went to prison, following his putsch attempt in that year. When he regrouped in 1925, the year in which the Storm Troops were given their brown, a new SS was formed, the Schutzstaffel

(Protection Squad), also wearing brown, but set apart by a black cap (with skull badge), black tie, and a black edging to the armband: a touch, as it were, of *distingué* black, signalling the fact that the Nazis *had* an élite. The distinction became total when in 1932 the new SS, now run by Himmler and expanded in numbers from hundreds to tens of thousands, adopted the famous all-black uniform. The brown shirt persisted for a time, but was later replaced by a white shirt, making the total effect severely smart, being black except for touches of white or silver (aluminium, rather) in collar-badges, shoulder-cords, stars, oak-leaves, eagle-and-swastika, and of course, still, the skull-on-bones.[8] Their black, then, was conceived and understood as élite black: the more so since the new SS uniform was in many respects an updating of the dress of a famous German cavalry regiment, the Black Bruns-wickers, the regiment raised in the early nineteenth century by Friedrich Wilhelm, *der schwarze Herzog*, the Black Duke of Brunswick. When planning his canvas *The Black Brunswicker*, Millais wrote '"Brunswickers" they were called, and were composed of the best gentlemen in Germany. They wore a black uniform with death's head and cross-bones, and gave and received no quarter.'[9] The SS were a more terrifying élite of course, since it was in peacetime, and to civilians, that they gave no quarter; and they were meant to be terrifying. Himmler remarked, chillingly enough, 'I know there are some people who get ill when they see the black tunic. We understand that and do not expect to be loved by too many people.'[10] The skull itself signified a readiness to die – the SS swore, in their initiatory oath, 'obedience unto death' – but it clearly threatened more deaths than their own, and indeed, grotesquely, the troops assigned to guard the concentration camps were explicitly named the Totenkopfverbände – the Death's-head Detachments. The SS were indeed the Third Reich's élite, not only a guard and a terror police, but a widely invasive governing agency, above the law themselves though awarded an embracing legal jurisdiction.

Drawn up in a guard of honour (illus. 78), the SS soldiers present arms with faultless regimentation. They wear metal helmets, as being ready to defend the Führer in any theatre of war; and of course the Waffen-SS provided the Wehrmacht with some formidably committed detachments. As their supreme commanding officer, and since the occasion is ceremonial, Himmler himself (to Hitler's right) wears the cap with skull and bones, and available regalia. Hitler, as Führer, wears not the black uniform of his élite guard, but the brown uniform of his SA and of the whole Nazi movement: he is the leader of all of them, and this difference in colour between him and Himmler does then give

234

78 Hitler and Himmler inspecting an SS guard of honour.

79 Hitler's personal bodyguard.

Himmler's black the aspect of the black worn earlier by king's ministers, whether or not the prince wore black (as for instance Thomas Cromwell wore black, though Henry VIII did not). That is, the black of the man devoted to being an implement of the will of his leader: and to being, vested with the leader's authority, an especially ruthless executant of that will on those under his command and surveillance.

As a fanatical personal guard grown to become a ruthless executive, the SS most recalls the Oprichniki, the black-clad Men Apart of Ivan the Terrible. The SS, too, were required to be men apart, foreswearing all loyalties except their absolute loyalty to the Führer, and submitting even their marriage plans for SS ethnic vetting. In the light of the Russian comparison, one may see an all-black uniform as the most complete and intense way of marking off a group of people from the polychrome ordinary mass: and indeed, with a different inflection, black had this value for priests, marking their separation – initially as hermits and monks – from the workaday community. Ivan chose black for the Oprichniki because of its allusion to the priesthood, and they were required, impiously, to have the total devotion to him that priests had to God. The SS too had something of this character. Himmler admired the disciplinary principles on which the Jesuits were organized, and was called by Hitler his Ignatius Loyola.[11] Indeed, the Jesuit command-structure had recommendations for both of them, for Jesuits were bound in total and absolute loyalty to the Pope, who might be seen as the Führer of the Church, and were absolutely at the command of the 'General' of the Society, who might then be read as somewhat corresponding to the Reichsführer-SS, SS-Oberführer Heinrich Himmler. And though the Nazis were hostile to Christianity – as a religion hardly devoted to 'Herrenbewusstsein' (master-consciousness) – SS recruits were still required to be *gottgläubig* (God-believing): a qualification that perhaps had a tactical component, since the SS recruited among both Protestants and some Catholics, but which also accommodated a need the Movement evidently felt to invoke for itself a religious sanction. SS rhetoric intermittently conjures an indeterminate God or Nature-principle or Will in the universe who has ordained the mastery of the master race. In the SS catechism the new recruit affirmed, when asked 'Why do we believe in Germany and the Führer?', 'Because we believe in God, we believe in Germany which He created in His world and in the Führer, Adolf Hitler, whom He has sent us.' The black uniformed young initiates – the mean age for the whole SS was twenty-eight – were the sworn ministers of a Germanic Messiah. They could thus displace responsibility for what they did; they were, in effect, trained to invite possession of their soul – an act of damnation in an older belief.[12] The supreme talisman they were trained to treasure was the black dagger, with nickel buckle, awarded to them on final full acceptance into the SS.

For they were at the same time holy knights, a consecrated Order like the Teutonic Knights, Templars, Hospitallers and other blessed Christian soldiers: a Schloss was made over to be their Camelot, where (at Wewelsburg) Himmler would dine at a round table, as the Nordic-British King Arthur used to, with his truest knights (of which there would be twelve, like Christian disciples). On these occasions they – this knightly, spiritual, military, ethnic, state-police élite – presumably wore the SS formal evening wear, a short black jacket like a bellboy's but with black silk lapels, and black trousers with white piping edged with aluminium braiding. The jacket had six non-functional silver buttons, with the SS runes on them, garnished with oak-leaves. All the available insignia were to be worn, including white shoulder cords, an aluminium cord aiguillette, and a white metal chest-badge with a skull on crossed bones.

Doubtless they exchanged mordant sallies and retorts: the tone perhaps raised, or lowered, by the knowledge that beneath the stone floor beneath the round table was a new-made stone crypt, where twelve pedestals awaited the urns containing the ashes of the noblest Obergruppenführer of all – or rather, the ashes of the new coats of arms that the SS commissioned for its knights. This Realm of the Dead was the SS holy of holies, though Himmler would also visit, once a year, the cathedral crypt where the remains of Heinrich I of Saxony lay (Himmler had arranged for their transportation there: he dealt in real skulls and real bones), Heinrich being dear to Himmler as a considerable killer of Slavs. Obviously not all the SS shared Himmler's deathly mysticism – his main lieutenant, Reinhard Heydrich, would seem to have been more fascinated with the pure efficient running of his black police executive machine – but a cult of dead Germanic heroes, a cult of heroic death, indeed a cult of death and killing, was built into SS ideology, making black, ancient colour of death, all too appropriately the colour they wore. Indeed, the image of black-uniformed skull-badged SS officers solemnly gathered in ancient stone crypts seems too like Hollywood kitsch to be true, though peculiarly chilling and appalling if true.

Noble as the Black Order was supposed to be, this was not a nobility tied to hereditary blue blood. Its nobility, on the contrary, was defined solely by intensity and effectiveness of loyalty, combined of course with a purity of German blood. In this sense the Order was open to any

German – of the appropriate height and facial conformation, it should be said (though these qualifications were later relaxed). This introduces a less outré aspect of SS black. For if the SS adopted black as the colour of the distinguished, and especially as the colour appropriate to an élite, still this was not an élite in situ, but rather a would-be or ascendant élite. And while black may be worn by an incumbent élite, where it pretends to a grave disinterested care in preserving the existing structure of advantage, still, as noted above apropos of rising merchants, black has a particular merit for insurgent or ascendant élites, in that being colourless it can pretend to be classless. It is clear that Himmler's SS was an especially potent and fast-action body of ascendants, growing with extraordinary rapidity in numbers, as, again with extraordinary rapidity, they took over more and more military, police and executive functions. Though the SS came in practice to welcome patricians, it is clear that it also welcomed Germans of all classes, and for instance recruited at least as many Germans of working-class background as of lower-middle or upper-class backgrounds, for all of whom it presented extremely good prospects. Indeed, for poor Germans, it was the only élite open to them, the only élite not closed by educational or hereditary barriers, and a real élite, *the* élite, too.[13] If one looks more closely at a black-coated SS guard, drawn up yet again for inspection by the Führer (illus. 79), one may be more struck (however ironic it may now appear) by their nervous youthful hopefulness, than by any visible keenness to kill.

It seems to me the key sociological aspect of men's black dress that it has a double effect: it steps outside, or sidesteps, the established grades of social class, while at the same time, by its gravity, it immediately creates its own dutiful-disciplinary élite. It is this double aspect that makes black an assisting condition not only for a strict assertion of power, but for the movement of power within a society. This point seems worth stressing, since power can sometimes be discussed as though it were distributed in a static social architecture, changing little until the structure is overthrown. But power exists as it is asserted and is always in motion, changing hands as stronger hands take it: it is a currency moving as currency moves, and tending to move *where* currency moves, in the constant anxiously effortful ferment of encroachment, ascendancy, arrogation, of thrust and counter-thrust of group within group – which shows on the surface as the history of fashion, which is the visible precipitation of new would-be élites. If black came to be a power colour through being an élite colour, that élite may originally have been purely spiritual (as with hermits and monks), but precisely through its equation with a spiritual élite, black offers both shelter and a reinforced magic for subsequent would-be and ascendant élites, and for ascendants generally. So it came finally to offer cover for the most obscene élite of all: an élite devoted to the belief in an élite race, and willing to commit not only to the subjugation, but to the extermination of another race. For it was, of course, the SS that took on itself that Nazi mission.

This last matter is so hideous, it seems beyond the scope of a disquisition on colour in dress: but colour is hardly irrelevant to racism, and if white racism has sometimes dressed itself in white – as with the Ku Klux Klan – it has also been willing to dress in black. It is not a matter only of the SS, for if the Spanish Inquisition was interested in heresy, it was mainly interested in the 'heresies' of – and mainly interested in burning – converted Jews and converted Moors. The question is obviously complex for many reasons, including the fact that as the Reich was increasingly involved in war, SS members more and more wore – for practical reasons – field-grey rather than jet-black uniforms. The SS none the less suggests, as the Black Friar Inquisitors earlier had, and Ivan's Oprichniki, that if black is fundamentally and intuitively felt to be death's colour, it can be a dangerous colour to surround oneself in wholly. It may complete our mourning and grieving, but it can help us be dead inside and death-dealing too. It can help us be willing to *be* death – to others – especially if we are not alone, but part of a black army, and especially again if the others are notably vulnerable, ethnically 'alien', and outnumbered. Of course anyone, and soldiers, may commit atrocities in any-coloured clothes; and it seems a cliché, even cheap, to dress evil men in black. But it does appear to be a datum of history that as black is lightless so it can be merciless. And that if it is a power colour, and death's colour too, it can assist, at least as an accessory, if one is on course to tamper with one's soul – to tamper with souls, with the human soul, with the soul of a people. It is not only in the cinema that black has been an accessory to evil.

Beside the SS, the British Fascists, Oswald Mosley's Blackshirts, might seem not much more than a chauvinistic pantomime. Indeed, Mosley seems a man of such mobile politics, a rich patrician become Labour MP, playing now to the Left and now to the Right, and again to the Left and again to the Right – while being personally such a peacock and popinjay – that one might suppose that in choosing the black shirt for the British Union there was at least a modicum of dandy black: the more so since, as Mosley recalled, 'soon our men developed the habit of cutting the shirt in the shape of a fencing jacket, a kindly little tribute to my love of the sport'.[14] Duelling was a patrician sport popular with Fascists, and encouraged by Himmler as the proper way for SS members to settle disputes since they could not go to court (they were above the courts). Reinhard Heydrich was another élite épéeist. The image of the Leader as dashing black fencing-master was natural to the stylishness that Mosley projected: in the words of an admirer, 'this new proud attitude to life, this ardour, this dash, this vivacity, was described by Mosley as panache, a word that seems entirely appropriate in both its senses' (that is, presumably, a swagger and a plume).[15] And Mosley's own black shirt was black silk. Mosley was not, of course, all mercurial dash and chameleonic oratory: if his main stress veered violently between Keynesian works and empire preference, and between riding the working class and crushing it, he did not veer at all in his belief that the nation needed, above all, strong leadership. In this sense, the British Union of Fascists was his natural terminus, rather than, what it might at first seem, one of many ports of call where he chanced to stay. The question then as to the blackshirt (as it was called, for the person was the garment and the garment the person) is to what extent it had the relatively innocent origin claimed for it, and to what extent it was, much more particularly, the sincerest form of flattery of Himmler's SS. Mosley's own account is on the neutral side:

We were faced with heavy odds . . . we had to wear some distinctive dress, a uniform in order to recognize each other. That is why people obliged to fight have worn uniforms of some kind or other from the earliest days of human history. We wore coloured shirts for the same reason, and black was chosen not only because it was the opposite of red but because at that time it was worn by no one else in the country.[16]

While it was important to Mosley that black was not red, this will hardly be the whole story, and Mosley had the precedent of the Italian Blackshirts. As to the SS, the precise degree of initial indebtedness is not fully clear, for the introduction of the blackshirt in Britain actually coincided with the move of the SS from black accessories to an all-black uniform: both occurred in 1932. It should be said that the blackshirt was orginally worn only by stewards: it was only after 1932 that it was worn by Mosley himself and by the movement as a whole, by which stage it is fully clear that the ideology of the shirt is, distinctly, SS ideology:

If you should join us, we will promise you this: when you have put on the Black Shirt, you will become a Knight of Fascism, of a political and spiritual Order. You will be born anew. The Black Shirt is the emblem of new faith that has come to our land. (*The Blackshirt*, 4 May 1934, p. 4)

It seems clear from the noble and knightly religiosity – with, even, its misapplied hope of a resurrection – that the faith that came to our land was in this instance at least, the faith of Himmler. The precedent was clarified when, the next year, the blackshirt was superseded, for senior members of the movement, by an all-black full uniform, all too manifestly modelled on the SS uniform. In fact it was a reach-me-down sort of SS privilege: below the senior echelons, the full uniform could be worn only by those willing to give the movement two nights a week. Those making a lesser contribution wore differing fractions of it – but could obtain additional garments, by, for instance, selling more copies of *The Blackshirt*. Though the movement was hardly yet an army, the implications of the uniform was unmistakable, at least as construed in Parliament: 'A uniform in politics symbolises force, to be used either now or in the future'[17] – a proposition one might apply to standardized dress generally, though as the dress is less military the force may be less physical (social uniforms mean social force, spiritual uniforms mean spiritual power). On the subject of the uniform, Mosley is character-istically disingenuous, and hardly fully leaderly – 'the men were keen to wear it as a mark of distinction, a party honour'.[18] He himself said the uniform was a mistake, and at all events it lasted barely a year, and was banned in a Public Order Act in 1936.

As a consequence of these changes, the British Union of Fascists was liable to appear in black but somewhat disparate array. Inspecting his forces on the day of the 'Battle of Cable Street' (illus. 80), Mosley himself, who takes the salute in a manner between a salute and a wave, wears the full black uniform in the particular high-waisted style he

80 Sir Oswald Mosley inspects his followers on 4 October 1936.

preferred. And Neil Francis-Hawkings to his left behind him, the Director-General of the British Union of Fascists, wears, like Mosley, the uniform and jackboots. Of the troops Mosley inspects, however, and who give him the 'Heil!' salute at discrepant angles, some wear the black uniform, some the fencing-style blackshirt with black trousers, and some the blackshirt with black jodhpurs and jackboots (these probably being members of the 'I' Squad, Mosley's own Praetorian guard). Of the flags they carry, the Union Jack alternates with the black banner of the British Union.

What is clear is that black was the colour of British Fascism – above all in the black shirt, worn first with grey trousers, then with black trousers or black riding-breeches.[19] As with the SS, the proposed knightliness of Mosley's 'Order' went with a pretence of classlessness. So, in *The Blackshirt*, an article on Fascist dress claims of the 'blackshirt':

It brings down one of the great barriers of class by removing differences of dress, and one of the objects of Fascism is to break the barriers of class. Already the Blackshirt has achieved within our own ranks that classless unity which we will ultimately secure within the nation as a whole. (24–30 November 1933, p. 5)

It may be that classless black has, elsewhere, served as a cover for ascendant élites. For the Blackshirts in Britain, ascendancy was hardly a foreseeable prospect: after the first electoral fiasco, Mosley started to speak of a 30-year struggle; and British Fascist black is more simply the black of a group that sees itself outside the existing class-categories, which it means to overthrow, for it means to take power, while in the meantime it will keep itself combative and fit. In this respect – as the colour of organized opposition to class – it has some of the same sense that it had in its association with Anarchist movements (in its use, for instance, combined with red, in the Anarchist flag). And there is an overlap in the rhetoric of 'classlessness' and 'struggle': but, of course, a deep difference in purpose, since the Anarchists and nineteenth-century dynamitards supported an ethic of sharing, theoretically without leaders or chains of command, while the ideology of Fascism went quite the other way. It was aggressively militaristic, disciplined and spartan: there was a headquarters in London (formerly White-land's Teachers Training College) that was called Black House – for the dark house of Britain's hierarchic severities finally took this literal form – where life was lived to bugle-calls, from reveille to lights out, with gymnastics, boxing and judo in between. An anti-class army was being trained in obedience and combat-relish (for Blackshirts could only be moulded 'through the furnace of the struggle for power'), while the familiar paradox of 'classless' élites shows when the new movement is associated by its excited sponsors with a revival of aristocracy: 'the democrats dread this classic figure more than anarchy – for it is the figure of the Leader, the natural aristocrat' behind whom stride 'the eternal *condottieri*'.[20]

What is disturbing about the striding *condottieri* (commanders), as with the SS, is their youth. They were mostly in their twenties (as were the two lead orators, after Mosley: William Joyce and 'Mick' Clarke). One might then speak of their susceptibility, especially if the British Union appeared to offer opportunities, and at all events offered promises, not otherwise available. There clearly was a generational aspect to the rise of Fascism. In Germany, disaffection with the generation that sent young men to be massacred in the trenches was compounded by disaffection in the following generation with the absentee fathers who were, precisely, away at the War – and, of course, by the disaffection of those seeking their first jobs in an economic Depression.[21] If the situation was less desperate in England, it was hardly happy. Both the SS and the Blackshirts are reminders of a further strong connection of black – a connection not irrelevant to the connections of black both with 'classlessness' and power – and that is the connection of black with youth.

That is one strong connection that has survived since the Second World War: and, interestingly, both the latterday revival of Fascism, and the revival of Fascist black, have been especially youth phenomena. The looser, revivalist use of Fascist motifs, involved in wearing swastikas, skulls and iron crosses here and there, has also been a youth fashion – indeed, a youth glamour, as the ruthlessness and cruelty of Fascist fact, in becoming a memory as those years recede, becomes a thing of fantasy: which becomes a fantasy of sadism, and so a fantasy-sadism, a sexual buzz. And not, after all, only for youth either, for there is a pornography for all ages that procures its fix not from putting on SS gear but rather from putting SS gear on women, from having a girl arrange a compromise between being naked and being dressed like an Obergruppenführer – as she fingers the implements of correction.

In the street or on the road, swastikas and iron crosses are still used as shock cosmetics, especially when attached to the easily decoratable surface of black leather: either the full leathers of a Hell's Angel on a Harley, or the more ubiquitous – the famous, the talismanic – black leather-jacket. Like the Fascist regalia, the black leather-jacket is a descendent of World Wars. It began as the leather flying-jacket worn by European air aces – and air forces – in the Great War, and then by air forces the world over in the Second World War. It was perhaps

81 Marlon Brando and Mary Murphy in a still from *The Wild One*, directed by
Laslo Benedek, 1953.

because of its service association, together with its protective and
comfortable but also combat qualities, that it passed into the use of
police forces – in America especially – where its supple mobility and
non-rip strength, combined with black's impersonality, allowed it to
work like a light-weight modern armour. Though the police have
traditionally worn blue, black has been so much used, historically, by
impersonal, tight-regimented, disciplining forces, that both black and
the police were perhaps only coming into their own in the development
of the twentieth-century black police jacket. (One might add, putting
the leather-jacket to one side, that some British police forces now,
though technically or officially wearing navy blue ('the boys in blue'),
have come to wear so deep a shade of blue, as to trousers, tunics,
helmets, that it is tantamount to black. Other forces, such as Cam-
bridgeshire's, do simply wear black.)

It seems too that bikers' black, at least as worn by Brando in *The Wild
One* (illus. 81), was in origin a mock version of police leather. For
Brando's own leather-jacket has black leather epaulettes, each with a
star, and he wears a peaked cap not unlike a police cap. In these respects
he is dressed differently from his co-bikers, and distinctly more in the
police style (indeed, if he wore dark jodhpurs instead of blue jeans, he
would look like a cycle-cop): perhaps indicating his authority, as leader
of the pack, also his virtue as hero, beneath the rough style. And the

bikers, like an anti-police, also are a coherent force, even in their anarchy. They break the speed-limit but in formation-biking, and (in films, anyway) heed the authority of the lead-biker. Their black leather is undoubtedly dangerous (I am taking as read the mere practical fact that leather is also, if you are riding a motor-bike, safe – the best thing to be wearing if you have to bail out). It is raw: a way of wearing on top of your clothes what normally is underneath them, skin – except that it is not so much skin as hide, but then it is stripped hide, hairless, naked. Also it is dead hide, the more dead or deadly because stained black. This nakedness with deadness, together with its animal associations, allows it to transmit its meanings intensely: which can be sinister (it is death-coloured) and violent (it is beast-skin). And if black leather was for a time a police uniform (for its police use has declined, as part of image-cleaning), it has also become the standard youth uniform, a means of putting on toughness in readiness to hit the street. It would seem, black leather, to be both black and powerful magic – an empowering magic, as if in putting on an extra skin, you put on you or in you an extra creature. It has become a folk intuition, that in putting on black leather you are putting on power: it may be the power that defies the law, it may be the power that enforces it.

Depending on who wears the black leather, and in what situations, it may use its death-power and animal-power combined to add danger and charge to sexuality, in a way that can overlap with the sex-abuse of Nazi insignia. Given the complicated relations of Eros and Thanatos in human sexuality in any case, it is not hard to understand how black, with its acquired associations with discipline, death and power, can be an efficient trigger and excitant, the more so when the practitioner, rapt in sexual mechanism, binds with black leather, or its deader-still surrogates black plastic or black rubber, the tender human body. Such practices have become an erotic imagery in the varying blacks of black-and-white photography, so masterfully modulated by (for instance) Robert Mapplethorpe.

Black and blackness, and dead materials, seem necessary ingredi-ents also of the dream that Evil is sexy: as if that fag-end of a failing religion, a sub-sub-Baudelairean eroticized demonism, were the last kick left in an atheist age. What is then grotesque – but maybe not so serious – is the way, in the further turning of fashion's wheel, a light touching on just these breathless clichés of sex-evil may add the desired slight hint of badness, of fearlessness, of travel beyond the bounds and back again, to chic light-weight jackets, displayed by stars and sold in stores to kids (black-jackets for the family) made of supple, black, unidentifiable materials.

This is not to suggest that street black, the youth sub-culture use of black, is necessarily fascistic, hell's angelic, or street-dangerous. The black leather-jacket, as the anti-uniform of rebels without causes, is associated not only with Brando but also with James Dean, in essence, or in myth, the non-violent, non-dangerous, tragic rebel soul. There may also be a play with respectable black: those Mods who in the Sixties wore – when riding their Lambrettas without their parkas – sharp black suits (girl Mods wore black-and-white) were assertively making a play-use of the middle class's 'decent black', of the black suit that goes back to the arrived Victorians. They were showing a confidence in being with it, and in having made it, to that degree that they could, at the weekend at least, be (at least) a style-élite. In this way they played off style against the wildness-élitism (black jackets, aluminium-studded) of the Rockers: whose big bikes showed that they too had some money, but either less hope or less comfortable illusions. Zest lay in getting head and headlamp side by side, and pushing the bike faster to no destination, other than the knife-edge state between extreme speed and death.

The motivation of the youth-cultures is a subject for proper sociological inquiry, so it is tentatively only that I suggest that in that world black carries, with markedly differing inflections, the value it has at times had in the past, as the uniform of a group which has either elected to be, or feels itself to be, outside the class hierarchy, but which has at the same time the aspiration or pretension of being some form of élite. It seems to me this may be said of both Mods and Rockers in the Sixties, and of Posers and New Romantics in the Eighties and Goths in the Eighties and now again in the Nineties: though the latter groups, playing all-black clothes against a white or whitened face, seem to echo at a distance the dandy's Hamletizing, and to be not only working the sexual thrill of death and evil, but to be turning to style and fearless show the real anxieties of what more and more is for youth a no-hope world. Of the major fears of recent decades, the Bomb had a remoteness, it was an Apocalypse on the horizon: but AIDS one can catch, and a life mainly of unemployment gets only more likely.

Whatever the anxiety, black still is for these groups smart and stylish, and mimics at its chosen distance older forms of arresting black: Goth black seems again to say, as black has at various points in the past, I am important. Whereas truly hopeless chic, which one might expect to wear black, does not necessarily do that. The Punk style of the Seventies and Eighties does seem to flaunt more aggressively a more real hopelessness as to going anywhere, and to meet it by going ugly, and guying, through exaggeration, the picture it believes the middle

82 Father Christmas in Trafalgar Square at the launch of a charity special offer, September 1986.

class has of it: spiked, pierced, brutalized, gobbing in the market, pissing in the park. Punk had true anarchy and used savage colour, in acid tones, to hit you in the eye. And Punk too, from the start, made its own use of striking black: it would use black T-shirts, black-leather or black-plastic jackets, black boots, black belts, black gauntlets, and its spears and peaks and crests of gelled hair, which might be crimson, chrome-yellow, grass-green, ice-blue, might also be jet-black.

Having attack and real energy, Punk could not escape becoming, in time, chic, and even as a street style becoming more friendly. In the scene of 1986 (illus. 82), where Punk meets Father Christmas in Trafalgar Square, the young couple have matching spikes and peaks and matching black leather-jackets. They sit close, and in the same posture, like a couple that are close in every way. Their zips are wherever possible undone, at the cuff as well as the jacket-front. She wears black tights, he wears black jeans (torn at the knee). Her eye make-up is at once jagged, and like smart glasses (which she doesn't need), and also makes a shadow to accentuate her eyes. An older convention of formal black-and-white survives in the white paint-spots on his jeans, which may also hint at his willingness to do the necessary DIY round the house later: maybe, too, the tiny padlock on a chain round his neck suggests a commitment to fidelity. He has an aggressive array of metal studs, but they are worn on his lapels, and so seem gestural, with again a kind of play formality (as it were of a Punk Liberace) rather than being seriously dangerous. Though he says on his upper arm that he means Business, he could also be read as the lover in black – not in grieving love either – and that identity, of the lover in waiting behind the violent man, is possibly the sub-text of a good deal of youth-culture street-black.

There is still, in the style itself, a residue of menace: and it is the hint of menace in street-black that makes it street-important. The higher style of important black also survives, and in the professions, where absolute reliability is at a premium, black retains its guaranteeing force. So City black will still be found, both old-style to match a rolled umbrella and worn with a different cut by yuppies. There is also intelligentsia black, associated not with suits but with sweaters, worn from the period of the Existentialists on, and claiming again serious-ness, the importance of thought, intellectual power. Though anti-formal – it is knitted, not machine-loomed – it is serious, representing the importance of thought, and claiming intellectual power, as it were of an informal, secular priest. There has even (not to be serious) been a kind of black garment for a thinker's eyes, in the heavily black-rimmed glasses of the Sixties (and dark glasses, shades, have of course been used dauntingly by a great many groups).

It is true that for many of the higher uses, black itself has come (finally) to be seen as old-fashioned, and, especially in suits, deep charcoal grey may now do duty for it: charcoal being not quite staid like black, though close enough in tone to engage allusively its values of gravity, weight, the authority of an impersonal expertise. It may be too that, with the twentieth century's change of style, black has come to be thought excessively formal, even sinisterly so, and thus has become to a degree taboo. It would be disturbing to be completely black-serious, while dark-toned suits are able to be at once important and 'natty' – a word that has been used of the suits Sir David Webster used to wear, attending functions at the Royal Opera House, and which he may be seen wearing in David Hockney's famous portrait (illus. 83). He sits as a person of considerable quiet authority. He sits as in a chair – a *cathedra* – of importance, though the design of thrones has so changed now that the tubular structure is invisible behind the skirts of his jacket. He seems to be seated almost on air, all we have is a manner of sitting – the 'seat', the posture, of authority. If gravity presumes to attract him downwards, he will not fall: he sits in stillness though he sits in space, being himself a centre of gravity.

The picture remains in its seatlessness, disturbing, a fact that may have some relation to Hockney's remark later, about his sessions with

83 David Hockney, *Sir David Webster*, 1971, acrylic on canvas. Royal Opera House, London, currently on loan to the National Portrait Gallery.

Webster: 'He was ill; I didn't know it then, but he was dying'.[22] The space beneath him may be a graver space – a grave space – and this portrait of a dark-clad man may be another painting that alludes through dark clothes to death. Death is recurringly relevant to dress. If black has been in abeyance in the later twentieth century, one must, I think, connect this with the way death itself takes, as it were, a lower profile. It is not just that we no longer wear black at a funeral, or wear black mourning at all, but that we are in general reluctant to be more aware of death than we can help. We do not want to remember our end, and our culture hardly has a right solemnity for death; and there are many incentives to think young.

To say this is not to desiderate a new Victorian mournfulness; nor may we simply connect the black fashions of previous times with a preoccupation with death. This study has been concerned with the many other factors involved. But one cannot, either, decouple black fashion from death: and, as noted above, the black fashions of several nations have coincided both with their highest point of international power, and with their elaborating cults of death. Especially this is so of fifteenth-century Burgundy, sixteenth-century Spain, and nineteenth-century England. It does seem that the nation that is aware of its power is liable also to be especially aware of death. I dare say it is not always so, and polychromatic empires may be cited: but still the black empires also exist. And though one may cite material explanations – for instance, that Victorians saw much of death, not only because of infant mortality, but also because the new big cities multiplied both the power and the visibility of disease; or that an imperial power needs for its agents to be more than normally willing both to kill and to die – still, the material explanations do not cover all the ground. It does seem, as suggested earlier, that humanity draws power from its awareness of death: that if there is a connection between Thanatos and Eros, there is also a connection between Thanatos and Kratos, between Death and Power. Even magic, which is abstracted power, seems vested in negotiations with the dead; and in religion transcendent power seems indissolubly connected with death, with the deaths of creatures, the deaths of people, the death of a god (eternal life is in another dimension). So in a secular, non-aristocratic empire, there still was Lenin's Mausoleum against the Kremlin wall, and it was on the roof of the mausoleum the salute was taken. Different nations use different myths and magics, and if America has lately been the world's most powerful nation, it has had its own many-coloured style (but there is black or dark dress in America too). And even in America there is a kind of cult of death, confirmed by the gun lobby, and hypostasized in the perpetual rediscussion and re-performance of the death of President Kennedy, and the slaughter of his assassin. The effect of the conspiracy theories is to make it clear this was not a wild act, but one emerging from the national life.

The idea of a nationwide conspiracy redoubles power, complementing the overt structure precisely with a covert structure, one that is the more menacing because out of sight and 'dark'. Conspiracy itself is reduplicated, as the McCarthyite fear of an invasive penetration by the Left is in turn complemented by the fear of industries, services and administrative agencies working to a concealed death-agenda of the Right. It is as if paranoia must be the dark side of a nation's thinking, if its daylight consciousness is of being a potent super-power (as, in individual psychology, paranoia is the obverse of convictions of grandeur). This whole multiple structure of extended intricated powers becomes a surreal political mystery-poetry in the novels of Thomas Pynchon, who has steadily extended his own black imagery, since, on the first page of *V*, 'Benny Profane, wearing black levis . . . happened to pass through Norfolk, Virginia'.[23]

In his major novel, *Gravity's Rainbow*, Pynchon is preoccupied both with a vast oppressive conspiracy, in which Fascism, international cartels, plastics and arms industries and indeed whole technologies shadowily cooperate – these being associated with dark rooms, black coats, black vehicles, darkened glass – and at the same time with secret networks of communication and opposition among the oppressed and exploited and disinherited. The part given to the 'Schwarzkommando', Hereros from German Africa, has the effect of introducing into an epic fiction of World War II Europe an oblique allusion to African Americans, the disinherited and abused under-race of America. In his previous novel, *The Crying of Lot 49*, the secret organization of the disinherited, the Trystero, is often, if and when it may be seen, clad in black. If two conspiracies and two paranoias intersect in Pynchon's work, it is because the world and human social life are felt to be profoundly ambiguous and menacing: values change and switch to their opposites, the Trystero itself is also a menacing organization, probably murderous, represented (possibly) in the closing pages of *Lot 49* by men who 'wore black mohair and had pale, cruel faces'. Indeed, it seems at times that in Pynchon's own imagination elements of Right and Left fantasy are merged. Both in his fiction – and also in the fiction on these themes by Don DeLillo – there is an unexpected uncertainty as to whether the shadowy subversive groupings, on which the plotting of the novels depends, are of the Right or of the Left. So DeLillo will refer in passing in *Mao II* to 'Left-wing death-squads', when 'death-squads', recently, have seemed rather to be of the Right. And though the black of the Trystero is associated at one point with a cartoon-film anarchist, the Trystero also resembles an early Fascist grouping (I acknowledge that such a literal-minded reading is likely to be contrary to Pynchon's intentions). I do not mean by these remarks to disparage the genius either of Don DeLillo, or of Thomas Pynchon, whose *magnum opus* – *Gravity's Rainbow* – is (among other things) the great twentieth-century meditation on black and blackness:

Deep, deep – further than politics, than sex or infantile terrors . . . a plunge into the nuclear blackness. . . . Black runs all through the transcript: the recurring color black. Slothrop never mentioned Enzian by name, nor the Schwarzkommando. But he did talk about the Schwarzgerät. And he also coupled 'schwarz-' with some strange nuns, in the German fragments that came through. Blackwoman, Blackrocket, Blackdream. . . . The new coinages seem to be made unconsciously. Is there a single root, deeper than anyone has probed, from which Slothrop's Blackwords only appear to flower separately?

Underlying the many blacknesses of the novel, from burnt bodies ('the slowly carbonizing faces of men he thought he knew') to excrement (Brigadier Pudding), the 'single root' of Pynchon's black does seem to be death, Thanatos, working as a perverse animating principle at the origin of the trajectories not only of rockets, but of lives, technologies, civilizations.[24]

Near or far, the figure of Death stands behind the man in black: an intuition reflected, usually in pop and debile form, in the modern mythology of Dracula. The original Dracula, in Bram Stoker's novel, was dressed all in black: there was no suggestion then of his shining a white shirt-front, or being debonair like Christopher Lee. He was grave, sepulchral, of the dead. Perhaps, in his bat-likeness and wolf-likeness combined, as in his preference for sucking out the blood of young women at night, he contained a certain vision of the nineteenth-century male not only as a negation of the womanly, but as a black parasite on the feminine. Dead within, dead at heart and soulless, the slave of a cannibal-erotic compulsion, he leaves a succession of women 'ruined', infected, become the living dead. Thus seen, he is like an exaggeration of those ageing, immobile, somewhat anonymous men in black predatorily haunting the *maisons* of the Impressionists' Paris. And it is as such a caricature that he has been especially perpetuated in the twentieth century: regularly now wearing full evening dress, complete with cape and every inch a Count, as it were the *ancien régime* in person, still sucking the blood of the respectable class, in the same act stealing their daughters (illus. 84). He seems the archetypal aristocrat of the folk imagination, handsome, erotically predatory, cruel; and presumably found frightening-thrilling in a way that adds class-masochism to the death-thrill. Francis Ford Coppola, offering to make him a tragic figure (and a faithful husband, in the very long term), has restored to him a dimension that, to a degree, he had at the start, of the melancholy man in black. In so far as he does, in his living death, stay popularly alive, it will probably be however for a different reason. For Dracula has a further dimension, one really that is very old, and both erotic and tragic – the Dance of Death and the Maiden. He is, perhaps, also the nearest approach we have now to a popular image of the Devil: another gentleman traditionally suited in black.

I should make it clear that I am not, in pursuing a recession of the significances of black, seeking to dramatize its workaday use, or to demonize the work-ethical values, sober, serious and busy, that black, dark and drab colours also have in our world. For black, or a shade of deep blue close to black, is our colour for large-scale impersonal service – for those serious services on which lives may depend – especially where they meet the public eye; as with the police, the fire service, railway staff, airline staff. And we would not be happy if planes and high-speed trains were piloted by harlequins. More at large in the

84 Bela Lugosi in a still from *Dracula*, directed by Tod Browning, 1931.

work-world, if black is not ubiquitous as it came close to being in the high nineteenth century, and if people wear bright colours – red, green, blue – still there is much drab and low-toned dressing, and a good deal of garments (trousers, jerseys, coats) still are black. Even if the work ethic is no longer to be found in its old Calvinist vigour, still there is a work-ethos that says, for instance, that it is work above all that gives meaning to living – an ethos that works with a particularly bitter and cruel effect as the number and kind of jobs available deteriorates. The work-ethos straddles political philosophies, dominating, with differing inflections, the capitalist countries, the socialist countries, and the ex-socialist countries: it is reflected in not dissimilar degrees of work-drabness in industrial Russia, agricultural China, and capitalist Japan.

Japan is an especially pertinent case, since there a feudal ethic of selfless service proved able to transform itself, almost overnight and with remarkable happiness, into one of the most formidable varieties of work ethic so far seen in the world: at the cost, it must be said, of many of the older silks and colours (though high-coloured festivals still survive). But the older Japan of the Shogunate had also asked its functionaries often to dress sombrely (magistrates wore black); and Meiji Japan in the nineteenth century adopted the black frock-coat and top-hat of the West. In recent years there has been a new fashion for black among young Japanese – smart black clothes, new black cars –

that, accompanying the frequent use of black in Japanese design (as in Tokyo *haute couture*), may amount to a new use of empire-black, as Japan makes public her sense of her station as the economically preeminent nation, with an apprehension at the same time that preeminence cannot last.

Of the West one might sometimes be tempted to say that the work ethic has seemed to give way to a play ethic. Really, of course, it is a work-and-play ethic, you both work and play hard, in a manner adjusted to the development of consumer products and leisure industries. There are offices and works to work in, and sports grounds and sports centres to play in, and it can even be the play places that are more deadly in earnest, especially if you go to them not actually to play, but rather to watch others play for you, in a way which is, for the players, work. The play ethic entails colours, but they are play colours, as in football shirts, track-suits, ski-wear: play more than display, signifying hygiene, physical vigour, and also the contained discharge of aggression, rather than play of feeling, emotional variety. Even in sport black reasserts its power, in the intimidating effect, for those opposing them, of such team colours as those worn by the All Blacks.

It is true that the asceticism that went with the work ethic is mitigated now, especially with the cult of good sex, which is associated (in magazines at least) with simple bright colours, rather than (as in traditional paintings of beauty) with rich colours or deep colours, or richly coloured shadows. In other words, there is an element of hopeful dream in the cult: it is not clear that our post-puritan world has in practice found it so easy to be full of good sex. And in other ways there is evidence, in these late-modern times, of ascetic strains still in us, and in our families and societies however they change; as the death-awareness that is hardly welcome to us is still not to be evaded, and indeed is a constant part of 'the picture' – at the distance involved in a news transmission. And in any case, the older asceticism is vigorous still, in old and new denominations of the scriptural religions. A good measure of heartlessness is structural to our economics, which depend on preserving a large pool of superfluous labour, and depend also like any lottery on having a great many more losers than winners. And on quite another level strains of self-punishment and self-damage are a part of sophisticated sensibility and show in the innovations of modernist art, with its high premium on fracture, breakage, friction, tension, discontinuity, jump-cut editing and contradiction, iconized in representations of the body that again is fractured, hurt, constricted, and very often has different parts of body or soul missing. But what, perhaps, finally has been our main characteristic has been precisely our belief that we could leave asceticism behind: so that where previous ages have believed in different virtues, and different nobilities, all to be achieved with cost and sacrifice, we have aimed to give up nothing. We have encouraged both an ideal and a rhetoric of wholeness, as though we had only to think of it to get it, though we also know that nothing comes on easy terms, and certainly not everything; while the ease with which we recognize the terribly damaged heroes in Beckett's novels and Francis Bacon's paintings means we also know we are or may be, within, that is to say psychically (not to say spiritually), crippled.

The painting of Francis Bacon with which I wish to close is his portrait of John Edwards (illus. 85), in which the damaged man – his form is cut as if bites have been taken out of it – is located within a blackness that seems, in its geometricality and intensity, to have at once a smart, a serious and a grim character. Perhaps also he is a man in black, in the sense that he seems half to wear, below his white collar, a black jersey or tunic. We cannot be sure because, as with other portraits reproduced in this study, the black garment is merged or absorbed in the surrounding jet-black dark. I say half to wear because he does at the same time seem to be naked, at least his shoulder, like his leg, is naked. In fact, the skin and inner rim of his shoulder is painted as though it came to a sharp edge, and had the clothing under it. It is painted as though the man in black were within the naked man: as though, to generalize, the men in black were inside us still. And while his shirt-collar looks modern, it could be older (for instance, it could be wanting a stiff collar to be fixed by a stud), and he has on his head what looks, from its widow's-peak and cheek-biting indentation, like the kind of older black cap men of the Elizabethan period used to wear. He seems, then, to have an affinity with those figures of Bacon's that are both of the past and of the present, such as his screaming clerics, and to be, if not a Pope, yet still to some extent a solemn or clerical figure, also alive now and not in orders, as if history carries through him into our time, like the black stream that descends behind him, and flexes and widens to take us in.

John Ruskin blamed his age's 'boast in blackness' on its 'want of faith'. This seems not a completely sound connection, when one thinks of the use of black by Christian, Jewish and Muslim clerics. And few people now will say Ruskin's faith is theirs. But still it may be that one universal message of the colour of clothes – the ineradicable communication underlying others – is the character of the faith of the people who wear them: and this must seem more likely if in a large part one takes faith – with no intention of underrating it – in a Durkheimian sense, and sees it as consisting of a society's solemn picturing of what

85 Francis Bacon, *Study for a Portrait of John Edwards*, 1988, oil on canvas. Private collection.

keeps it together. Of course society is not only social, and one thing that keeps a group together, and sustains its members when alone or desperate or dying, is a sense of the nature of the place one occupies in the universe, however vast and frightening and forbidding one may see the universe as being. With these provisos made, one might want to say, somewhat more along the lines of Ruskin, that without a faith – or without an outlook that acknowledges the needs faiths used to try to meet – neither life nor clothes will have colours rich and deep.

I should try to make clearer what I conceive I have been saying. It seems to me one visible fact, in the history of the millennium that is shortly to end, has been – unevenly and in waves and abeyances – the darkening, the blackening, of men, of what they wear: a development that grew to be most engulfing in the mid- to late nineteenth century, when men's dress was most different from the dress of women. We live now in the aftertow of the black wave's latest rise and breaking. And black has many values, because all statements made by clothes are ambiguous, and even one colour will have different meanings; so that much of what one says is inevitably conjectural. But still one may say that if there is a dominant meaning in the widespread use of black, that meaning is associated at once with intensity and with effacement: with importance, and with the putting on of impersonality. Alone or in ranks, the man in black is the agent of a serious power; and of a power claimed over women and the feminine. Black may be a shadow fallen on the feminine part of man. The ultimate allusion of black is to death, and in the high-black periods, the power the men in black have served has been dead- or death-serious both at home and in the state: the most hideous extreme of this has occurred in the twentieth century. But originally the fashion derived from the use of black in churches, where it was associated with a kind of spiritual grieving: with a spirituality that placed humanity in an infinite abandonedness and depth of need. This black relates to the older black of mourning, for grief is another way of discovering, as it were behind the daylight, a universe of absence and insatiable want. And this black – one could think of it as Hamlet's black – is not to be wished away in some easy move for colour (as the Impressionists airily turned their backs on black, and Cézanne is important because he brought the black opacity of substance back). All of which is to say that, in spite of the 'dark' values black has often had, one would no more want it cut out of clothing than one would want people to have no weight or no shadow. Which is as well for the many people who, without being ascetic or power-assertive or spiritual, happen still to look best in black, having in themselves a colour, an intensity, a light.

References

Introduction

1 Alison Lurie, *The Language of Clothes* (London, 1982), p. 5.
2 Roland Barthes, *The Fashion System*, trans. Matthew Ward and Richard Howard (New York, 1983), pp. 64–5.
3 Barthes on black, *The Fashion System*, p. 173. Nathan Joseph, *Uniforms and Nonuniforms: Communication Through Clothing* (New York, 1986). For a discrimination of differing 'readings' of dress, see Michael R. Solomon, ed., *The Psychology of Fashion* (Toronto, 1985); Eco's 'under-coding' (see Umberto Eco, *A Theory of Semiotics*, Bloomington, IN, 1979) is discussed by Fred Davis, 'Clothing and Fashion as Communication', in Solomon, *Psychology of Fashion*, pp. 15–27.
4 Susan B. Kaiser, 'The Semiotics of Clothing: Linking Structural Analysis and Social Process', in Thomas A. Sebeok and Jean Umiker Sebeok, eds., *The Semiotic Web 1989* (New York, 1990), p. 616.
5 Ann Hollander, *Seeing through Clothes* (London, 1988), p. 366. Hollander's fifth chapter (pp. 365–90) includes a magnificent discussion of black dress, one that I took into account in my own researches only, I am afraid, on the book's British publication in 1988 (it had appeared in the USA in 1978).
6 See Peter Bogatyrev, *The Function of Folk Costume in Moravian Slovakia*, in 'Approaches to Semiotics', ed. Thomas A. Sebeok, No. 5 (The Hague, 1971). On old and married black, pp. 67–8; on wealthy black, p. 49; on black breeches, a percolation of black fashion from higher society, versus the older bright blue breeches still worn by millers, pp. 46–7.
7 The position of Herbert Blumer is lucidly epitomized in Fred Davis, *Fashion, Culture, and Identity* (Chicago, 1992), especially pp. 113–20. For Davis's own developed theory of identity ambivalence see, especially, chapter 2 ('ambivalence management', p. 25).
8 Georg Simmel, 'Fashion', *International Quarterly* (1904), reprinted *American Journal of Sociology*, 62 (May 1957), pp. 541–58; see also Grant D. McCracken, 'The Trickle-Down Theory Rehabilitated', in Solomon, *Psychology of Fashion*, pp. 39–54.
9 Judith Butler, *Gender Troubles: Feminism and the Subversion of Identity* (London, 1990), p. 25: 'gender proves to be performative . . . gender is always a doing . . .'. On changing inflections of gender in dress see Aileen Ribeiro, *Dress and Morality* (London, 1986), also her works cited below in chapter 1 n. 2, and Chapter 4 nn. 3, 9; other salient works, cited later in this book, are Valerie Steele, *Paris Fashion: A Cultural History* (Oxford, 1988), and Juliet Ash and Elizabeth Wilson, eds., *Chic Thrills: A Fashion Reader* (London, 1992). 'Ambivalence management': Fred Davis, *Fashion, Culture, and Identity*, p. 25. On shoulders, see Claudia Brush Kidwell, 'Gender Symbols or Fashionable Details', in Claudia Brush Kidwell and Valerie Steele, eds, *Men and Women: Dressing the Part* (Washington DC, 1989), especially pp. 129–43.
10 Luce Irigaray, *Sexes and Genealogies*, trans. Gillian C. Gill (New York, 1993); see especially 'Flesh Colours' (pp. 153–65).

11 Luce Irigaray writes on angelic veiled white in 'Belief Itself', *Sexes and Genealogies*, pp. 25–53. Nancy Chodorow, *The Reproduction of Mothering: Psychoanalysis and the Sociology of Gender* (Berkeley, 1978), especially pp. 180–90. On masculine negations, one might recur also, as Kathy Ferguson has done, to Hegel's assumption that male consciousness is isolated, doomed, antagonistic and dominant: Kathy Ferguson, *The Man Question: Visions of Subjectivity in Feminist Theory* (Berkeley, 1993), pp. 36–68.

12 Marjorie Garber, *Vested Interests: Cross-Dressing and Cultural Anxiety* (London, 1992), on Michael Jackson, p. 185; on representation, p. 374.

13 Elizabeth Wilson, *Adorned in Dreams: Fashion and Modernity* (London, 1985), p. 120. I quote Vivienne Westwood from Juliet Ash, 'Philosophy on the Catwalk', in Juliet Ash and Elizabeth Wilson, eds., *Chic Thrills: A Fashion Reader* (London, 1992), p. 171.

14 Jo B. Paoletti and Claudia Brush Kidwell, Conclusion in *Men and Women: Dressing the Part*, p. 158.

15 'The way in which we dress may assuage that fear ['of not sustaining the autonomy of the self'] by stabilizing our individual identity', Elizabeth Wilson, *Adorned in Dreams*, p. 12.

16 'Status demurrals': see Davis, *Fashion, Culture and Identity*, p. 57; Joseph, *Uniforms and Nonuniforms: Communication through Clothing*, p. 42.

1. Whose Funeral?

1 'Ce vêtement noir que portent les hommes de notre temps est un symbole terrible; pour en venir là, il a fallu que les armures tombassent pièce à pièce et les broderies fleur à fleur. C'est la raison humaine qui a renversé toutes les illusions, mais elle en porte elle-même le deuil . . .': *La Confession d'un enfant du Siècle* (Paris, 1880), p. 11.

2 The *Journal des tailleurs* is quoted from A. Ribeiro, 'Concerning Fashion – Théophile Gautier's "De la Mode" ', *Costume*, 24 (1990), pp. 55–68.

3 'Nous célébrons tous quelque enterrement', Baudelaire, 'The Salon of 1846', Chapter XVIII; I quote from *Baudelaire: Selected Writings on Art and Artists*, trans. P. E. Charvet (London, 1972), p. 105; the text of 'Salon de 1846' may be found in the *Oeuvres Complètes*, ed. Claude Pichois (Paris, 1976), II, pp. 415–96 (esp. p. 494). For Balzac see *Oeuvres Diverses* (Paris, 1935), I, p. 345. Page references to the novels of Charles Dickens are to the Oxford Illustrated Dickens, since the Clarendon Edition is not yet complete. The dates given at the first mention of a Dickens novel are those of the original serial publication. *Great Expectations* (1860–1), ch. XXI, pp. 162–3, ch. XX, p. 154; *Dealings with the firm of Dombey and Son* (1846–8), ch. XIII, p. 169.

4 *Great Expectations*, ch. XXXV, p. 266; 'Mugby Junction' (1866), in *Christmas Stories*, p. 476.

5 Baudelaire, *Selected Writings*, p. 105.

6 Issue of 12 April 1842, quoted in Philip Collins, ed., *Dickens: Interviews and Recollections* (London, 1981), I, pp. 54–5.

7 J. C. Flügel, *The Psychology of Clothes* (London, 1930), pp. 111–12.

8 Edward Bulwer-Lytton, *Pelham, or The Adventures of a Gentleman* (London, 1828). The text was substantially revised: I quote from the First Collected Edition, but add in parentheses the corresponding references in the first edition: maternal advice, ch. 4 (I, ch. IV, pp. 27–8); Cheltenham, ch. 39 (II, ch. II, p. 12); Maxim VII, ch. 44 (I, ch. VII, pp. 63–8); chain and ring, ch. 28 (I, ch. XXVII, p. 244). In a disquisition on dress in chapter VII of the first edition, later cut, Pelham again commends the combination of black waistcoat, coat and trousers. He says that as to colour there is no 'certain or definite rule' adding 'among all persons, there should

be little variety of colour, either in the morning or the evening.' (II, pp. 65–8).

9 Thomas Carlyle, *Sartor Resartus: The Life and Opinions of Herr Teufelsdröckh* (London, 1904), I, pp. 220–22. Beau Brummell's life and practices were recorded by his friend, William Jesse in *The Life of George Brummell, Esq., commonly called 'Beau Brummell'* (London, 1886). On cravats see also James Laver, *Dandies* (London, 1968), p. 36; on the whole large phenomenon of dandyism see especially Ellen Moers, *The Dandy: Brummell to Beerbohm* (London, 1960).

10 Brummell's coat, however, was normally blue, and his later attitude to devotees of his admirer Bulwer-Lytton was ironical; so he greeted his biographer-to-be, Captain William Jesse, when he appeared in the new fashion of pure black and white, 'My dear Jesse, I am sadly afraid you have been reading *Pelham*; but excuse me, you look very much like a magpie'. Quoted in Moers, *The Dandy*, p. 82.

11 Quoted by Moers, *The Dandy*, p. 24. It is clear Brummell's phrase means his father kept himself *in* his place. Brummell's father had been secretary to Lord North; his grandfather may have been a confectioner or tailor, or a valet. His mother was minor gentry. Brummell *père et mère* were sufficiently arrived in 1781 to commission a portrait by Reynolds of their two sons (exhibited in the Royal Academy in 1783 as 'Children'). In the portrait, now in Kenwood House, the very young beau may be seen sweetly lisping childish numbers dressed in spotless white.

12 The Delacroix is from *Oeuvres Littéraires* (Paris, 1923), II, p. 159; on Delacroix's admiration for Lawrence, see Lee Johnson, *The Paintings of Delacroix: A Critical Catalogue* (Oxford, 1981), I, pp. 54–5. On d'Orsay and Disraeli, see Moers, chs. IV, VII, and Laver, pp. 51–61. The young Disraeli might also be met in 'green velvet trousers and a canary-coloured waistcoat' or in a black velvet coat and purple trousers with a gold band down the seam. In such clothes, however, he was called not so much a dandy, as a popinjay or coxcomb (see Moers, *The Dandy* pp. 96–100). For Turveydrop, see *Bleak House* (1852–3), ch. XIV, p. 190.

13 Quoted in Valerie Steele, *Paris Fashion: A Cultural History* (Oxford, 1988), p. 83.

14 Brummell and *liaisons*, in Moers, *The Dandy*, p. 36; Camilla Toulmin, in Moers, p. 161. The whole subtle question of the dandies and identity is discussed by Jessica R. Feldman in *Gender on the Divide: The Dandy in Modernist Literature* (Ithaca, NY, 1993).

15 *Bleak House*, ch. XIV, pp. 190–1. *Sartor Resartus*, p. 219. On Brummell's washing, teeth-cleaning and tweezerings, see Moers, *The Dandy*, pp. 32–3.

16 See Moers, *The Dandy*, p. 111, and Captain Rees Howell Gronow, *Reminiscences and Recollections* (London, 1900), I, pp. 68–86.

17 S. T. Coleridge, *Biographia Literaria*, ed. James Engell and W. Jackson Bate (London, 1983), I, pp. 180–1.

18 *Bleak House*, ch. XXVIII, p. 393.

19 Charles Darwin, *The Descent of Man* (London, 1871), II, pp. 206–7.

20 Charlotte Brontë, *Jane Eyre*, ed. Q. D. Leavis (Harmondsworth, 1966), ch. 17, pp. 200–3.

21 *Great Expectations*, ch. XXVI, p. 202.

22 *Jane Eyre*, Brocklehurst as pillar, ch. 4, p. 63; at speech-day, ch. 7, pp. 94–7.

2. Black in History

1 Victor Turner's discussions of the use of white, red and black pigments, found very widely through the world, are especially well known: see, for instance, 'Colour Classification in Ndembu Religion', in M. Banton ed., *Anthropological Approaches to the Study of Religion* (London, 1966). James Faris, in *Nuba Personal Art* (London, 1972), is wary of too much read-in meaning, and stresses the mainly aesthetic purpose of much decoration. Recording that a deep rich black is an especially sought-after and beautiful colour – permitted by the Nuba only to men over twenty

– he still notes that black also is the colour of witches and witchcraft, and that good and bad magic are regularly described in white and black terms. On water-bearing, fertile black see (for instance) Alfonso Ortiz, *The Tawa World* (London, 1969).

2 Since the subject has been little referred to in discussions of black dress, I attach some notes on Chinese black prepared by a Chinese scholar, Xuejun Sun. The colour black in China is associated with Heaven, whose true colour is that of the darkness before dawn. Below his black tunic (which was usually embroidered) the Emperor wore a full-length yellow skirt, yellow being the colour of earth. The Emperor wore these clothes for formal and sacrificial occasions; they were also recommended by Confucius for weddings ('If heaven and earth do not have intercourse, nothing will grow'). It was in the Chou Dynasty (11th century BC to 774BC) that the emperor wore black leather and his ministers black linen when they convened formally in the morning; in the afternoon, less formally, his ministers could wear white. In the Han Dynasty (206BC to 24AD) the Emperor stipulated that his officials wear seasonal colours, blue in spring, red in summer, yellow in autumn, black in winter; but when called to royal audience they should always wear black. Though imperial dress later brightened, the Emperor continued to wear black for sacrificial occasions until the Manchurian Qing Dynasty came to power in the seventeenth century. The Qing emperors did not wear black, but the heir to the throne had the right to wear black, while other princes could wear blue. Also during the Qing Dynasty (1644–1911) Buddhist and Taoist monks were required to wear black – a colour which had in any case been gaining ground in the priesthood (as against the original saffron robes of the Buddhists), probably because of its sacrificial associations. As in Russia, monks would be referred to as 'men in black'. And black was increasingly to acquire associations of humility and lack of status, while merchants and the leisured class tended to wear white (which was also, in China, the colour of mourning – so in China, as in the West, merchants and the prosperous were to wear the mourning colour). The bright colours were reserved for officials.

3 Lines 10–12, 24–31. I quote affectionately from Theodore Alois Buckley, *The Tragedies of Aeschylus, literally translated* (London, 1882). The following quotations translate lines 1048–50.

4 One is familiar with the devil in black from nineteenth-century fiction, for instance in Poe's 'The Devil in the Belfry' (1839): 'His dress was a tight-fitting swallow-tailed black coat . . . black kerseymere knee-breeches, black stockings, and stumpy-looking pumps, with huge bunches of black satin ribbon for bows' *Poetry and Tales* (Cambridge, 1984), p. 303. But in *A Hundred Mery Talys* (1526), a tailor wearing black is mistaken for the Devil: see Derek Brewer ed., *Medieval Comic Tales* (Cambridge, 1972), p. 52. And the Devil wears a tight-fitting black garment (with, on his shoulders, a gold cape) in Ambrogio Lorenzetti's 'Allegoria del Cattivo Governo' of the 1330s or 1340s in the Palazzo Pubblico, Siena. For earlier black devils see P. du Bourget, 'La couleur noire de la peau du démon', *Actae del VIII Congreso Internacional de Arqueologia Cristiana* (Citta del Vaticano and Barcelona, 1972), pp. 271–2.

5 *The Eumenides*, lines 55–6.

6 I take the quotation from G. S. Tyack, *Historic Dress of the Clergy* (London, 1897), pp. 7, 15. In general on this subject I have consulted Janet Mayo, *A History of Ecclesiastical Dress* (London, 1984).

7 *The Letters of Peter the Venerable*, ed. Giles Constable (Cambridge, MA, 1967), I, Letter 28, p. 57; the following two references are first from Letter 28, p. 57, and, second, from Letter 111, p. 289 – the letter with the fullest discussion of black-and-white.

8 It is beyond the scope of the present study, and beyond my knowledge, to discuss the role of black in the Islamic world. A Muslim commentator on the Koran is

quoted by Winthrop D. Jordan as saying: 'Black is the colour of darkness, sin, rebellion, misery; removal from the grace and light of God'; see *White over Black: American Attitudes toward the Negro, 1550–1812* (Chapel Hill, NC, 1968), p. 39.

9 The general work of the Inquisition was entrusted especially to two orders, the Dominicans and the Franciscans, since these mendicant orders, travelling through the world vowed to poverty, had a good rapport with the laity. The Dominicans were more regularly trained as theologians, and were noted for their enthusiasm for the work. It was the Dominican provincial of Toulouse who was ordered (in 1233) to appoint members of his order to make inquisition for heresy in Narbonne, Bourges, Auch and Bordeaux. See Bernard Hamilton, *The Medieval Inquisition* (London, 1981), especially pp. 36–9, 60–3.

10 Of the mendicant Orders, black was also worn by some divisions of the Franciscans (who otherwise, in the medieval period, wore grey), notably by the Friars Minor Conventual. Of the military Orders, those of our Lady of Montjoie (twelfth century), the Hospitallers of St Thomas of Canterbury at Acre (twelfth century) and the teutonic Brethren of the Sword (founded 1204) all wore white and followed the style of the Templars.

11 See Michèle Beaulieu, 'Le costume français, miroir de la sensibilité (1350–1500), *Cahiers du léopard d'or: I, Le Vêtement*, ed. Michel Pastoureau (Paris, 1989), especially pp. 268–9, and the illustration to this article, 'Un lépreux d'après Vincent de Beauvais', fig. 9, p. 283.

12 Lines 443–9. All quotations are from *The Riverside Chaucer*, ed. Larry D. Benson, 3rd edn. (Oxford, 1988).

13 Eustache Deschamps, quoted in J. Huizinga, *The Waning of the Middle Ages* (London, 1924), p. 250.

14 'In the fourteenth century, in the period of Ladislas Jagellon and Queen Hedvig, the court wore grey on ordinary days and black clothes on *jours de fête*. At the Polish-Hungarian assembly at Sacz, in February 1395, the Polish court wore clothes that were elaborately decorated with pearls and precious stones, but were of the colour black. . . . The shade of black and the quality of the material were of great importance', translated (abridged) from Malgorzata Wilska, 'Du symbole au vêtement: fonction et signification de la couleur dans la culture courtoise de la Pologne médiévale', *Cahiers du léopard d'or: I. Le Vêtement*, pp. 316–17. As in Spain, the distinctive use of black in Poland continued through several centuries. Though fashions, including colour-fashions, travelled internationally, it is also true, to a degree, that nations were colour-coded: see the discussion of French White in chapter 4 below, especially n. 1. On later Polish black – especially the black caftan – and its influence on Jewish black, see n. 23 below.

15 Cited by Huizinga, *Waning*, p. 12; see also pp. 40–41.

16 'Declaration of all the noble deeds and glorious adventures of Duke Philip of Burgundy', quoted (and translated) by Richard Vaughan, *Philip the Good: The Apogee of Burgundy* (London, 1970), p. 127.

17 See Margaret Scott, *Late Gothic Europe, 1400–1500* (London, 1980), p. 62.

18 Scott, *Late Gothic Europe*, p. 100.

19 *Le Blason des Couleurs en Armes, Livrées et devises par Sicille héraut d'Alphonse V, Roi d'Aragon, publié et annoté par Hippolyte Cocheris* (Paris, 1856), p. 87, see also pp. 43–5. Jehan Courtois is identified as the author by John Gage, *Colour in Culture* (London, 1993), p. 82; he was Sicily Herald to Alfonso, King of Aragon, Sicily and Naples, and is often referred to as 'Sicille' or 'Sicily Herald'.

20 The quotation is from Donne, 'Holy Sonnets', Sonnet IX.

21 Both the tradition of the divine darkness, and the tradition of its visual representation, are discussed in some detail by Gage, *Colour in Culture*, pp. 59–60.

22 The first passage is from Lynn White Jr, 'Death and the Devil', in Robert S. Kinsman ed., *The Darker Vision of the Renaissance* (London, 1974), p. 26; the second

from Huizinga, *Waning*, p. 124.

23 Quoted in Alfred Rubens, *A History of Jewish Costume* (London, 1973), p. 184. The 'high' period of the distinctive Jewish hat was from the twelfth to the fifteenth centuries. Though the Jews anciently had a black dye, it was used much less than red and green dyes. The Chapters of Exodus on (high-) priestly dress (XXVIII and XXIX) mention precious stones, violet braid, violet, purple and scarlet stuff, but do not mention black; nor does Josephus (quoted by Rubens, pp. 180–83). In Egypt in 1004 the mad Caliph Al-Hakim ordered Jews and other non-Moslems to wear black clothes and black turbans, as a way of annoying his enemies, the Abbasids, who wore black (Moslem black, in mourning for Ali). Otherwise there was scant use of black before the fifteenth century AD. The use of black by rabbis was influenced by Christian clerical and academic dress, and especially, from the sixteenth century, by the black Geneva gown and white bands of the Calvinist Church; though the high black round-topped hat worn by rabbis shows the assisting influence of Orthodox Christendom. Especially from the sixteenth century onwards, lay Jews in Poland adopted the black caftan that was part of a native tradition of black wear (see n. 14 above), and by the eighteenth century they regularly wore wide brimmed black felt hats, or hats edged with sable, rather than the yellow hats they had earlier (in the sixteenth century) been required to wear. Jews in Germany, in the eighteenth century, were known by their black dress (see Rubens, p. 121). The later movement westward of these communities reinforced the habit of wearing black in Jewish communities in Western Europe.

24 The quotations and references are from Vespasiano da Bisticci's 'Life of Alfonso, King of Naples': see *Renaissance Princes, Popes, and Prelates*, ed. Myron P. Gilmore (London, 1963), pp. 60–73.

25 See Stella Mary Newton, *The Dress of the Venetians, 1495–1525* (Aldershot, 1988), pp. 9–16; the final citation is from Pietro Casola, *Journey to Jerusalem*, quoted in W. Carew Hazlitt, *The Venetian Republic, its Rise, its Growth, and its Fall* (London, 1900), II, p. 748.

26 See Newton, *Dress of the Venetians*, p. 22.

27 Quoted in Hazlitt, *Venetian Republic*, II, p. 746.

28 Quoted in D. S. Chambers, *The Imperial Age of Venice, 1380–1580* (London, 1970), p. 112.

29 *The Merchant of Venice*, III. ii. 269–74.

30 Jacob Burckhardt, *The Civilization of the Renaissance in Italy*, trans. S.G.C. Middlemore (London, 1929), p. 82.

3. *From Black in Spain to Black in Shakespeare*

1 Baldassare Castiglione, *The Book of the Courtier*, trans. Sir Thomas Hoby [1561], ed. J. H. Whitfield (London, 1974), p. 116.

2 Quoted in Geoffrey Parker, *Philip II* (London, 1979), p. 177.

3 Parker, *Philip II*, pp. 50–51.

4 Tennyson's *Queen Mary* was published in 1875 and, cut to half its length, produced in 1876 with Henry Irving as Philip; see Leonée Ormond, *Alfred Tennyson: A Literary Life* (London, 1993), pp. 177–83. Philip on the 'autos' is quoted by Parker, *Philip II*, p. 100.

5 On Russia, I draw especially on Ian Grey, *Ivan the Terrible* (London, 1964); also on Prince A. M. Kurbsky's *History of Ivan the Terrible*, ed. and trans. J.L.I. Fennell (Cambridge, 1965).

6 Brian Reade, *The Dominance of Spain, 1550–1660* (London, 1951), p.10.

7 Antoine de Brunel, 'Voyage d'Espagne', *Revue Hispanique*, 30 (1914), pp. 119–375.

8 Peter the Venerable, Letter 111, p. 289.

9 On the black painting of armour, see Claude Blair, *European Armour: circa 1066 to*

circa 1700 (London, 1958), p. 172. As to the Black Prince, David Hume refers to 'the heroic Edward, commonly called the Black Prince, from the colour of his armour', in *The History of England from the Invasion of Julius Caesar to the Accession of Henry VII* (London, 1762), II, ch. XVI, p. 232; and another John Harvey notes that there is 'some rather shadowy evidence that the Black Prince was described in French as clad at the battle of Crecy "en armure noire en fer bruni", a phrase Harvey translates as "in black armour of burnished steel", though "bruni" here, rather than meaning polished, may be closer to its original meaning, to make brown (or dark): see *The Black Prince and his Age* (London, 1976), p. 15. Hubert Cole, in *The Black Prince* (London, 1976), refers somewhat indeterminately to 'the sable banners that had given him the name by which he was to be known to history' (pp. 9–11). Barbara Emerson notes more cautiously that 'in 1563 the chronicler Grafton was the first to refer to [Edward of Woodstock] as the Black Prince' (*The Black Prince*, London, 1976, pp. 1–2), and the name was given currency by Shakespeare when, in *Henry V*, the Archbishop of Canterbury urges Henry to emulate his 'great uncle . . . Edward the Black Prince' (I. ii. 105). The Clown in Shakespeare's *All's Well That Ends Well* merges Edward of Woodstock and another black and black-clad prince: 'The Black Prince, sir, alias, the Prince of Darkness, alias, the Devil' (IV. v. 45–6).

10 See John W. O'Malley, *The First Jesuits* (Cambridge, MA, 1993), p. 45; O'Malley notes that '*praepositus generalis* is the technical Latin term'.

11 See, for instance, the entry on Luther in F. L. Cross, *The Oxford Dictionary of the Christian Church* (Oxford, 1958), pp. 831–3.

12 A Letter from Beza and Others, quoted, with other relevant material, by James L. Ainslie, *The Doctrines of Ministerial Order in the Reformed Churches of the 16th and 17th Centuries* (Edinburgh, 1940), p. 36.

13 See Ainslie, *Doctrines*, pp. 36–7.

14 Revd Hastings Robinson, ed., *Zurich Letters: 2nd Series* (Cambridge, 1845), p. 357.

15 Calvin's sermon on Micah, and prayer before work, are cited in Alastair Duke, Gillian Lewis and Andrew Pettegree, ed., *Calvinism in Europe, 1540–1610* (London, 1992), pp. 30–35.

16 Simon Schama, *The Embarrassment of Riches* (London, 1987), p. 569.

17 See 'Massachusetts Dress Ways' in D. H. Fischer, *Albion's Seed* (New York, 1969), pp. 139–46.

18 See Roy Strong, 'Charles I's clothes for the years 1633 to 1635', *Costume*, 14 (1980), pp. 73–89.

19 *Hamlet* (I. ii. 77–86). Shakespeare quotations are from the Arden Edition of the Works of William Shakespeare: *Hamlet*, ed. Harold Jenkins (London, 1982); *The Merchant of Venice*, ed. John Russell Brown (London, 1959); *Othello*, ed. M. R. Ridley (London, 1958); *Titus Andronicus*, ed. J. C. Maxwell (London, 1953).

20 See Huizinga, *Waning*, p. 12 and pp. 40–41.

21 My remarks on Alfonso's jests draw not only on Vespasiano da Bisticci (see chapter 2 n. 19) but also on conversations with Dr Anthony Close, of the Modern and Medieval Languages Faculty at Cambridge, who is at present editing a Spanish jest-collection.

22 Goethe and Schlegel are quoted in the Casebook, *Shakespeare: Hamlet*, ed. John Jump (London, 1968), pp. 26–7. In D. H. Lawrence's *Twilight in Italy* (first published 1916) see chapter 3, 'The Theatre'; the quotation is from p. 75 in the Penguin edition (1960).

23 'Yonder melancholie gentleman . . . his long cloake, or his great blacke Feather', lines 1 and 15, 'Meditations of a Gull', *Epigrammes*, 47, *The Poems of Sir John Davies*, ed. Robert Krueger (Oxford, 1975), p. 150.

24 On colour at resurrection, *The Athenian Oracle: Being an Entire Collection of the Valuable Questions and Answers in the Old Athenian Mercuries* (London, 1703), I,

pp. 435–6, quoted in Joseph R. Washington Jr, *Anti-Blackness in English Religion, 1500–1800* (New York, 1984), p. 19. Sir Thomas Browne, *The Works of Sir Thomas Browne*, ed. Charles Sayle (Edinburgh, 1912), II, pp. 383–4. *Ben Jonson*, ed. C. H. Herford Percy and Evelyn Simpson (Oxford, 1941), VII, 'The Masque of Blacknesse', pp. 169–80.

25 T. S. Eliot, 'Shakespeare and the Stoicism of Seneca', *Selected Essays*, 3rd edn (London, 1951), p. 130; F. R. Leavis, 'Diabolic Intellect and the Noble Hero', *The Common Pursuit* (Harmondsworth, 1962), p. 152.

26 *The Origins of Shakespeare* (London, 1977), p. 78.

27 I take these quotations from the very full presentation of many aspects of attitudes to Africans in Winthrop D. Jordan's *White over Black* (Chapel Hill, NC, 1968), pp. 33–5.

4. *From Black in Art to Dickens's Black*

1 Since discussions of French White are (in my experience) hard to find, I cite at length from an authoritative article. 'Le blanc . . . prend peu à peu de l'importance au cours de la première moitié du XIV siècle et joue un grand rôle à partir du règne de Jean II. . . . Le blanc est souvent associé à la reine, notamment à Isabeau de Bavière . . . Les habitants de Tournai, en 1382, lors de l'entrée de Charles VI, portent du blanc en signe de pureté. . . . C'est aussi le symbole de l'humilité. Un bel exemple est donné par l'entrée de Louis XI à Tournai en 1464, où les habitants sont vêtus de blanc pour signifier cette attitude. Ce peut être le symbole de la *Libéralité*. Cette personnification est vêtue de blanc lors de l'entrée de Louis XII à Paris en 1498. . . . Le blanc enfin triomphe à la fin du XVe siècle à la cour de France. Dans une miniature des *Vigiles du roi Charles VII* de Martial d'Auvergne, offert à Charles VIII, *France* est vêtue de blanc fleurdelisé d'or.' Christian de Mérindol, 'Signes de hiérarchie sociale à la fin du moyen âge d'après le vêtement méthodes et recherches', *Cahiers du léopard d'or, I. Le Vêtement*, ed. Michel Pastoureau (Paris, 1989), pp. 201–2. The discussion of colour-meanings in this article (which is confined to France) makes scant reference to black, merely noting that it is sometimes but not always used for mourning, and that black is a colour of ill fame in Italy, where 'les courtisanes portent un mantelet noir' (p. 201). It should be said that the colour red was massively used in the medieval period (most of all in the fourteenth century) by French monarchs and their servants. The royal accounts of 1387 mention specific colours the following number of times: red 197, green 96, blue and violet 66, white 35, pink 29, grey 2, black 2 (p. 195).

2 On the feast of Hades at Versailles, see André Félibien, *Relation de la Feste de Versailles* (Paris, 1668). In *À Rebours*, at 'a funeral banquet in memory of the host's virility, lately but only temporarily deceased', there were 'paths . . . strewn with charcoal, the ornamental pond . . . filled with ink. . . . The dinner itself was served on a black cloth. . . . Dining off black-bordered plates, the company had enjoyed turtle soup, Russian rye bread, ripe olives . . . caviare, mullet botargo, black puddings . . . truffle jellies, chocolate creams, plum-puddings. . . . And after coffee and walnut cordial, they had rounded off the evening with kvass, porter, and stout': Joris-Karl Huysmans, *Against Nature* (Harmondsworth, 1959), ch. I, p. 27. Huysmans says Des Esseintes's 'funeral feast' was 'modelled on an eighteenth-century original'. If one made a connection with the excremental black death-eating in Pynchon's *Gravity's Rainbow* (London, 1975), pp. 232–6, 715–7) one might see Western tradition as punctuated by the anti-sacrament or death-sacrament of the black meal.

3 On gowns and wigs, as well as the (breeched) three-piece suits, see Aileen Ribeiro, *Dress in Eighteenth-century Europe, 1715–1789* (London, 1984), especially pp. 27–31.

The eighteenth-century hat, normally carried if a wig was worn, was black.
4 The English visitor is Arthur Young, quoted by Ribeiro, p. 86; on the other
   countries mentioned, see Ribeiro, *Dress in Eighteenth-century Europe*, pp. 70, 71,
   130, 135.
5 G. Baretti, *An Account of the Manners and Customs of Italy* (London, 1769), II, pp.
   205–6.
6 The contemporary observer is Madame du Bocage, *Letters Concerning England,
   Holland and Italy* (London, 1770), I, p. 140, quoted by Ribeiro, *Dress in Eighteenth-
   century Europe*, pp. 163–4, where a full vivid account of masquerade dress is given.
7 Daniel Roche, *The Culture of Clothing* (Cambridge, 1994), a translation of *La
   Culture des Apparences* (Paris, 1989), see especially Table 11, p. 127, and Table 15,
   p. 138. The basis for Roche's figures are the inventories of personal wardrobes
   which the law required on a person's death: normally the notaries set down
   colours. Amalgamating two of Roche's tables, one can see how colours changed, in
   the clothes of different classes, between his two chosen dates.

Colours and patterns calculated as percentages of the wardrobes
of both sexes in 1700/1789.

	Nobilities	Professions	Artisans & Shopkeepers	Wage-earners	Domestics
Black	33/23	44/37	28/32	33/12	29/13
Brown	27/7	10/13	14/9	18/6	23/4
Grey	5/12	13/11	16/23	10/21	20/17
White	21/19	14/28	12/17	9/32	6/28
Red	8/38	8/11	9/19	12/29	13/38
Blue, Yellow (Misc. other 1700*)	6	11	21	18	9
Stripes	48/67	63/75	6/44	88/66	75/60
Flowers	10/27	24/20	20/36	6/18	12/25
Checks & Misc.	42/6	13/5	4/20	6/14	13/15

*Roche includes for 1700, but not for 1789, a category of miscellaneous other colours, which I cite to complete the percentages for 1700.

It is of course a delicate task, deciding how to 'read' such quotients. Unfortunately for my purposes, Roche's colour-figures do not distinguish between the clothes of men and women, though it is clear from other sources that the predominance of darks and blacks is in men's dress, the predominance of whites and colours in women's. One must allow too that 'nobility' includes the nobility of 'la robe', the judicial and legal nobility, who made a large use of black (though also a good use of red). The use of black by all classes would be affected by the need, in a period when clothes were expected to last, to have in one's wardrobe a fair stock of garments that could be worn when mourning. In the dyeing trade in these years the largest demand was for black-dyeing: and these clothes could not be dyed light again though they must continue to be worn. On dyeing in this century, see Alan Mansfield, 'Dyeing and cleaning clothes in the late eighteenth and early nineteenth centuries', *Costume*, I/2 (1968), pp. 24–8.
   As to the professional class, at the start of this period nearly half their clothes are black, and at the end of it well more than a third still are black – more, that is, than for any other group at either date in this table. They also make the smallest increase in the use of bright colours, brightening from eight to eleven percent, an increase of a third or so, when all the other classes 'colour up' by well more than 100 per cent, and the aristocrats by 400 per cent. One would have to note too that the professionals' use of brown increases, while everyone else's goes down. So all

in all, though the use of white increases also (white being an un-coloured colour, like black), it is the professionals who are the truly dark birds on the branch.

The artisans and shopkeepers are also interesting, since they are the only group whose use of black increases. In 1700 they have the same proportion of black clothes as those in domestic service; and in 1789 they have the same proportion of black clothes, as the nobility itself had had in 1700. They are also, after the professionals, the class that makes the smallest increase in bright colours. One could be tempted to conclude that it was this class in particular that had a rising serious sense of dignified standing, as they rose from being providing servants to being serious professionals of provision. Darkening when all others were growing more coloured, the artisans and shopkeepers may have been a serious biding presence.

8 Description by Arthur Young, 25 October 1787, quoted in J. M. Thompson, ed., *English Witnesses of the French Revolution* (Oxford, 1938), p. 131.

9 The instructions, and popular responses to them, are cited in Aileen Ribeiro, *Fashion in the French Revolution* (London, 1988), pp. 45–8. My paragraphs on the French Revolution are greatly indebted to Ribeiro's book.

10 The comments are by an English bystander, Edward Rigby, quoted by Thompson, *Witnesses*, p. 59.

11 The 'young people of the first fashion . . .' are described in Thompson, *Witnesses*, p. 94; the reference to those in black 'pour mourir . . .' is from the *Chronique de Paris*, 6 December 1789; the quotation from the *Journal de la Mode et du Goût* is from its first issue, 25 February 1790.

12 Description by H. R. Yorke in Thompson, *Witnesses*, p. 224; the Duc d'Orléans wore blue; some were open-necked.

13 On the dress of suicides, see Richard Cobb, *Death in Paris* (Oxford, 1978), pp. 76–7.

14 Elizabeth McClellan, *Historic Dress, 1607 to 1800* (London, 1906), p. 328.

15 There was a sub-language, or dialect, in the placing of the black beauty spot by women or men: Le Camus found a patch 'at the exterior Angle of the Eye . . . killing', one 'in the midst of the Forehead, Majestic', while a patch on the nose demonstrated daring: *Abdeker, or The Art of preserving Beauty* (London, 1754), p. 151, quoted by Ribeiro, *Dress in Eighteenth-century Europe*, p. 109. The beauty-spot was made of 'black Taffety . . . cover'd with Gum Arabic'.

16 F. Chenoune, *A History of Men's Fashion* (Paris, 1993), p. 319 n. 33; Daniel Roche, *The Culture Of Clothing*, pp. 58–9.

17 Chenoune, *History*, p. 19.

18 *Daniel Deronda*, introduction by F. R. Leavis (New York, 1961; a facsimile of Blackwood's 1878 edition), ch. XI, p. 79.

19 See, for instance, *The History of Sexuality: An Introduction*, trans. Robert Hurley (Harmondsworth, 1984), pp. 122–31.

20 On Gautier and Baudelaire, see nn. 2 and 3 to ch. 1 above; for Ruskin, see *Modern Painters*, III, ch. 16, sec. 9. As to Oscar Wilde, his letter to *The Daily Telegraph* of 2 February 1891 (published 3 February 1891, p. 5) observed that 'the uniform black that is worn now, though valuable at a dinner-party, where it serves to isolate and separate women's dresses, to frame them as it were, still is dull and tedious and depressing in itself. . . . At present we all have more than a dozen useless buttons on our evening coats, and by always keeping them black and of the same colour as the rest of the costume we prevent them being in any way beautiful.' He notes, too, the tendency of black clothes *not* to change: 'For the dress of 1840 is really the same in design and form as ours'.

21 For example: 'Certain it is, however, that this great power of blackness in [Hawthorne] derives its force from its appeals to that Calvinistic sense of Innate Depravity and Original Sin, from whose visitations, in some shape or other, no

deeply thinking mind is always and wholly free', Herman Melville, 'Hawthorne and his Mosses', 'Uncollected Prose', *The Library of America: Herman Melville* (New York, 1984), III, p. 1159.

22 Gustave Flaubert, *Madame Bovary*, trans. Alan Russell (Harmondsworth, 1950), part I, chapter 7, p. 53; part III, chapter 5, p. 288.

23 *Little Dorrit* (1855–7), Book the First, ch. III, pp. 31–5; the black figurines are in ch. V, p. 54.

24 *Dombey*, ch. III, pp. 22–3.

25 *Dombey*, ch. VIII, p. 93.

26 *The Personal History of David Copperfield* (1849–50), ch. II, p. 22.

27 *Bleak House*: Kenge, ch. III, p. 18; Lord Chancellor, ch. III, p. 30; Mr. Tulkinghorn, ch. II, p. 11; Mr. Vholes, ch. XXXIX, p. 549.

28 The thirteenth century saw the beginnings of a civil legal profession, taking over in many areas from the ecclesiastical courts, and through the fourteenth and fifteenth centuries a fully organized legal profession developed throughout Europe. Judges might exercise the royal prerogative, and hence wore splendid and noble dress. The judges in Genoa wore black because they were senators, and their black robes were richly voluminous, damask or velvet.

   The dress at the English Inns of Court had been standardized, between 1558 and 1611, in a series of measures of good protestant character. Ruffs were forbidden, gowns must be 'sad coloured', hair must be short, and curling was prohibited. From the end of the sixteenth century, staff and students at the English Inns of Court wore black gowns, decorated with silk tufts. King's Counsel wore, from their effective initiation in the early Seventeenth Century, an open black silk gown, of the type generally worn by men of dignity and learning; solicitors also wore from that period a long open black gown. Barristers, those lawyers who were trained by attending cases in court, had at first worn lay dress. By the early sixteenth century, they regularly wore the lay Tudor black gown. In the seventeenth century this became a full gown, closed in front with buttons, but by the following century the gowns of all lawyers were open.

   In the dress of advocates, there were of course national variations. Spanish advocates, by the eighteenth century, had come to wear a black apron and black cloak. Earlier, advocates in several countries had worn colours, for instance if they wore the livery of their King; so French advocates in the fifteenth and sixteenth centuries might wear scarlet robes, as did French judges. In England, the original advocates (serjeants-at-law) were known by the white coif they wore, as well as their parti-coloured, normally blue/green, robes. The parti-coloured robe itself (changed now to purple and 'murrey' – mulberry-coloured) was last worn, at the ceremony of the creation of a new serjeant, in 1762, thereafter being laid aside for the black silk gown worn in normal court practice. In the late Seventeenth Century, lawyers, like others, adopted the wig which, surviving beyond the general period of the wig, became a new head-armour of the legal brain, as it were a later form of coif. I draw especially on W. N. Hargreaves-Mawdsley, *A History of Legal Dress in Europe* (Oxford, 1963).

29 *Bleak House*, ch. II, p. 11.

30 Henry VIII's Act for the Reformation of Excess of Apparel, of 1533, enforced sober dress on people of private standing, but allowed scarlet to those of position and dignity: codifying, for England, a 'rouge et noir' differentiation general in Europe, witness the patricians and senators of Venice. The histories of the different gowns and gown-colours are recorded in W. N. Hargreaves-Mawdsley's *A History of Academical Dress in Europe until the end of the Eighteenth Century* (Oxford, 1963). The relative humility of the black gown was not always accepted, and in Paris, in the eighteenth century, the assistant professors (*agrégés*), possibly moved by a proto-Revolutionary spirit, chose to wear the red robes of full professors

(*antécesseurs*), and persisted in doing so until allowed to by law (pp. 46–7). The general tendency however was from variety of colour to black. Rank still was indicated in the different forms of black gown, and (in England) those whose gowns were spare and sleeveless were able to assume the appearance of higher standing by wearing the full-sleeved mourning gown. The mourning gown was 'exactly the same as the canonical gown of the Church of England in the seventeenth and eighteenth centuries' (p. 104). The mourning gown was worn by all at an academic funeral – except for the dead professor himself, laid out in the red robes of his prestige (p. 51).

31 *The Life and Adventures of Nicholas Nickleby* (1838–9), ch. IV, p. 31; *Dombey*, ch. XI, p. 142: *Copperfield*, ch. XVI, p. 238.

32 The mildly clerical doctor, *Middlemarch*, Book II, ch. XVIII, p. 181; Lydgate, Book I, ch. X, p. 92; Dr Parker Peps, *Dombey*, ch. I, p. 4; Mr Chillip, *Copperfield*, ch. I, p. 9. The physician of few words is in *The Life and Adventures of Martin Chuzzlewit* (1843–4), ch. XXV, p. 416, the momentary surgeon in ch. XVIII, p. 307. On the undertaker's establishment, and 'suit of black', see Mr Mould, again in *Chuzzlewit*, ch. XIX, pp. 321–5.

33 Henry Fielding, *Joseph Andrews*, ed. Martin C. Battestin (Oxford, 1967), ch. XVI, p. 73. Anthony Trollope, *The Warden* (first published, 1855), ed. Richard Church, (Oxford, 1961), Mr Harding, ch. I, p. 4, Dr Grantly, ch. 5, pp. 60–61. *The Mystery of Edwin Drood* (1870), Mr Sapsea, ch. IV, p. 31, Revd Crisparkle, ch. VI, p. 49.

34 *The Fitz-Boodle Papers* (first published in *Fraser's Magazine*, 1842), *The Biographical Edition of the Works of William Makepeace Thackeray* (London, 1898), IV, pp. 341, 342, 357. Elizabeth Wilson, *Adorned in Dreams* (London, 1985), p. 136.

35 'A glance up the high street of the town on a Candlemas-fair day twenty or thirty years ago revealed a crowd whose general colour was whity-brown flecked with white. Black was almost absent. . . . Now the crowd is as dark as a London crowd.' Hardy goes on to specify the proportion of corduroy trousers, black trousers, black canvas overalls, faded black suits etc. 'The Dorsetshire Labourer', *Longman's Magazine*, 9 (July 1883), p. 258.

36 *Little Dorrit*, Book the First, ch. XXI, p. 249.

37 *Little Dorrit*, Book the First, ch. X, p. 111.

38 Jaggers, *Great Expectations*, ch. XVIII, p. 129; Merdle, *Little Dorrit*, Book the First, ch. XXI, p. 247; Turveydrop, *Bleak House*, ch. XIV, p. 190; Gradgrind, *Hard Times* (1854), Book the First, ch. I, p. 1; Headstone, *Our Mutual Friend* (1864–5), Book the Second, ch. I, p. 217.

5. England's Dark House

1 *Great Expectations*, ch. XXV, p. 198; ch. LI, p. 394.

2 Letter to Forster of (?)15 March, 1844, *The Letters of Charles Dickens*, IV, ed. Kathleen Tillotson (Oxford, 1977), p. 74; see also John Forster, *The Life of Charles Dickens* (London, 1908), I, p. 325.

3 For the Overs/Dickens correspondence, and a highly pertinent discussion of it, see Sheila M. Smith, 'John Overs to Charles Dickens: A Working-Man's Letter and its Implication', *Victorian Studies*, XVIII/2 (1974), pp. 195–217.

4 'Fourth Quarter', *The Chimes* (1844), *Christmas Books*, p. 149; for the Macready reference see Smith, 'John Overs to Charles Dickens', p. 216.

5 *Bleak House*, ch. XIX, p. 271.

6 The phrase concludes Dickens's description of the London railway-station being built in *Dombey and Son*, ch. VI, p. 63.

7 *Little Dorrit*, Book the First, ch. X, p. 116.

8 *Our Mutual Friend*, Book the First, ch. XI, pp. 128–33; Book the Second, ch. IV, p. 255.

9 *Dombey*, ch. XXIII, p. 320; *Bleak House*, ch. LVIII, p. 786; *Little Dorrit*, Book the First, ch. X, p. 110.

10 *Dombey*, ch. XXIII, p. 319; *Great Expectations*, ch. XI, p. 78.

11 *Bleak House*, ch. XVI, p. 220; ch. XXII, p. 310; ch. III, p. 28; ch. I, p. 1; *Great Expectations*, ch. XXI, pp. 162–3; *Little Dorrit*, Book the First, ch. III, p. 28; *Our Mutual Friend*, Book the First, ch. XII, p. 145.

12 *Hard Times*, Book the First, ch. V, p. 23; Book the Second, ch. I, p. 110.

13 *Great Expectations*, ch. LIV, p. 416.

14 Evidence of Thomas Bennett, *Report of the Select Committee on Factory Children's Labour* (1831–2), quoted in Oliver MacDonagh, *Early Victorian Government, 1830–1870* (London, 1977), p. 31.

15 *The Storm Cloud of the Nineteenth Century, Two Lectures delivered at the London Institution February 4th and 11th, 1884* (Orpington, 1884), pp. 48–51.

16 Letter to Charles Collins, 6 July 1853, quoted in Mary Lutyens, *Millais and the Ruskins* (London, 1967), p. 61; see also the discussion of this painting (cat. No. 56, pp. 115–17) in *The Pre-Raphaelites* (Foreword and Introduction by Alan Bowness), published by the Tate Gallery, London, 1984).

17 It would have to be said that the few sentences where Booth extends his imagery to the 'natives' do refract a sense of social difference through racial difference and sub-difference: 'That is the forest. But what of its denizens? . . . Of these pygmies there are two kinds; one a very degraded specimen with ferretlike eyes, close-set nose, more nearly approaching the baboon than was supposed to be possible, but very human; the other very handsome, with frank open innocent features, very prepossessing. . . . The two tribes of savages, the human baboon and the handsome dwarf, who will not speak lest it impede him in his task, may be accepted as the two varieties who are continually present with us – the vicious, lazy lout, and the toiling slave. They, too, have lost all faith of life being other than it is and has been.' *In Darkest England and the Way Out* (London, 1970, first pub. 1890), pp. 10–12. On the dark forest, Hell and abyss see Part I, 'The Darkness'; on the Salvation Ship and emigration see, for instance, pp. 152–7.

18 'Doré's *London*: Art and Evidence', *Art History*, I/3 (1978), pp. 341–59.

19 *London*, pp. 142, 144, 145, 145, 145, 146.

20 *Bleak House*, ch. XVI, pp. 220–2; ch. XXII, pp. 310–14.

21 As to the police: Jo, lit up by the police bull's eye, is seen 'trembling to think that he has offended against the law in not having moved on far enough'. Cf. Alan Woods on Doré's illustration 'The Bull's Eye': 'We see a group of the poor; and we see the police. . . . Once more we have an image of social control. . . . The Bull's Eye . . . shines on a group of six figures, and is directed particularly at the only figure in the group who is standing. . . . Only one of the other five looks towards him, apprehensively; the others look anxiously at the police as they crouch fearfully against the wall. The police tower above them. . . . The central policeman . . . looks stern . . . the one on the left seems to be enjoying his power.' Woods, 'Doré's *London*', p. 352.

22 'The Praise of Chimney-Sweepers', *The Works of Charles and Mary Lamb*, ed. E. V. Lucas, II: *Elia and the Last Essays of Elia* (London, 1903), p. 109. Citing Lamb, I should mention too, in the Last Essays, 'The Wedding', as touching both on authorial black, and on an occasion when formality was not expected to be black: 'She was pleased to say that she had never seen a gentleman before me give away a bride, in black. Now black has been my ordinary apparel so long – indeed I take it to be the proper costume of an author – the stage sanctions it – that to have appeared in some lighter colour would have raised more mirth at my expense, than the anomaly had created censure' (pp. 241–2). As to *The Water-Babies*, though soot is not sin for Tom, it is so for his master, Grimes, and only his own penitence can cleanse it – 'his own tears did what his mother's could not do, and Tom's could not

do, and nobody's on earth could do for him; for they washed the soot of his face and off his clothes': *The Water-Babies: A Fairy Tale for a Land-Baby*, new edn illustrated by Linley Sambourne (London, 1885), p. 359 (first publication was in 1863).

23 Ruskin, *Storm Cloud*, pp. 46–58.

24 Much funeral furniture may be seen reproduced in John Morley, *Death, Heaven and the Victorians* (London, 1971), where mortality figures are also quoted: 'By the third decade of the century *The Lancet* could cite the fact that mortality in city dwellers was forty per cent higher than amongst the rest of the population; in London, in 1830, the average age of death was estimated at forty-four years for gentry, professional persons, and their families; at twenty-five years for tradesmen, clerks and their families; and at twenty-two for labourers and their families' (p. 7). The *Quarterly Review* commented on the first *Annual Report of the Register of Births, Deaths and Marriages*: 'Are cities then necessarily the graves of our race?' (Morley, p. 34). If not black, funeral palls might be violet, and high Anglo-Catholics 'might use violet in place of black for funeral vestments' (p. 29) The Mayhew passage, from *The Shops and Companies of London and the Trades and Manufacturers of Great Britain*, is quoted on p. 63.

25 'Going to see a man hanged, July 1840', originally published in *Fraser's Magazine*, *Works*, III, pp. 645–6. Albert Borowitz, *The Woman who Murdered Black Satin* (Columbus, OH, 1981), p. 296. Forster is quoted on p. 264, the account of satin bankruptcies by Charles Kingston on p. 290, the review of Madame Tussaud's, from *Punch*, on pp. 286–7. Borowitz discusses Dickens's use of Maria Manning in chapter 19, pp. 297–311.

26 I take my information from, especially, L. Taylor, *Mourning Dress* (London, 1983); see, in particular, chapter 10, 'The Colours of Mourning'.

27 See especially Yoshio Abe, '"Un Enterrement à Ornans" et l'*habit noir* baudelairien. Sur les rapports de Baudelaire et de Courbet,' *Etudes de Langue et Litterature Francaises*, I, (1962), pp. 29–41.

28 *Great Expectations*, ch. XXXV, pp. 264–6; *Middlemarch*, ed. Rosemary Ashton (Harmondsworth, 1994), ch. XXXIV, pp. 324. *Bleak House*, ch. LIII, pp. 713; *Vanity Fair*, ch. XLI, *Works*, I, pp. 406, 405. On Wellington's funeral see, for instance, Morley, *Death, Heaven and the Victorians*, ch. VII; the funeral car itself, shorn of its pillars, draperies and armaments, is now in the crypt of St Paul's Cathedral.

29 E. M. Forster, resuming the notebooks of his aunt Marianne in *Marianne Thornton, 1797–1887* (London, 1956), p. 71, quoted in Philip Collins, *From Manly Tear to Stiff Upper Lip: The Victorians and Pathos* (Wellington, 1974), p. 4. Philip Collins's lecture deserves to be better known for its study of the Victorian cult of grieving, and the later inhibiting of this cult. 'Private feeling and private grief should not be displayed in public', urged an etiquette book of the 1890s (Collins, p. 5).

30 'The Princess', IV, in *The Poems of Tennyson*, ed. Christopher Ricks (London, 1969). All citations are taken from this edition. As to white mourning: Mrs Gaskell (1859) advised that 'pure entire white is mourning for girls in an evening', Morley, *Death, Heaven and the Victorians*, p. 72.

31 Quoted by Leonée Ormond in her discussion of *Enoch Arden*, and of Browning's objections to its close, in her excellent and invaluable *Alfred Tennyson: A Literary Life* (London, 1993), p. 159.

32 'The Charge of the Light Brigade', II. 14–17.

33 The uniform of the Rifle Brigade (the 95th Foot, established 1800, previously Colonel Coote Manningham's Experimental Corps of Riflemen) has traditionally been green. It is a further instance of mid-nineteenth-century blackening (though a practical one) that, due to the variable hues of green dyes, the cloth for the uniform of Riflemen was from 1830 dyed black. The practice was discontinued, and green resumed, with the introduction of mineral dyes in 1890. See P. W.

Kingsland and Susan Keable, *British Military Uniforms and Equipment: Volume I* (London, 1971); the pages are unnumbered, but see closing paragraphs in the section on The Rifle Brigade.

34 Leader, *The Times*, 1 August 1854.

35 'Hatred and vengeance, my eternal portion,' *The Poems of William Cowper*, I, ed. John D. Baird and Charles Ryskamp (Oxford, 1980), p. 209. *The Poems of Gerard Manley Hopkins*, ed. W. H. Gardner and N. H. MacKenzie, 4th edition (Oxford, 1970), p. 98.

36 *More Nonsense*, 1872, reprinted in *The Complete Nonsense of Edward Lear*, ed. Holbrook Jackson (London, 1947), p. 167.

37 *The Complete Prose Works of Matthew Arnold*, ed. R. H. Super, VIII, *Essays Religious and Mixed* (Ann Arbor, 1972), pp. 294–5. The essay had been an address to the Royal Institution, delivered 8 February 1878 and first published, as 'Equality', in the *Fortnightly Review*, March 1878. In fairness to Arnold, one should note his prior distinction: 'our middle class divides itself into a serious portion and a gay or rowdy portion'. This 'gay or rowdy' portion he associates with popular jingoistic songs and 'the modern English theatre, perhaps the most contemptible in Europe'. He concludes however that 'the real strength of the English middle class is in its serious portion', and proceeds to describe its self-imprisoned puritanism.

38 *Drood*, ch. II, p. 5.

39 *Copperfield*, ch. XV, p. 219, ch. XVI, pp. 234–5, ch. XVII, pp. 253–4; *Little Dorrit*, Book the First, ch. X, p. 118.

40 On Dickens's personal form of dandyism, seen at the time as having a 'Cockney' inflection, see Moers, *The Dandy*, ch. X, especially pp. 220–22. For Dickens's more general thoughts on dandyism see *Bleak House*, ch. XIII – 'Dandyism of a more mischievous sort, that has got below the surface. . . . Dandyism – in Religion, for instance . . .'. Many comments by contemporaries on Dickens's dress are included in Philip Collins, *Dickens: Interviews and Recollections*, 2 vols (London, 1981). For instance, Dickens was 'rather inclined to what was once called "dandyism"' (I, p. 14), his taste in dress was 'intolerable' (I, p. 20). Later he gave less offence: in the period from 1853 on 'he was always well dressed, frequently wearing a black velvet waistcoat' (II, p.240). But still, in the period from 1860 on, 'he was always theatrically dressed' (II, p. 274), and from 1865 on: 'He was a toff, he was; he always used to wear a white bowler hat and a cutaway coat' (II, p. 272).

41 *Bleak House*, ch. III, pp. 17, 18; *Little Dorrit*, Book the First, ch. II, p. 23; see also Book the Second, ch. XXI, 'The History of a Self Tormentor', pp. 663–71.

42 *Little Dorrit*, Book the Second, ch. XXX, p. 777.

43 *Great Expectations*, ch. VIII, p. 59; ch. XLII, p. 332.

44 *Our Mutual Friend*, Book the Second, ch. I, p. 217; Book the Second, ch. VI, p. 288; Book the Third, ch. X, p. 544.

45 *Drood*, ch. II, p. 8; ch. XIX, pp. 219, 223.

6. Men in Black with Women in White

1 Fred Davis's remarks are addressed to the quality, to 'the aristocracy, and . . . the upper Bourgeoisie who emulated it': *Fashion, Culture, and Identity* (Chicago, 1992), p. 38. On Russian women's blackened teeth see A. Ribeiro, *Dress in Eighteenth-century Europe, 1715–1789* (London, 1984), p. 109.

2 Nancy Chodorow, *The Reproduction of Mothering: Psychoanalysis and the Sociology of Gender* (Berkeley, 1978), esp. pp. 180–90.

3 The father is Mr Gibson in *Wives and Daughters*, ed. Angus Easson (Oxford, 1987), p. 59; the ashamed ladies are in *North and South*, ed. Angus Easson (Oxford, 1982), I, ch. I, p. 9; the silent ladies in the same novel, ch. II, p. 162; the fashion talk in *Mary Barton*, ed. Edgar Wright (Oxford, 1987), ch. IX, p. 112. I am indebted for

these references to Simon Parkin.

4 *North and South*, I, ch. XX, p. 161; *Middlemarch*, ch. LXXX, p. 789; Jo Baraclough Paoletti, 'Ridicule and Role Models as Factors in American Men's Fashion Change, 1880–1910, *Costume*, 19 (1985), pp. 121–34.

5 *Felix Holt*, ed. Peter Coveney (Harmondsworth, 1972), ch. I, p. 86. On round shoulders and narrow waists, see Claudia Brush Kidwell, 'Gender Symbols or Fashionable Details?', especially the section 'The Hourglass Shape for Men and Women', in Claudia Brush Kidwell and Valerie Steele, eds, *Men and Women: Dressing the Part* (Washington DC, 1989), pp. 126–9, where also a nineteenth-century commentator is quoted: John F. Watson, 'Men and women stiffly corseted; long unnatural-looking waists; shoulders and breasts stuffed and deformed . . . and artificial hips' (*Annals and Occurrences of New York City and State, in the Olden Time*, Philadelphia, 1846, p. 247).

6 *Jane Eyre*: travelling dress, ch. X, p. 121; cloak and bonnet, ch. XII, p. 146; black stuff and silk, ch. XIII, p. 151.

7 The first version of Richard Redgrave's painting was exhibited at the Royal Academy in 1843 under the title 'The Poor Teacher'; it did not include the children, who were added, at the request of the buyer, John Sheepshanks, to the new version, reproduced here, which was exhibited at the Academy in 1845 under the title 'The Governess'. The catalogue quotations are from Susan P. Casteras and Ronald Parkinson, *Richard Redgrave 1804–1888* (London, 1988), p. 112.

8 Frances Hodgson Burnett, *Little Lord Fauntleroy* (Harmondsworth, 1994, originally 1886): black velvet skirt, p. 10; black cloth suit, p. 20; black velvet cap, p. 73; black velvet suit, pp. 78, 82, 86, 133; with vandyke lace, p. 172.

9 *Middlemarch*, ch. LXXIV, pp. 749–50.

10 *Daniel Deronda*: black silk, ch. XXVII, p. 220; riding dress, ch. XXIX, p. 244.

11 *Notes on England*, trans W. F. Rae (London, 1872), pp. 68–9.

12 *The Letters of Peter the Venerable* (see ch. 2, n. 7 above), I, Letter 111, p. 289.

13 Elizabeth Gaskell, *North and South*, II, ch. XIX, p. 378. Wilkie Collins, *The Woman in White*, ed. Julian Symons (Harmondsworth, 1974; originally published 1859–60), the meeting with the Woman in White, pp. 47–55.

14 *The Woman in White*: Anne Catherick told to wear white, p. 84; Laura Fairlie in white, pp. 74, 80, 82; Marian Halcombe described, p. 58. There is also in the novel a man in white, Mr Fairlie, who has a dark coat but a 'waistcoat and trousers of spotless white' (p. 66): but he is a spoilt selfish recessive hypochondriac. He has feet 'effeminately small' and also is sexless and virginal: in other words he allows Collins to represent the bad side of women's blanched white purity.

15 Already in the late eighteenth century, as Daniel Roche has recorded, with specific figures as to France, a wife regularly spent twice as much on clothes as her husband: see *The Culture of Clothing*, p. 116.

16 *Little Dorrit*, Book the First, ch. XXI, p. 247.

17 From *Mosses from an Old Manse* (1846); I cite the text of the Centenary Edition, as reprinted in *Hawthorne: Tales and Sketches*, ed. Roy Harvey Pearce (Cambridge, 1982), p. 1005.

18 *Middlemarch*, ch. I, p. 13. On the over- and under-estimation of Victorian sexual inhibition see Valerie Steele, 'Clothing and Sexuality', in *Men and Women: Dressing the Part*, p. 51.

19 *Jane Eyre*, ch. XIII, p. 151; *Middlemarch*, ch. XIX, pp. 188–9.

20 *Middlemarch*, ch. XXVIII, pp. 273–4.

21 *Middlemarch*, ch. LXXXIII, p. 810.

22 *Middlemarch*, ch. XLII, p. 424.

23 *Daniel Deronda*: nereid, ch. I, p. 5; archery meeting, ch. XI, p. 84; black silk, ch. XXVII, p. 220; white shawl, ch. LVI, p. 518; last meeting, ch. LXIX, p. 607.

24 Leopold von Sacher-Masoch, *Venus in Furs*: the text is published, together with

Coldness and Cruelty by Gilles Deleuze in *Masochism* (New York, 1991); *passim*, but
especially pp. 153–66. It is true that Wanda sometimes wears ermine; mainly she
wears sable. She may, again, be assisted by 'three slender young Negresses, like
ebony carvings, all dressed in red satin and each with a rope in her hand.'

25 'Sorcière au flanc d'ebène . . .' is from Poem XXVI ('Sed non Satiata'), the 'jour
noir' from Poem LXXVIII ('Spleen'), 'Les Fleurs du mal: Spleen et Ideal', *Oeuvres
complètes*, ed. Claude Pichois (Paris, 1975), I, pp. 28, 74. 'Spleen' ends thus: 'et
l'Angoisse atroce, despotique, / Sur mon crâne incliné plante son drapeau noir'.
Cf. in another 'Spleen' poem, Poem LXXVI (p. 73), 'Je suis un cimetière abhorré de
la lune'. Nerval, 'Je croyais voir un soleil noir dans le ciel désert et un globe rouge
de sang au-dessus des Tuileries. Je me dis: "La nuit éternelle commence . . .",
Aurelia, part 2, IV, *Oeuvres complètes*, ed. Jean Guillaume, Claude Pichois *et al.*
(Paris, 1993), III, p. 734. 'En cherchant l'œil de Dieu, je n'ai vu qu'une orbite /
Vaste, noire et sans fond, d'où la nuit qui l'habite / Rayonne sur le monde et
s'épaissit toujour', Le Christ aux Oliviers II, *Les Chimères: Exégèses de Jeanine
Moulin* (Paris, 1949), p. 68. Baudelaire, the most black of dandies, at one point
summarized his position as 'La femme est le contraire du dandy. / Donc elle doit
faire horreur . . . / La femme est *naturelle*, c'est-à-dire abominable. / Aussi est-elle
toujours vulgaire, c'est-à-dire le contraire du dandy'; quoted in Jessica Feldman's
discussion of the dandy's simultaneous attack on women, and appropriation of
women's characteristics, in *Gender on the Divide* (Ithaca, NY, 1993), p. 6ff. On
Baudelaire's dress and dandyism see Feldman, p. 110ff., also Enid Starkie,
Baudelaire (London, 1957), pt. I, ch. 3, 'The Dandy'.

26 'Je suis le ténébreux, – le veuf, – l'inconsolé, . . .', 'El Desdichado', *Les Chimères*,
p. 5.

7. *Black in our Time*

1 'Having started as . . . dazzlingly sinister, it [black] became turned into daylight
respectability and began to share in the flavour of null black,' Anne Hollander,
Seeing through Clothes (London, 1988), p. 380. Though this movement occurred,
both men and women's evening-wear use of black continued rich and smart and in
its own way dazzling, witness not only many paintings of the late-century (e.g.
Manet, Degas, Tissot, Sargent) but Du Maurier's *Punch* cartoons which recur,
with a mildly satiric exhilaration, to the tall splendid figures black-suited men cut.

2 The specifications for the suit are from *New York World*, 4 May 1882, cited by
Richard Ellmann, *Oscar Wilde* (London, 1987), p. 177n.; the companions suit
commissioned from Wirtz of New York was to be 'couleur du lac au clair de la
lune'. On the other colours, see Ellmann pp. 4, 22, 84, 201, 268; on evening-dress,
see pp. 37, 225. The colour of sin and the mourning bed, *The Picture of Dorian
Gray* (London, 1993; first published, 1890): ch. 2, p. 25; ch. 11, p. 116. Wilde's
letter appeared in *The Daily Telegraph* on 3 February 1891, p. 5 (and see n. 20 to
ch. 4 above).

3 The suggestion is Hans-Thies Lehmann's; see Mark M. Anderson, *Kafka's Clothes*
(Oxford, 1992), p. 35. The last sentence quoted of 'Excursion into the Mountains'
reads in the German 'Versteht sich, dass alle im Frack sind.'

4 *The Trial*, translated by Willa and Edwin Muir (Harmondsworth, 1968), p. 7.

5 K in turn, it should be said, treats his clients at the Bank with a small-scale version
of the enigmatic and contradictory behaviour of the Court: they must wait all day
and then be disappointed, though he is there for them and no one else, just as the
man 'Before the Law', in the novel's climactic parable, waits all his life at the law's
gate and never can enter, though that gate exists for him and no one else. The
Kafka references in the following paragraphs are: *The Trial*, landlady, p. 27; guilt,
pp. 73–4; Leni, pp. 122–3; gloves, p. 245; dog, p. 251. *The Castle* (trans. Willa and

Edwin Muir, Harmondsworth, 1957): market-place, p. 34; mother and child, p. 18; Barnabas, p. 27; Klamm's clothes, p. 167; official clothes, p. 164; great books, p. 169. As to Castle dress, there is, in addition to Klamm, the official Erlanger: 'he wore a black fur coat with a tight collar buttoned up high' (p. 255). The landlord of the Herrenhof Inn, where officials from the Castle repair, is 'dressed in black and buttoned up as always' (p. 264).

6 Since there are many causes for any choice of clothes, I mention that a historic hero of Mussolini's home-town of Forli (nearest large town, that is, he was born at Predappio, fifteen kilometres south of Forli) was Giovani dalle Bande Nere, John of the Black Bands, son of Caterina Sforza and Giovanni de Medici, who, in the early sixteenth century, headed the papal forces, later fighting under black banners both for the French and for the Emperor out of life-long mourning for his patron-relative Pope Leo X.

7 On shirts, see Heinz Höhne, *The Order of the Death's Head* (London, 1969), p. 24. On liberation black, see Robert Lewis Koehl, *The Black Corps* (Wisconsin, 1983): 'The "Black Corps" (Das schwarze Korps) was adopted as the name of the SS magazine in 1935 because the romantically inclined wished to make a parallel between the Schutzstaffel as a paramilitary unit in black uniforms and the similarly attired free corps volunteers of the 1813 War of Liberation' (p. xxiiin). As to Greek black, I should mention parenthetically that the traditional men's dress of Crete has long consisted of a black scarf, black shirt, black breeches and stockings.

8 On the detailed development of the SS uniform, see Andrew Mollo, *Uniforms of the SS, Vol. 1: Allgemeine-SS 1923–1945*, 4th edn (London, 1991).

9 John Guille Millais, *The Life and Letters of Sir John Everett Millais* (London, 1899), I, p. 350.

10 Quoted by Herbert F. Ziegler, *Nazi Germany's New Aristocracy: The SS Leadership, 1925–1939* (Princeton, 1989), p. 8.

11 See Ziegler, *Nazi Germany's New Aristocracy*, p. 7.

12 On the catechism see Höhne, *Order of the Death's Head*, p. 148; on the age-structure of the SS, see Ziegler, especially pp. 62–5.

13 See Ziegler *passim*, especially pp. 103–6.

14 Sir Oswald Mosley, *My Life* (London, 1968), p. 302.

15 Edmund Warburton, quoted in anon., *Mosley's Blackshirts: The Inside Story of the British Union of Fascists, 1939–1940* (London, 1986), pp. 51–2.

16 Mosley, *My Life*, p. 290.

17 House of Commons Debates, vol. 317, col. 1388; quoted by Robert Skidelsky, *Oswald Mosley* (London, 1975), p. 417.

18 Mosley, *My Life*, p. 303.

19 It should be said that Mosley had plans for a force of Brownshirts also, to consist of industrial workers; and for Greyshirts too, who would be probationary members. Women members of the movement wore black blouses, skirts and berets. See Colin Cross, *The Fascists in Britain* (London, 1961), pp. 75–7.

20 The first quotation is from *Fascist Quarterly*, quoted by Skidelsky, *Oswald Mosley*, p. 312; the second from 'James Drennan' (W.E.D. Allen), quoted in Skidelsky, p. 313.

21 See Ziegler, *Nazi Germany's New Aristocracy*, pp. 74–9, where the generational claim is tested and given a quaified recognition.

22 David Hockney, *David Hockney*, ed. Nikos Stangos (London, 1976), p. 204.

23 Thomas Pynchon, *V* (London, 1975), p. 9.

24 Thomas Pynchon, *Gravity's Rainbow* (London, 1975), pp. 390–1, 351, 232–6.

Photographic Acknowledgements

The author and publishers wish to express their thanks to the following sources of illustrative material and/or permission to reproduce it (excluding those sources credited in the picture captions):

Agence Photographique de la Réunion des Musées Nationaux, Paris: nos. 35, 42, 56, 67, 69, 71, 72 and 73; Arquivo Nacional de Fotografia/Jose Pessoa: no. 16; Associated Press: no. 80; Associated Press/Topham: no. 77; Osvaldo Böhm: no. 19; British Film Institute, London: nos. 81 and 84; British Library, London: no. 74; Cambridge University Library: nos. 2, 3, 6, 33, 44, 45, 50, 53, 58 and 64; Hulton Deutsch: no. 57, 78 and 79; Det kongelige Bibliotek, Copenhagen: no. 26; Pamela Lister: no. 63; The Mansell Collection: nos. 4 and 9; Marlborough Fine Art, London: no. 85; Metropolitan Museum of Art, New York: Bequest of Miss Adelaide de Groot, no. 70, Arthur H. Hearn Fund, no 75, Bequest of Edith Minturn Phelps Stokes, 76; National Gallery of Art, Washington, DC (© 1994, Board of Trustees): Harris Whittemore Collection, no. 65, Rosenwald Collection, no. 68 and Widener Collection, no. 37; Press Association/Topham Picture Library: no. 82; Royal Collection Enterprises (© 1994 Her Majesty the Queen): no. 17.

Index

italic numerals refer to illustrations